Painting for My Life

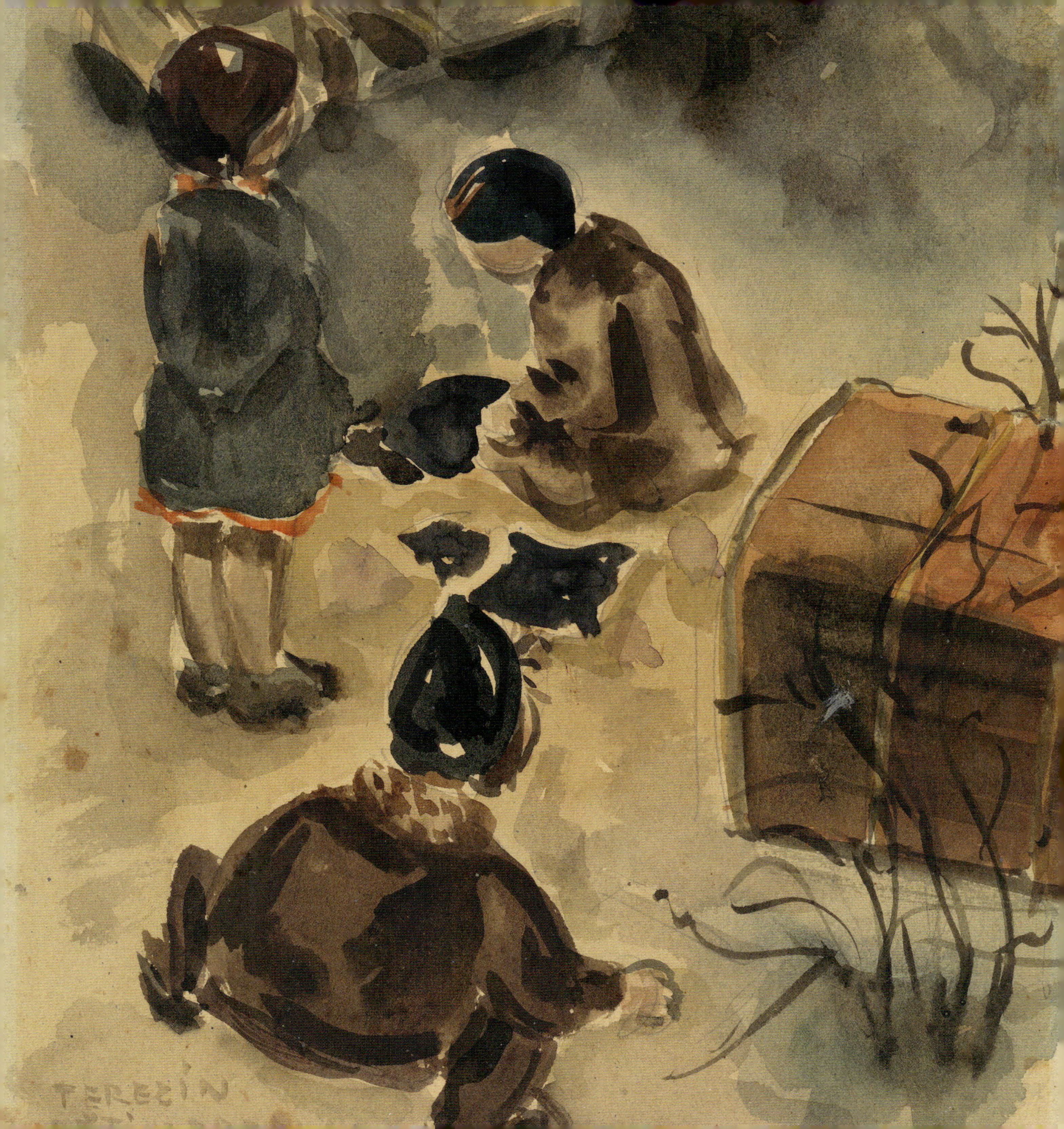

TEREZIN

Painting for My Life

The Holocaust artworks of Marianne Grant

Jo Meacock

Peter Tuka

Paula Cowan

Deborah Haase

Glasgow Museums Publishing

First published in 2021 by Glasgow Museums Publishing, part of Glasgow Life

More information about Glasgow Museums' collection may be found at
http://collections.glasgowmuseums.com

ISBN 978-1-908638-30-4

Designed by Caroline and Roger Hillier, The Old Chapel Graphic Design
Edited by Susan Pacitti
Photography by Maureen Kinnear and Alan Broadfoot
Map by John Westwell

Printed in Scotland by J Thomson Colour Printers, Glasgow
Cover printed on 350gsm Galerie Satin; text printed on 150gsm Galerie Satin

Front cover image: *Girl with Yellow Star*, 1942/43, Marianne Grant, PP.2005.38.21
Frontispiece: *Children at the Ashes*, 1943, Marianne Grant, PP.2005.38.16

Contents

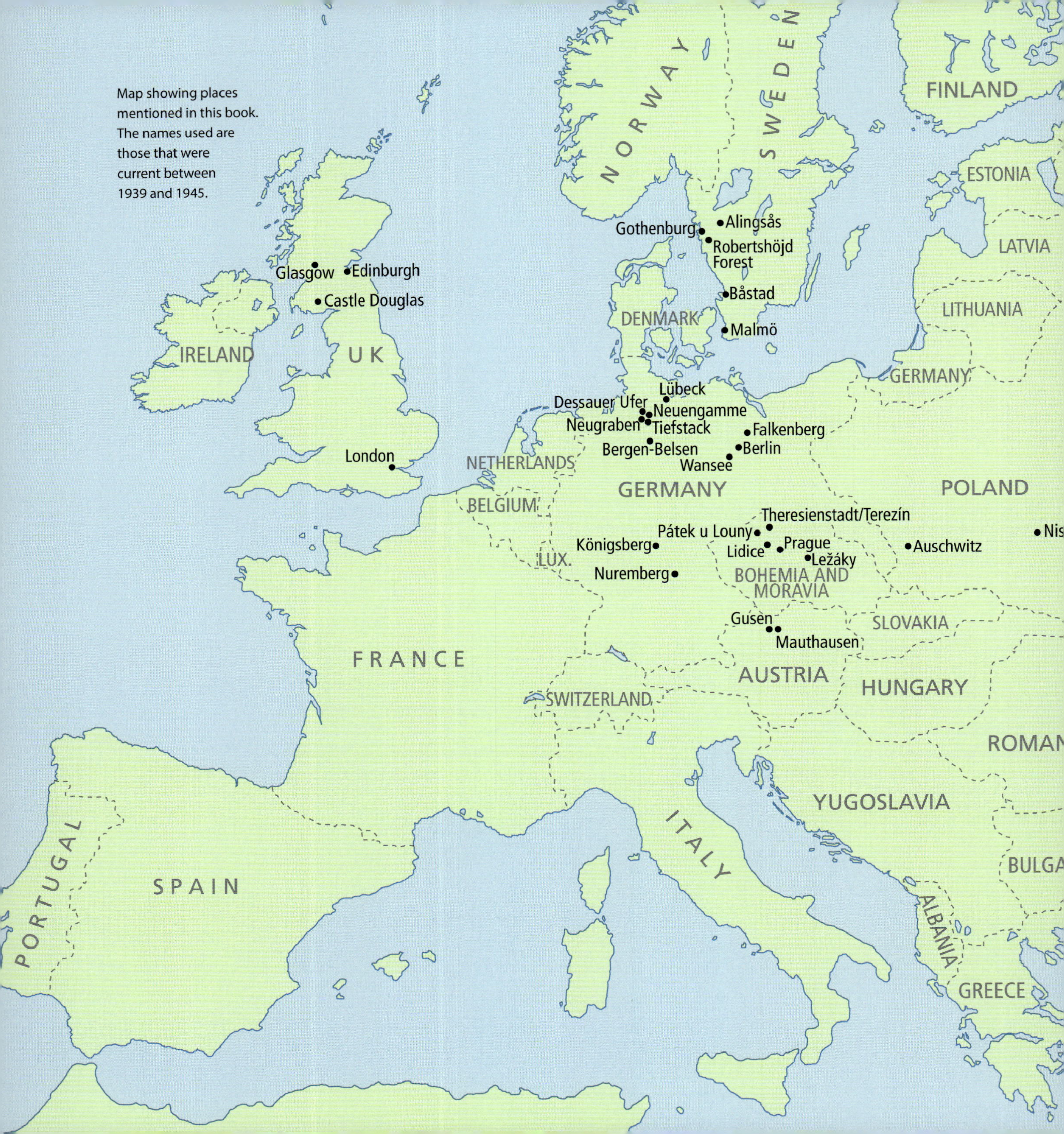

Map showing places mentioned in this book. The names used are those that were current between 1939 and 1945.
NORWAY
SWEDEN
FINLAND
ESTONIA
LATVIA
LITHUANIA
GERMANY
Gothenburg
Alingsås
Robertshöjd Forest
Båstad
Malmö
DENMARK
Glasgow
Edinburgh
Castle Douglas
IRELAND
UK
London
Lübeck
Dessauer Ufer
Neuengamme
Neugraben
Tiefstack
Falkenberg
Bergen-Belsen
Berlin
Wansee
NETHERLANDS
GERMANY
POLAND
BELGIUM
LUX.
Theresienstadt/Terezín
Pátek u Louny
Königsberg
Lidice
Prague
Auschwitz
Nis
Nuremberg
Ležáky
BOHEMIA AND MORAVIA
Gusen
SLOVAKIA
Mauthausen
FRANCE
AUSTRIA
HUNGARY
SWITZERLAND
ROMAN
YUGOSLAVIA
ITALY
PORTUGAL
SPAIN
BULGA
ALBANIA
GREECE

This book is dedicated to

the memory of the 22 members of Marianne's family

who were murdered in the Holocaust

Acknowledgements

The authors would like to thank:
Victoria Rudebark for assistance with contacting Swedish archives and accessing Swedish online resources; Martin Linde, Collections Management Systems and Photo Archive, Swedish National Maritime and Transport Museums for information on M/S *Rönnskär* and other Swedish Red Cross ships; Yael Fried, Curator, Jewish Museum, Stockholm, whose grandmother was on the same boat as Marianne and had a similar journey through the camps; Anette Sarnäst, archivist, Malmö City Archives, Isabel Larruy Bergqvist, archivist at Sigtuna Foundation, and Roman Wasserman Wroblewski of the Swedish Holocaust Memorial Association for information on Jewish refugees and sanitoria in Sweden; Tereza Maizels, Archive Manager and Curator, Beit Terezin, for her assistance with enquiries about Marianne's artworks; Iva Gaudesová, Curator, Terezín Memorial, for assisting with enquiries about locations Marianne depicted in her Theresienstadt artworks; Martina Šiknerová, Collection Department, Terezin Memorial, for assistance with images; Dita Kraus and Eva Erben for kindly sharing their memories of Marianne; Robyne Calvert and Clémence Aycard for assistance in contacting French archives and collections; Ann Evans, Maureen Kinnear and Alan Broadfoot for their help with images; Susan Pacitti for her patience, perseverance and good humour throughout; Helen Watkins and Rebecca Quinton for their sharp eyes and wise counsel; Hannah Wilson for her enthusiastic advocacy; Deborah Haase and Harvey Kaplan, Scottish Jewish Archives Centre, for their insight, experience and support; Howard Singerman, Gathering the Voices Association, for his encouragement; and, most of all, Geraldine Shenkin for her involvement, support and enthusiasm for this project.

Funders

We are grateful to the following for their generous funding, without which this publication would not have been possible.
In appreciation to the Conference on Jewish Material Claims Against Germany (Claims Conference) for supporting this publication. Through recovering the assets of the victims of the Holocaust, the Claims Conference enables organizations around the world to provide education about the Shoah and to preserve the memory of those who perished.

The Alma and Leslie Wolfson Charitable Trust; The Clive Jay Berkley Foundation; The Esterson Trust; The Glasgow Jewish Community Trust; The Harold Hyam Wingate Foundation; The Netherlee and Clarkston Charitable Trust; The Queens Park Charitable Trust; Talteg Ltd; The Grant, Shenkin, and Slater families, in ever-lasting memory of Marianne Grant; Judy Norman; and other generous individuals who donated.

Preface

Marianne Hermann, a young Jewish artist and Holocaust survivor from Prague, came to live in Glasgow in 1951, joining German Jewish refugee Jack Grant, who had already settled in Battlefield on the southside of the city, having arrived in 1939 as part of the Kindertransport rescue missions. Marianne had spent seven gruelling years experiencing firsthand the Nazis' ideology of hate, interred in a succession of concentration, labour and extermination camps. Then as a registered displaced person after the war in 1945, she had found a safe haven in Gothenburg, Sweden, before finally making Glasgow her home.

This year marks not only the centenary of the birth of Marianne Grant, but also the seventieth anniversary of the UN Refugee Convention. Despite the horrors of the Holocaust, lessons have not been learnt, and since World War II we continue to see conflict, human rights abuse and genocide. Glasgow has prided itself on welcoming the displaced, whether East Asians expelled from Uganda in 1972, Chileans fleeing General Pinochet in 1973, Vietnamese boat people escaping brutal oppression in the 1980s or Bosnian and Kosovan refugees fleeing ethnic cleansing in the 1990s. In 1999, the year the Scottish devolved parliament opened, Glasgow became Scotland's first asylum dispersal city, with asylum seekers arriving from Columbia, Croatia, Nigeria, Somalia, Romania, Sri Lanka and Iraq, and most recently Libya, Syria, Democratic Republic of Congo and Afghanistan. We must acknowledge that there has been racism and anger from some; however, like Marianne Grant, these New Scots have brought a multitude of professional and creative skills to the city and have enriched our communities and cultural life. Projects and charities like Refuweegee and Maryhill Integration Network, both of which Glasgow Museums has been privileged to work with, were specifically set up to welcome and help families integrate into local communities. Glasgow is honoured to now be a city of immense cultural diversity and vitality.

In 2004, thanks to generous grants from the National Lottery Heritage Fund, Art Fund and National Fund for Acquisitions, Glasgow Museums was able to acquire the Marianne Grant Holocaust Artworks Collection for posterity. In December 1941 Jews within the Protectorate of Bohemia and Moravia had been forbidden from visiting museums and galleries, but now there is a permanent display of Marianne's artwork in the 'Conflict and Consequence' gallery in Kelvingrove Art Gallery and Museum. Sadly, Marianne passed away in 2007 at the age of 86, but her story and her voice still ring out today, her artwork being an integral part of Glasgow Museums' Holocaust learning workshop for primary and secondary students and the annual Holocaust Memorial Day schools project, for which we have been collaborating with a school in Glasgow's twin city of Nuremberg, the very city where

Nazi racial laws were ratified and military tribunals were held after the war.

The researchers writing this book were privileged to have access to new archival material, previously unpublished, made available by Marianne's family and translated by Peter Tuka. Marianne's daughter Geraldine Shenkin has shared family information and memories, and Deborah Haase, Honorary Curator at the Scottish Jewish Archives Centre, knew Marianne well. Contact made with Marianne's friends from the Nazi camps and with Jewish museums and heritage organizations internationally has enriched our understanding of Marianne's Holocaust journey and her incredible courage and resilience. It is astounding that her unique artwork, made within the Nazi camps, has survived. The collection carries immense potency today, representing a challenge and reminder to our visitors about the value of the individual, the need for community and hope in the darkest hour.

Duncan Dornan, Head of Museums and Collections, Glasgow Life, November 2021

Foreword

Marianne Grant's Holocaust artworks, words and memorabilia are a unique record of the Holocaust. Her artworks were made between 1938 and 1945, when Marianne, with her mother, endured the Nazi occupation of her country, forced labour, the concentration camps at Theresienstadt and Auschwitz-Birkenau until she was ultimately liberated from Bergen-Belsen Concentration Camp.

How did she survive in the midst of such terrors?

She painted when she could, creating extraordinary artworks that give us, firsthand, her intimate insights into the Holocaust as she was experiencing it. From her later testimony and letters she reveals not just how her practical and artistic skills were exploited, but how they also helped sustain her, and shed light on her personality and her endearing character.

Chance brought Marianne to settle in Scotland in 1951, but it was over 50 years until her story was told. Once she started to speak about her experiences Marianne was determined that her story was recorded accurately. She went on to speak at Holocaust Memorial Day events and to schoolchildren. She wanted us all to learn from her experiences so we can be better equipped to grasp the complexities of the Holocaust and to grapple with the fundamental questions it asks of all of us.

The Scottish Jewish Archives Centre and others in Scotland have been ingathering collections, archives and testimony from formers refugees and survivors. The Marianne Grant Holocaust Artworks Collection held by Glasgow Museums forms one of the most outstanding of these collections. Holocaust education and research in Scotland is now supported by these exceptional collections, allowing the history of this period to be understood in a Scottish context.

It's almost 20 years since Marianne's Holocaust pictures were exhibited in Kelvingrove accompanied by the catalogue *I Knew I was Painting for My Life* and a film interview. Since then the Scottish Government has funded an education pack for schools based on Marianne's artworks and testimony, and Marianne is celebrated in an artwork by Shauna McMullan in the Scottish Parliament. She is represented in the collections in the Scottish Jewish Archives Centre and features in the new Scottish Holocaust-era Study Centre.

Public, scholarly and educational interest in Marianne's artworks and her story continues to grow, so it is very timely and welcome that Glasgow Museums is now publishing a new edition of the catalogue of Marianne's artworks and her story. This is an enriched volume, which benefits from new academic research into hitherto unknown documents, and fascinating evidence gleaned from letters Marianne wrote after the war to her close friend, confidant and fellow survivor Petr Erben. The letters were only recently discovered in family papers left by Marianne.

Scholarly convention would have Marianne described in this catalogue as 'Grant'. However, all the contributors refer to her as Marianne; those working on the book who had not met her felt so connected through the close involvement of Geraldine and myself they chose this style. I think Marianne would have approved.

Dr Jo Meacock, Curator of British Art at Glasgow Museums, assesses Marianne's pictures in the context of the Holocaust and war artists. Her examinations interpret Marianne the artist, a woman artist, an artist painting for herself, for her personal sustenance and survival, giving us firsthand testimony. Peter Tuka, postgraduate researcher in History of Art at the University of Glasgow, takes us to Prague and reveals the significance for Marianne of the Association of Jewish Youth. He brings into focus issues around personal identity and he spotlights the importance of friendship bonds:

> … Many of them [young Czech Jews] grew up in families with Czech traditions and customs, and with an awareness of Czech nationalism. With the occupation, Nazism did not only take their homeland, but by diminishing them, by making them lesser and unwanted members of society, also took away their sense of belonging. Suddenly, these Jewish youngsters found themselves surrounded by a society, in which there was no place for them. (p. 51)

Dr Paula Cowan's thought-provoking contribution brings us up to date on developments in Holocaust education in Scotland, and lets us reflect on the ongoing need for learning about the Holocaust.

Despite the horror of the Holocaust Marianne went on to rebuild her life, to have her family, and, to allow us to benefit from her experiences so that we – wherever we are – can help shape the world to be a better place. Marianne s a true hero of our times.

Deborah Haase, Hon. Curator, Scottish Jewish Archives Centre, Glasgow, November 2021

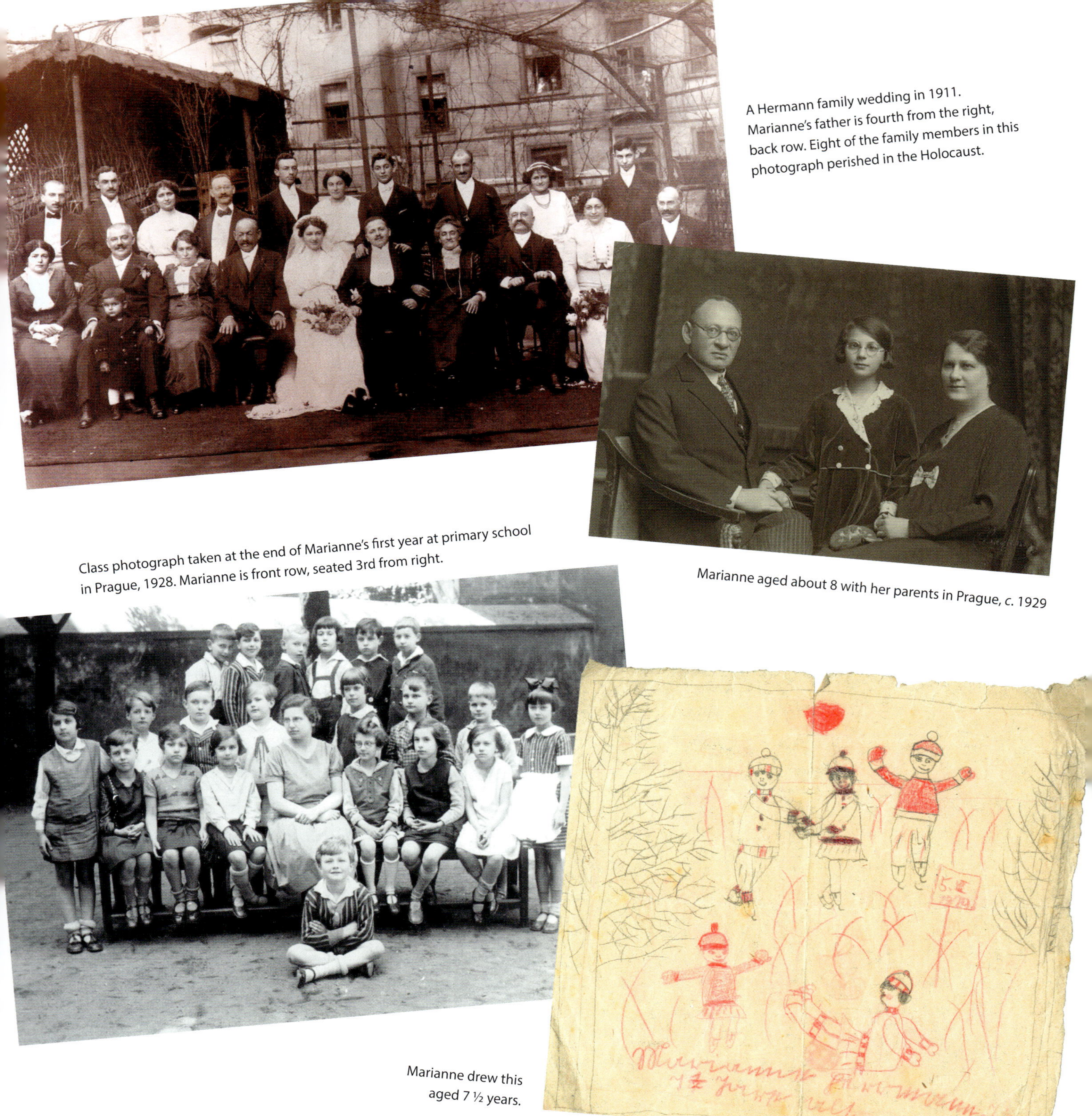

A Hermann family wedding in 1911. Marianne's father is fourth from the right, back row. Eight of the family members in this photograph perished in the Holocaust.

Marianne aged about 8 with her parents in Prague, c. 1929

Class photograph taken at the end of Marianne's first year at primary school in Prague, 1928. Marianne is front row, seated 3rd from right.

Marianne drew this aged 7 ½ years.

My Story

Marianne Grant (1921–2007)

My Family

MY NAME IS MARIANNE GRANT, née Hermann, nicknamed Mausi,[1] from Prague [in the Czech Republic]. My father came from a small village, Syřema, near Žatec,[2] in the Sudetenland,[3] North Bohemia. He was the son of hop farmers, from a family of ten children. From the age of eight, he lodged with a *Chazan*[4] in Prague in order to get a proper education. He became the foreign exchange manager of the Bohemian Union Bank in Prague, and met my mother, the youngest of three sisters, when he was sent to a branch in Bielsko, which after World War I became part of Poland. She was the daughter of a *Chazan*, Moritz Rosner, and his wife Cecelia, from Brno, Moravia. My mother Anna was a milliner and she married my father in 1920. They settled in Prague. I was born in September 1921. We lived in the centre of the town in a small flat for seven or eight years. Then we moved to new flats built by the bank for their employees near vast, beautiful parks.

Schooling

I went to primary school and a girls' high school. After that I did one year at an English private grammar school. After persuasion by my father's three sisters and my mother, my father relented and gave me permission to attend the famous Rotter Schule of fashion and graphic design in Prague.

Occupation

In April 1938 my father died – a few months before the occupation of Czechoslovakia by the Germans. We had to leave our flat in that good district, which was now used only by ethnic Germans. We had to move into a small flat across the river Vltava in Smíchov. Most of our relations lived there, so that was not too terrible. My mother purchased a *Kapitalisten* Certificate which paid for two years in Jerusalem's famous Bezalel Art School. I did not want to leave my mother, and as I cried and cried, we gave the chance to another person.

Under Hitler the Council of the Jewish community had to provide volunteers for agriculture, as the farmers were taken to the mines as slave labour. I went out with a Jewish group called El Al to which I belonged. We were sent to various large farms in Bohemia and Moravia. At the end of the season in autumn 1941 we all had to wear the yellow star with *Jude* on it. I taught teenage Jewish girls fashion design privately at home, went to a sculptor secretly, and learned how to sew lingerie (also on the quiet), at some risk to the proprietor.

Transport AO593: Theresienstadt
28 April 1942–December 1943

On 28 April 1942 we were taken in great haste (although we had been preparing for it for months) to the Exhibition Centre in Prague, where we were kept on the floor overnight. The next day we were sent by normal trains to what we did not know at the time was the ghetto[5] of Theresienstadt. This was a fortress built by the Empress Maria Theresa and used to this day by the Czech Army.[6] We were put up in the military barracks vacated by the soldiers. We were allocated a room, 40 of us lying on the floor, each having a space of 3ft by 6ft. I chose to work in agriculture as I was told it was more lucrative than the Art Department. I could exchange second-class vegetables for bread or other rations. I became second in charge of the youth garden where girls aged 12 to 17 worked.

In my spare time after work I went sketching and painting with a friend, Gert, whom we met when we were gathered in the Exhibition Hall. Gert and I went to the mock cafés and drew the old Austrian and German Jews, who thought they were coming to a retirement home. Most of them perished from typhoid and enteritis through malnutrition. I also painted my surroundings, particularly the outside of the ghetto walls, as we felt very shut in.

When they moved the entire Czech population out of Theresienstadt because of the overcrowding, the empty houses were used for the Jews. The girls of my youth group got one of these empty houses. To begin with we had no bunk beds, so we improvised furniture with the suitcases we had. When Heydrich was murdered in Prague[7] the entire population of the ghetto was marched outside. We had to stand at roll call from early morning till night to be counted and shouted at by the German commanders. Many fainted. Some died.

DS457 Auschwitz Concentration Camp
18 December 1943–July 1944

The Jewish Council in the ghetto was pressurized to summon 1,000 people every day to go on the cattle trains to the east. My mother was summoned three times and I managed to get her released, but the fourth time it was not possible, and she was taken onto a cattle wagon. I rushed back to the house, left my artwork with a friend, grabbed a few belongings and jumped on the train, but not into the same wagon as my mother. It took days – no food, no drink, just a bucket in the corner to relieve ourselves. When the trains stopped in darkness we were surrounded by SS with killer dogs, black Dobermans, shouting '*Raus! Raus!*', Out! Out! I searched for my mother all night in the concrete blocks where we were kept. Eventually I found her at dawn.

Selection

The next day we were taken to a building where Polish women shouted orders at us to strip off all our clothing. Then we were herded outside in the bitter cold of the Polish winter. There were German SS officers in their uniforms and black high boots. We were ordered to walk past them naked. Afterwards I found out that one of them was the notorious Dr Josef Mengele. He held a leather whip and with this pointed to the left and right. The ones who went to the left were condemned to death to be gassed in the gas chambers. The others were spared and sent to transit blockhouses. Men and women were separate.

Czech Family Camp in Auschwitz-Birkenau

We were sent to the Family Camp Auschwitz-Birkenau and settled in one of the long cement and brick blocks with timber walls. We slept on planks with straw mattresses. We took our shoes off every night: one morning mine were missing from under my sleeping plank. I received thin canvas clogs and my toes got frozen and were black and septic. This was sheer agony in the winter temperature, especially as we sometimes had to stand for hours for *Appell* (roll call).

I was called upon to look after the children, who were separated from their mothers and put into the Children's Block with the children of the previous transport. One block was without bunk beds, and this was where we entertained the children. We secretly taught them. I taught them painting and nature study. The Germans kept the Children's Block in comparative comfort. They had a thicker soup and we were given all sorts of materials like paper, pens, paint, and so on. There were even tables and rough benches – the height of luxury!

The SS came frequently to visit and amuse themselves with the children, as they were bored stiff in this desolate part of the world. One of these SS was a Slovak collaborator who spotted my drawings. He commissioned me to make hand-painted fairy tale books for his children, and he took me to the gypsy camp where I had to paint an oil of a beautiful gypsy girl for his wife. When he came to look for me again at the Children's Block and I was not there he found me lying ill with pleurisy and awful boils on my bunk bed with my mother. He demanded to see the Jewish doctor on our block. As she had no medication to give me, he brought me whatever was necessary and bread and butter, and so he actually saved my life.

Dr Mengele

News travelled fast, and I was ordered to Mengele, the notorious SS doctor who did different medical experiments with inmates. I was ordered to draw two girls, twins, who had certain skin markings on their bodies. Next time I was told to do research in the dwarf camp. I was taken by an SS man with a motorbike and sidecar. Afterwards I was called to Mengele again, in a hut with a Persian carpet on the muddy floor. He handed me an architect's toolset and I had to draw the family tree of one of the Hungarian dwarf families in black ink. He paced up and down in his high leather boots without a word. I was shaking. If I had made a blob or mistake, I would have been finished. At this time I knew I was painting for my life.

I received permission and materials to paint on the wall of the children's block for the benefit of the Red Cross. I did Mickey Mouse, Bambi the deer, all kinds of children of the world – Chinese, Indian, Eskimo[8] – and trees, flowers and mushrooms. It was partly educational and also to brighten the environment. I redid this in 1997 for the exhibition *No Child's Play. Children of the Holocaust* in Yad Vashem, Jerusalem (see fig. 4.15, p. 110).

The children and adults who came with the transport before us were taken away on 8 March 1944. The whole camp went numb. You could not hear a sound and there was no motion when they stood in line. The *Schreiber* (literally, the one who writes), a privileged Jew or Kapo [a Jewish person employed by the Nazis as a guard] in his grey and blue pyjama suit and striped cap, took note of each person's tattoo. There was no selection.

The gas chamber ovens worked all night. We could smell the stench of burning flesh and hair.

Slave Labour in Germany
Early July 1944–April 1945

We were taken again to the sauna (gas chambers), stripped of everything. The SS women who were checking our tattoos secretly belonged to the Communist Party and assured us we would get through selection and not be gassed. After the showers the SS began the selection: the able ones to one side, the children and weak to the other. The able ones were given overalls, put on trains and sent to Germany as slave labourers.

We reached the waterside at Hamburg Dessauer Ufer. We were housed in former grain stores in the harbour. We collected old bricks from the bombsites and put them on barges. During an air raid attack we had to run to the air raid shelter, but I did not jump far enough from the barge to the quay and fell into the water in my overalls and heavy boots. A friend, Vera, stopped and pulled me out. The German supervisor was kind and let me use the site hut, where I could dry my clothes during the air attack on a small iron stove.

We were under the supervision of the SS of the Neuengamme Concentration Camp. When we were in Neugraben work camp a few of the women were sent back to Auschwitz and death because they were pregnant. One managed to stay, as she worked in the SS office. She gave birth to a healthy baby boy who was instantly put to sleep by our Jewish doctor Goldie by SS order. We were all in shock and mourning.

In Neugraben, near Hanover, we were digging trenches for sewage, gas and electricity, and foundations for housing and air raid shelters. We were bombed and some people were killed. We ran to the air raid shelter. The ground was sprayed with air raid mist. We could only crawl underneath it. A Russian prisoner of war threw me a sandwich as I crawled past. We actually went to the same shelter as the Germans, just a little apart.

As we were digging the foundations for new houses a young German mother befriended me. She sometimes handed me a sandwich or an apple. I made a caricature of the woman, her baby in the pram and me and gave it to her as a thank you (see fig. 4.17, p. 113). A copy of the picture appeared after the war in the local housing association's twenty-fifth, fortieth and fiftieth anniversary magazines.

A few other girls and I could make toys, and we were ordered to the German headquarters to make dolls for Christmas out of scraps of material. As I was a painter I was asked to decorate the walls of the officers' dining hall with beer jugs and sausages. I was allowed to keep all the paints and pens, which came in very useful later. I was given a job inside after Christmas, cleaning rooms. After the bombing we were shifted to other places.

Bergen-Belsen Concentration Camp 5 April 1945

With the British Army approaching we were moved to Bergen-Belsen Camp, partly by train and partly on foot. We were greeted by the sight of dead bodies, typhoid, lice and starvation. When we arrived, the SS were wearing white armbands as a sign of surrender. We were shocked to see piles of dead bodies everywhere. We found a place in a wooden hut in which people were dead and dying from typhoid. In order to protect ourselves we had to check our clothes every day to make sure we were free of lice, as they were the carriers of the disease. The kitchens were not functioning anymore, and we had to fend for ourselves. We tried to raid the potato and beetroot pits, and the Hungarian militia who were housed in brick houses just by the barbed wire shot at us, just for fun, killing many people. My mother and I shared one beetroot per day between us. There were no rations, no bread, no soup. I went on painting dead bodies. Between the young birches a beautiful young red head caught my eye (cat. 31).

For days the earth was trembling. It was the British army tanks under Field Marshal Montgomery, who liberated Bergen-Belsen on 15 April 1945. The British soldiers were in shock. They had never experienced such human misery. Through their kindness in distributing their own rations they killed many, as the emaciated people could not digest the rich food and many perished.

Liberated by the British Army 15 April 1945

As I spoke English, I was immediately made an interpreter to the army. I also got an office job and among other duties it was my task to hand out the cigarette rations to the British soldiers and officers. My mother got typhoid and was taken to an isolation hospital that was created by the army. Meanwhile I was rehoused with other survivors in the brick-built barracks that were originally occupied by the Hungarian soldiers.

My mother was looked after by an Irish volunteer doctor named Sean Styles. He befriended us and came for meals which my mother cooked when she became better. He also took me to the British headquarters for a party and introduced me to Field Marshal Montgomery. I declined the offer of a drink, but I had a dance and an interesting talk with him.

The British Army had orders to burn the whole of Bergen-Belsen as it was so infectious. This was the ceremony of burning the last hut block (cat. 42).

Dr Styles decided that my mother was too undernourished to survive if we went back home to Prague, as food was very scarce on the continent. He put us on a Red Cross boat from Hamburg to Sweden filled with very ill and weak people.

Sweden July 1945–1951

I was a helper on the Red Cross boat and met my first Swedish girl, a nurse, on the boat (cat. 43). I befriended a young Jewish Dutch girl. She was in the terminal stage of tuberculosis (cat. 44). We landed in Malmö in Sweden in summer 1945. All of us and our meagre belongings were disinfected with DDT dust before disembarking. We were put up in a school. The Jewish community took an interest: some of us were invited to their homes and we even put on an improvised show for them. From Malmö we were taken to a camp of wooden chalets in Robertshöjd Forest near Gothenburg (cat. 45). My mother was taken to a sanatorium where she was nursed back to health.

I made friends with a shoe manufacturer called Herbert Sterner who came with his oldest daughter Myrre – with whom I became life-long friends – to visit the refugee camp. I managed to get work making all sorts of stuffed animals like yellow giraffes and teddies, which I loved. In November 1945 I also had my first exhibition of the Bergen-Belsen drawings and watercolours and I sold the stuffed toys there as well. There were very good reviews in the Gothenburg newspapers. Then I worked in a graphics studio and I did stage design. My mother joined me in the camp and got a job as a milliner in a large store. Between us we had enough money to keep ourselves and we settled in Gothenburg. Eventually we moved to a lovely flat just outside the city where I established my own studio, designing hand-painted Christmas mats and table decorations. I even employed a few girls. My mother gave up work and looked after me.

To Glasgow in 1951

I made a lot of friends. My friend Margit's German-born husband Helmut had died. Margit travelled to Glasgow to show her young son to his grandmother, Mrs Silberman, who lived in Braemar Street in Battlefield. In Glasgow Margit met a German Jewish refugee who lodged with Mrs Silberman. She gave him my address and we started to write to each other. He came to visit me in summer 1951 and we went with my mother for a holiday to Båstad on the coast. We got engaged on that vacation. In autumn 1951 I came to Glasgow with my mother and we married in London, as we had family there. We spent a weekend on honeymoon in Bournemouth at the Cumberland Hotel, and then came back to Battlefield, where we later raised our family.

Marianne Grant, 12 December 2001

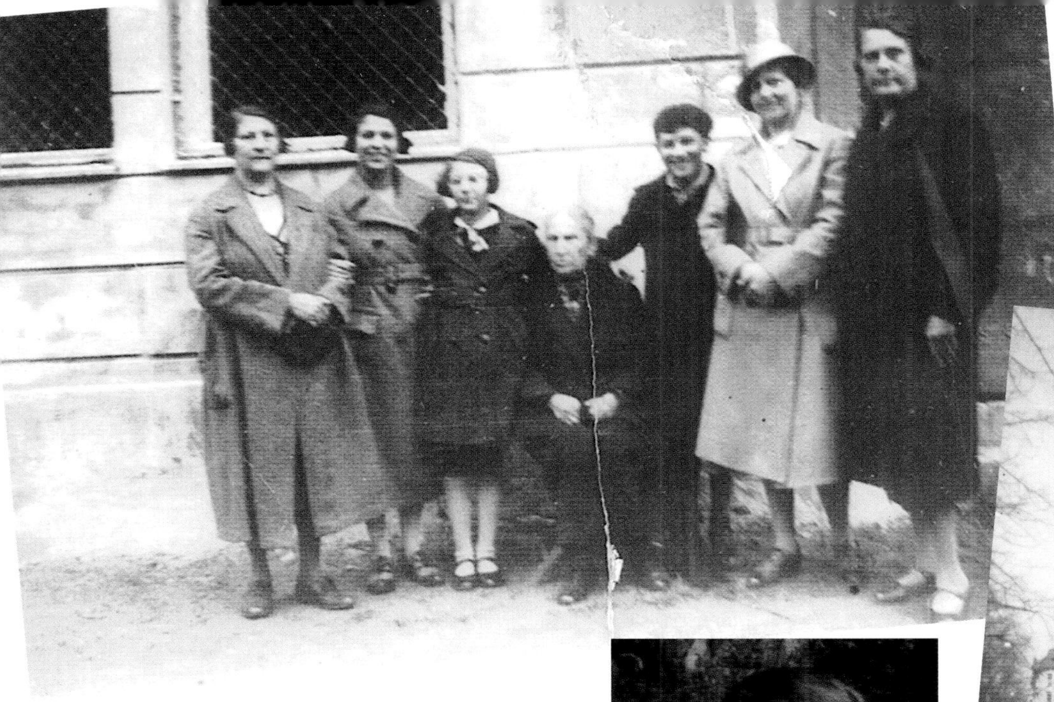

Marianne outside her maternal grandmother's home, Bielsko, 1935

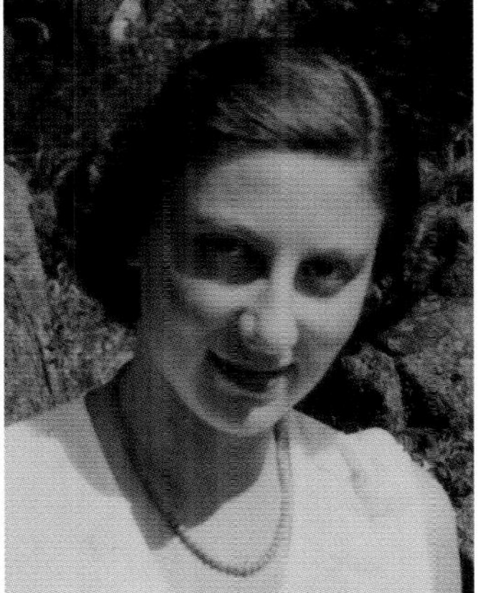

Marianne, about 1947, in Gothenburg

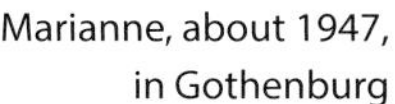

Marianne and Anna in Gothenburg, early 1946

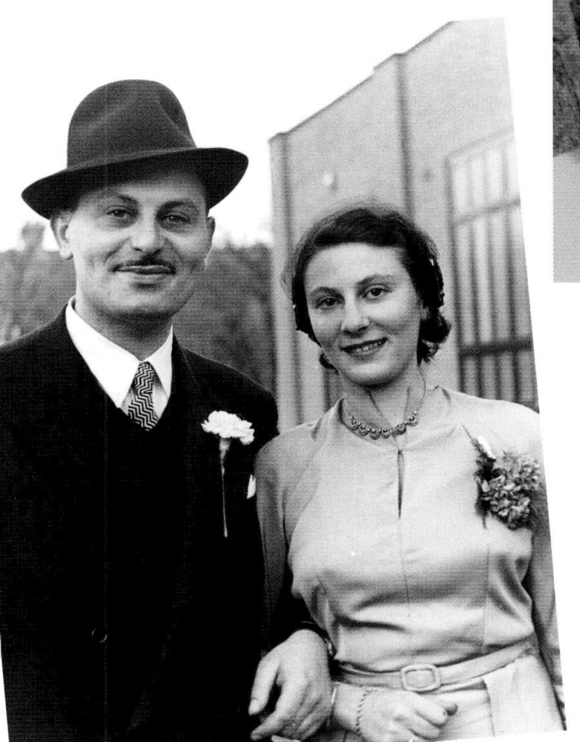

Marianne and Jack's wedding photograph, London, 1951

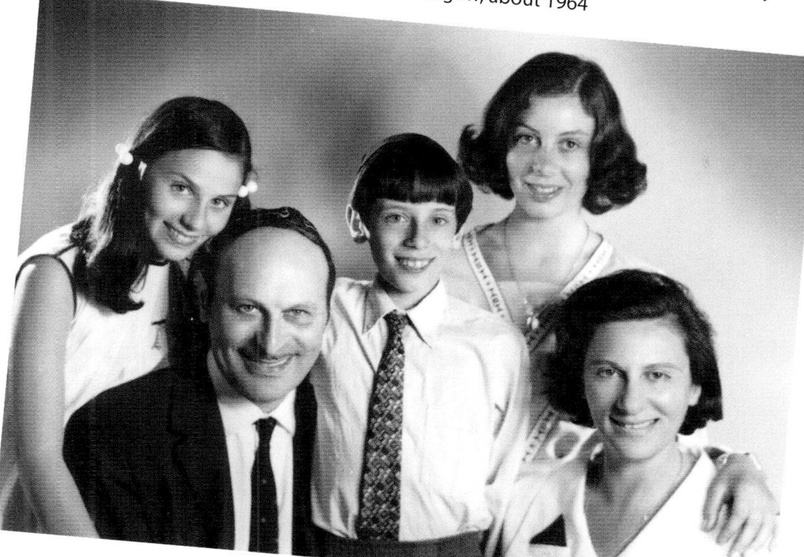

Marianne and Jack with their children Geraldine, Gary and Susan, Glasgow, about 1964

Marianne's Story from 1951 Onwards

Deborah Haase

Well I survived with my art. It helped me, very much so… In Auschwitz it saved my life and I got food. In the work camps I was also helped with my art. I got an apple now and then. An apple a day was fantastic.

Marianne Grant, 2001

IN 1946 AND 1947 Marianne travelled to Prague from Sweden, recovering precious belongings, including her student artwork exercises. She and her mother Anna had given these to family for safekeeping before they were deported. Marianne had already been reunited with her Theresienstadt artworks, which had been sent to her in Gothenburg in November 1945 by her friend Petr Erben.

In Sweden Anna was able to recuperate and Marianne, drawing on her art skills, began to build a new life and to earn a living. They settled in Gothenburg.

However, as Marianne described in *My Story,* all this changed after her friend Margit, when in Glasgow, gave Jack Grant, a German Jewish refugee, her address. The two corresponded, and when Jack went to meet Marianne in Sweden in the summer of 1951 they agreed to marry.

Jack (1921–1986) born Jaakov (Horst) Grodszinsky in Königsberg in East Prussia, was also a Holocaust survivor. He had escaped the Nazis in early 1939 on a Yeshiva Kindertransport;[9] his parents Frieda and Eric, and his brother Sigfried, all perished in the Holocaust. In 1941, Jaakov was teaching young Jewish refugees who had been evacuated to Ernespie House in Castle Douglas, a town in Dumfries and Galloway in Scotland. Back in Glasgow, he changed his name to Jack Grant and became a naturalized British citizen in 1948.

Marianne and Jack set up home, along with Anna, in Battlefield Avenue, Glasgow. Daughter Susan was born on 25 December 1952 followed by twins Geraldine and Gary in May 1957.

From the 1950s to the 1970s marriage, family and community life were the main focus of Marianne's life. Community life became more significant when in the early 1960s the family moved to Newton Mearns, a suburb in the south of Glasgow. Jack had become the minister for the then fledgling Newton Mearns Hebrew Congregation. He also continued working as a *cheder* teacher, serving as *shochet* and *monel*[10] for the Glasgow Jewish community and as honorary chaplain to the Jewish branch of the British Legion. Marianne fully supported Jack in his role in the community. The family was a regular presence at synagogue services and Marianne participated in community and synagogue life.

Marianne had gone to evening art classes at The Glasgow School of Art, but Jack was not enthusiastic about her having to accept a lift to get there so she did not continue with them. However, daughter Geraldine recalls Marianne always enjoyed drawing and painting, mostly in watercolours. At their home in Newton Mearns Marianne had her easel and paints set up in the back porch and when the children left home, she used a bedroom as a studio. Her paintings – flowers, landscapes and 'doodles' of her always-beloved Mickey and Minnie Mouse – were hung in the house and later gifted to children and grandchildren. Marianne used her graphic skills to create table plans for congregation members' Barmitzvah and wedding celebrations. She encouraged her children to paint and draw. Anna sewed and embroidered for the family.

Through these years, the trunk storing Marianne's student art exercises, her artwork from Theresienstadt, and her paintings and memorabilia from Prague and from her time in Sweden all stayed, untouched, in the attic. Daughter Susan remembered:

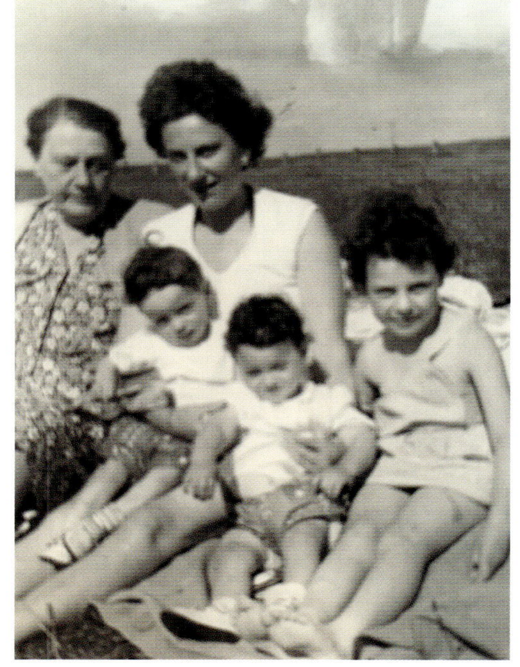

Anna, Marianne and the children, about 1958, Barassie Beach, Troon, Scotland

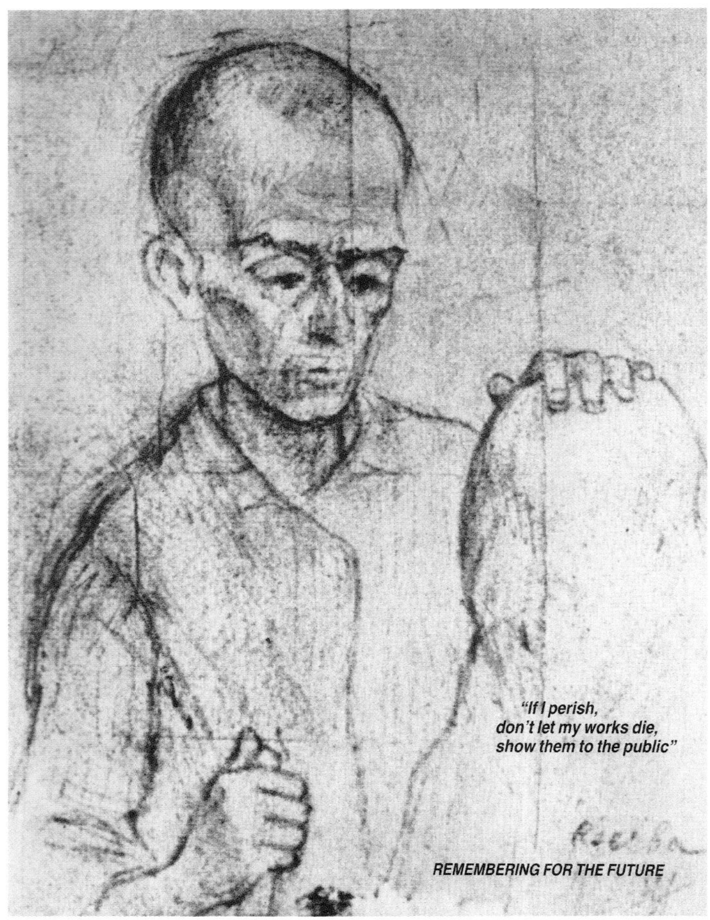

Cover of the catalogue *Remembering for the Future,* 1988. The artwork is *Auschwitz, 1940* by Włodzimierz Siwierski. Auschwitz Memorial Museum

Although the Holocaust had made a tragic impact on both my parents' lives, they decided to shield us from it. Mausi's art was locked away in a trunk upstairs and they never ever spoke to us about what had happened. However, even as children, we suspected something had occurred in their past. Not a morsel of food was ever wasted.[11]

Daughter Geraldine recalled:

Throughout our childhood and all her life Mum kept and reused newspapers, cards, scraps of paper and all kinds of things in case they could be useful. When we were young, at home, our parents spoke in German and in Yiddish, and later Mum encouraged us to study German, saying they could help us with that.[12]

After Jack died, Marianne accepted an invitation to show her Holocaust artworks and after this she also began to speak in public about her Holocaust experiences. In 1988 she lent some of her Holocaust pictures for an exhibition and catalogue of original drawings and reproductions from concentration camps and ghettos by victims of the Holocaust.[13] The exhibition was at the Royal Institute of British Architects, London, and at Renfield St Stephen's Parish Church in Bath Street, Glasgow, in November 1990.

In 1997 Marianne recreated from memory the wall drawings from the Children's Block in Auschwitz for an exhibition *No Child's Play: Children in the Holocaust –*

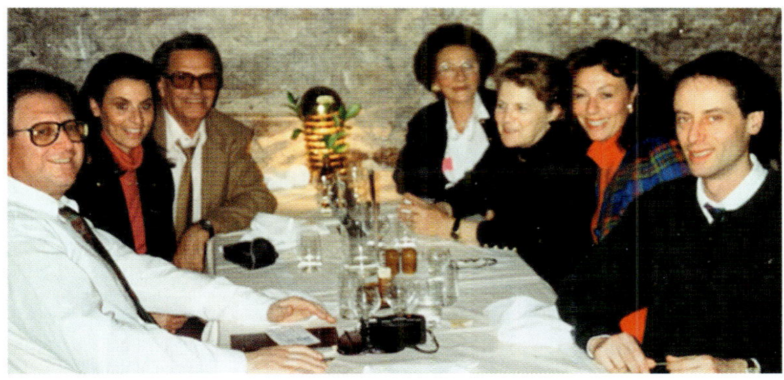

left
The family with Petr
Erben and his wife Eva,
Prague 1993

Creativity and Play at Yad Vashem, the World Holocaust Remembrance Center, in Jerusalem. Around this time, Marianne began to speak about her Holocaust experiences to her family. Significantly, she took the family to Prague. Daughter Geraldine recollected:

below
Watercolour *Hibiskus*,
signed 'Marianne
Aug. 94'

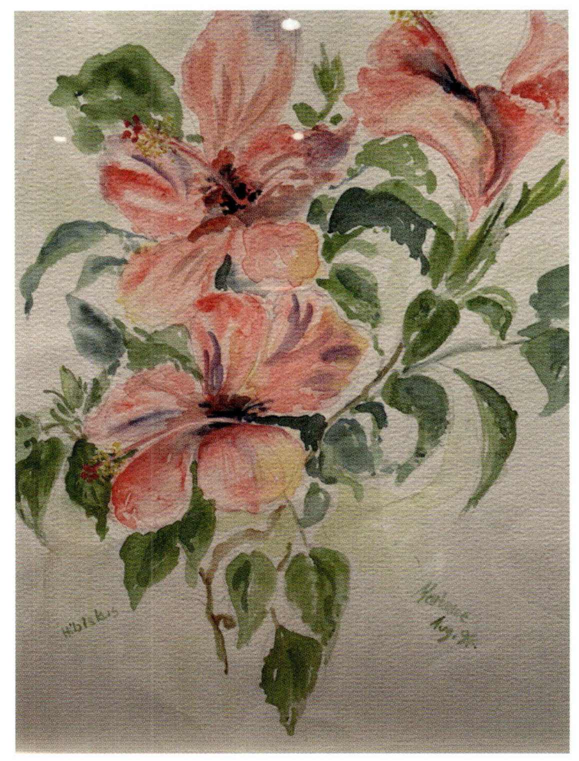

Mum – she cried when we landed at the airport. Most times she was very controlled at home and in public but the emotion of being in Prague was overwhelming for her and for all of us. She wanted all her children to see her Prague, to see where she came from. She was very pleased we were able to see the flat where she lived with her mother and father. She took us to pay respects to the Hermann family buried in the main Jewish cemetery in Prague. Characteristically when we went to one of the very old synagogues for a Shabbat service, Mum stayed while Susan and I had to leave, as the room for the women was so claustrophobic! She took us to Theresienstadt to visit the concentration camp and ghetto. She never went back to Auschwitz.

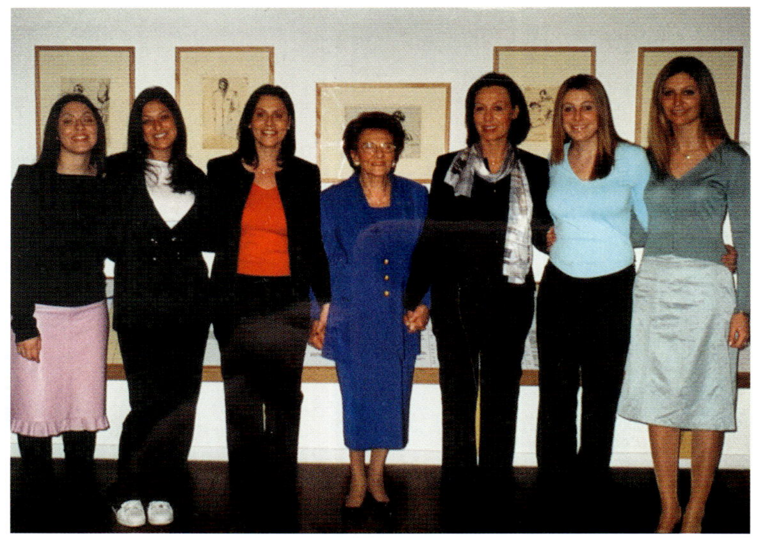

Marianne with her daughters and granddaughters, Kelvingrove Art Gallery and Museum 2002

In 2001 Marianne agreed to being interviewed and filmed by Glasgow Museums for an exhibition of her Holocaust artworks with an accompanying catalogue. The following year *I knew I was painting for my life: The Holocaust artworks of Marianne Grant* was displayed in Kelvingrove Art Gallery and Museum. The exhibition was also shown in Edinburgh City Art Centre in 2003. The Scottish Executive produced a teaching pack based on Marianne's filmed interview, which was distributed to every secondary school in Scotland.

Marianne participated in the Holocaust Memorial Day ceremony in The Glasgow Royal Concert Hall in 2002 and in the years following. She also contributed to a number of Yom HaShoah commemorations.[14] Marianne was awarded the Freedom of East Renfrewshire, the region of Scotland in which she lived, in 2003. Provost Betty Cunningham said: 'Marianne richly deserves this honour. She is an example to all of us and her busy life has been all about service to others, her family and her faith, values which have sustained her.'

In 2004, the Marianne Grant Holocaust artworks collection was purchased by Glasgow Museums with grant aid assistance from The National Lottery Heritage Fund, The Art Fund and The National Fund for Acquisitions.

In 2005, Marianne attended the reception for Holocaust survivors hosted by the Queen at St James's Palace. A year later she met the Queen again at the re-opening of Kelvingrove Art Gallery and Museum, where her story and a changing selection of her pictures (rotated annually) are on display in the exhibit *The Holocaust: Remembering for the Future*.

Marianne died on 11 December 2007. At her funeral in Glasgow she was mourned by hundreds from the Jewish and wider community, by those who knew her personally and by those who had encountered her through her Holocaust artworks and her testimony.

Obituaries celebrated her contribution to Holocaust education and her artistic talents. They also reflected on her many engaging characteristics and qualities; her charm, her love of colour, her smile, her compassion for others, her bravery and her spirited determination which made her such a life force for creativity and for good, even in the direst of circumstances.

To me, Marianne was a remarkable artist, generous, warm and loyal, a very smart woman who was a stickler for detail – getting things correct really mattered. Geraldine illustrated this by recalling a visit with Marianne to the cinema to see the film *Schindler's List*. At the end of the screening everyone sat still. Geraldine was in tears. Marianne leant over to her and said: 'Very good but no smell'.

Marianne becoming a Freeman of East Renfrewshire in 2003

Marianne was always very clear: we need to know about the Holocaust so that we never forget what happened and we can work to ensure it does not happen again. Through her legacy, her artworks and her words – her hope carries on.

As Susan said, 'Mausi was never bitter or vindictive about what had happened to her. She was always at pains to find the good in others, irrespective of their religion. She was a compassionate listener, broad minded and always interested in the lives of others.'

And Geraldine recalls, 'I always remember my mum saying it doesn't matter what colour you are – pink, yellow, black or white we are all the same and we should all love and respect each other.'

Today, Marianne's artworks are known, her words recorded and celebrated, and her art and words continue to inspire and educate people of all ages. Since Marianne passed away, Geraldine has spoken about Marianne to primary and secondary schools in Glasgow and South Lanarkshire, and with pupils at Glasgow Museums Resource Centre. In 2015 she contributed an interview about Marianne to the *Gathering the Voices Project* (which gathers stories of Holocaust refugees who escaped Nazi persecution and settled in Scotland).

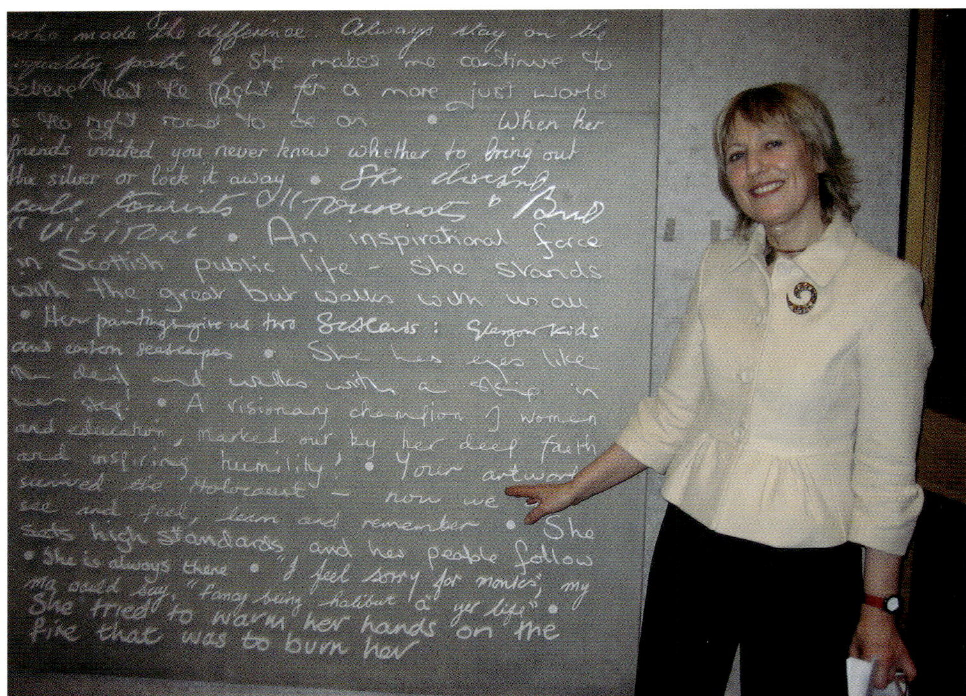

Deborah Haase at the Scottish Parliament unveiling of *Travelling the Distance*

Marianne features in the Scottish Jewish Archives Centre collections and displays, and in the Scottish Holocaust-era Study Centre display and digital catalogue.[15] In 2021 Education Scotland updated the Marianne Grant learning pack as an online teaching resource.

I was fortunate to have known Marianne all my life. Then I had the privilege as a curator with Glasgow Museums to work with Marianne to bring her Holocaust artworks and her story to a wider audience. I remember many special moments we shared. Foremost, of course, that day in 2001 when we went to the attic and she opened the trunk – the beginning of another chapter in Marianne's journey through life and the start of a new extraordinary journey for all of us. In 2006, when I was invited to contribute to *Travelling the Distance*[16] I paid tribute to Marianne, artist and Holocaust survivor, with the words 'Your artworks survived the Holocaust – now we can see and feel, learn and remember'.

My thanks to Geraldine Shenkin who helped with this biographical account, and to all the family for their support which would have meant so much to Marianne.

Notes

1 Marianne signed most of her artworks. She used a range of attributions, including MH, M Hermann, M. Hermannová, Mausi.
2 Place names given are Czech names: Syřema = German Surau, Žatec = German Zaats.
3 The Sudetenland is a historical German name referring to the regions along the northern, western and southern border of the present-day Czech Republic, which were largely inhabited by Sudeten Germans.
4 A chazan. In Judaism, this is the man who leads the congregation in prayers by singing in a synagogue.
5 Historically 'ghetto' was the term for the area of a city where the Jewish population was forced to live. The Nazis set up ghettos in major Eastern European cities, separated by walls and gates to keep Jewish people apart from inhabitants in the rest of the town.
6 Since Marianne wrote this, Theresienstadt (Terezín) is no longer in use by the army. It is an ordinary town, with people living in the townhouses where thousands died. The barracks are now mostly empty; some belong to the Theresienstadt Memorial Museum, with displays dedicated to ghetto life.
7 In September 1941, Reinhard Heydrich (1904–1942) became Deputy Reich Protector of Bohemia and Moravia. He was the German Commander of the Czech Protectorate, and an attempt to assassinate him was made in Prague on 27 May 1942. He died on 4 June as a result of his wounds.
8 Indian and Eskimo were terms previously in common use but have now been recognized as names imposed by non-indigenous people. The preferred terms today are Native American and Inuit.
9 Yeshiva Kindertransport – a lifesaving Kindertransport that rescued a number of young men studying in Orthodox Jewish schools known as Yeshivas.
10 *Cheder* is the religious school for children, where they are taught the basics of Judaism and the Hebrew language. *Shochet* is the person specially trained and licensed to perform *Shechita*, the Jewish religious and humane method of slaughtering permitted animals and poultry for food. *Mohel* is a devout person trained to perform the ritual Jewish circumcision.
11 Susan Slater (née Grant; 1952–2020) speaking at Woodside Park Synagogue in 2014.
12 Geraldine Shenkin (née Grant) speaking with the author.
13 Elizabeth Maxwell and Roman Halter, *Remembering for the Future* (conference, exhibition and publication), London and Boston: Little, Brown, 1988.
14 Yom HaShoah is the annual Jewish Remembrance Day for victims of the Holocaust.
15 Part of the Scottish Jewish Heritage Centre.
16 *Travelling the Distance* is a sculpture by Shauna McMullan commissioned by the Scottish Government, installed in the Scottish Parliament in Edinburgh alongside a photographic and digital exhibit which was added in 2019.

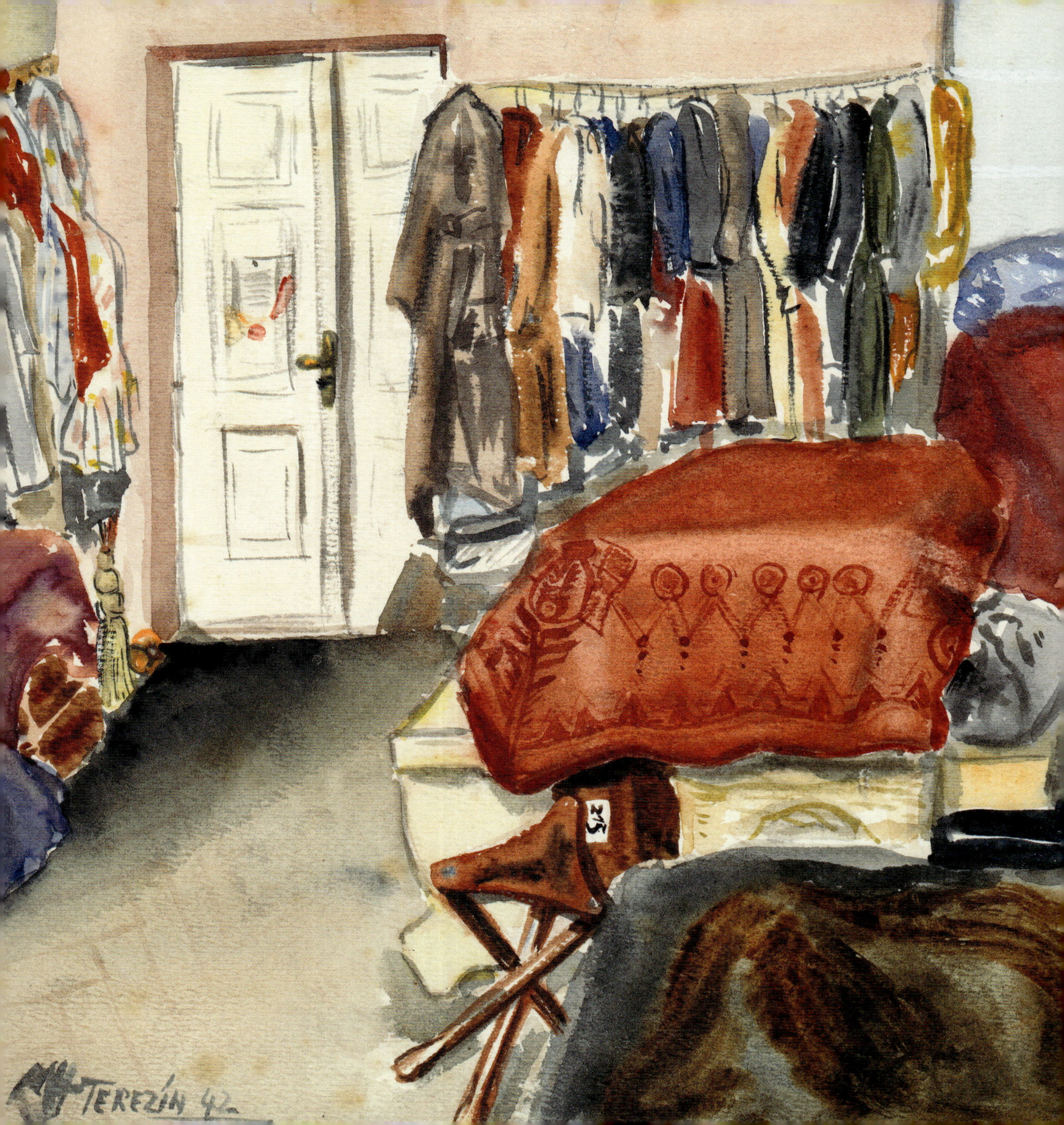
Terezín 42

Art as Witness Statement and Survival

Jo Meacock

THE PAINTINGS AND DRAWINGS of Holocaust survivor Marianne Grant occupy a unique place in the history of twentieth-century art. Marianne was no artistic trailblazer and was rather conservative in her aesthetic tastes. 'In general, I hate those hypermodern things', she declared in a letter to her friend Petr Erben (1921–2017) in October 1945. 'In my opinion, an artwork is truly art only when it expresses something, or when it speaks to people – either through its mood, or its narrative, or its beauty'.[1] Marianne's skill lay in seeing beauty in small things, despite desperate circumstances. This is evident in the art she produced in Theresienstadt concentration camp-ghetto, in the Children's Block at Auschwitz-Birkenau, in the German slave labour camps around Hamburg, and even in the extreme suffering and misery that was Bergen-Belsen. For Marianne, art was a gift that she used instinctively and resourcefully in times of immense fear and physical hardship. It not only gave her the will to live but ensured her survival. Tragically most artists did not survive the ghettos or the slave labour, concentration and extermination camps. For some, art was their downfall, bringing unwanted attention and punishment; in contrast, Marianne asserted 'it saved my life'.[2] Made inside the camps, from lived experience, Marianne's drawings have a power and authenticity that cannot be matched by the more artistically accomplished or psychologically penetrating compositions produced by official war artists commissioned by the Allies to record the camps at their liberation, or by artists processing the horrors of the Holocaust retrospectively. The significance of Marianne Grant's art lies in its status as first-hand testimony

Youth Room, 1942
(cat. 6, detail)

Art as life and hope

Marianne had felt the impulse to draw from a young age: 'I just drew from the day I was able to hold a pen or a pencil. It was just in me.'[3] Her mother Anna, was not only a milliner, but also an amateur artist, drawing watercolours of flowers and designing embroideries. Her father Rudolf too had an artistic eye, as a small-scale collector of ceramics and Persian carpets. He used to take Marianne to visit Prague's famous churches, such as the magnificent St Vitus Cathedral with its medieval paintings, mosaics and sculpture. From childhood, Marianne's artistic talents had been encouraged. Aged six she sent drawings as gifts to her eye specialist, whom she saw about a squint, and he had them published in a local daily paper. She believed in the power of her artistic talents, claiming she only passed geometry because her teacher liked her nature studies and animal drawings. In 1937 Marianne began attending the renowned school of graphic arts in Prague, Studio Rotter, set up by Jewish graphic designer Vilém Rotter (1903–1978), which had an excellent reputation, particularly for its courses in commercial art. There Marianne studied graphics and then fashion design, and started to paint in watercolours and oils.

The art that she made during imprisonment was an important connection for Marianne to her previous life, before the world had been turned on its head. Drawing helped to restore a sense of normality, offering rare moments of personal space and autonomy within the constraints of camp life. Writer, academic and Holocaust survivor Ruth Klüger (1931–2020), who had been a child in Theresienstadt, described it in her memoirs as 'a place so overcrowded, that it was virtually impossible occasionally to find a corner where you could talk to someone else'.[4] Marianne's watercolours of the living quarters in Theresienstadt reveal her determinedly clinging on to a semblance of 'home' (cats. 5 and 6). Consciously cheerful and optimistic, they contrast dramatically with the deprivation and lack of privacy highlighted by other artists, such as Charlotta Burešová (1904–1983). In *Mr Scheuer Visits his Wife* (fig. 1.1) she shows a cramped interior in which a young woman dresses, politely ignored by the other inmates, including a stooped old man visiting his sick wife, and an elderly woman, propped up on a suitcase, trying to focus on her devotional reading.

As for other Holocaust artists, drawing gave Marianne purpose, created resilience and enabled her to cope with the emotional strain of her circumstances. For a moment the daily reality of overcrowding, insanitary conditions, hunger, queues, illness (Marianne was seriously ill with hepatitis in Theresienstadt and pleurisy in Auschwitz), fear and deportation were forgotten. Her drawings express the wish that life might return to what it was, and her early drawings in Theresienstadt in particular convey hope for the future – her nude study of the actor Nava Shean (1919–2001; cat. 23) is a case in point. Nudes are very rare in Holocaust art because of the way people were routinely degraded and dehumanized by being forced to undress. However, at this point, when the horrors of Auschwitz, of naked men, women and children made to stand in the biting wind and rain waiting selection, were still to come, Marianne was thinking about improving her figure drawing skills, which she recognized as a personal artistic weakness, thinking of a life, a career in art, beyond the camps.

The first person Marianne had seen when she arrived in Auschwitz was a young boy she knew, Gusta, pushing a cart full of corpses. She wrote in 1945 that, 'I am still being possessed by memories that I cannot get rid of, and at night I dream about the worst kinds of things'.[5] Yet she chose not to paint these horrors. The fairy tale books Marianne created (cat. 14 and p.110) and the Disney characters she painted on the walls of the windowless

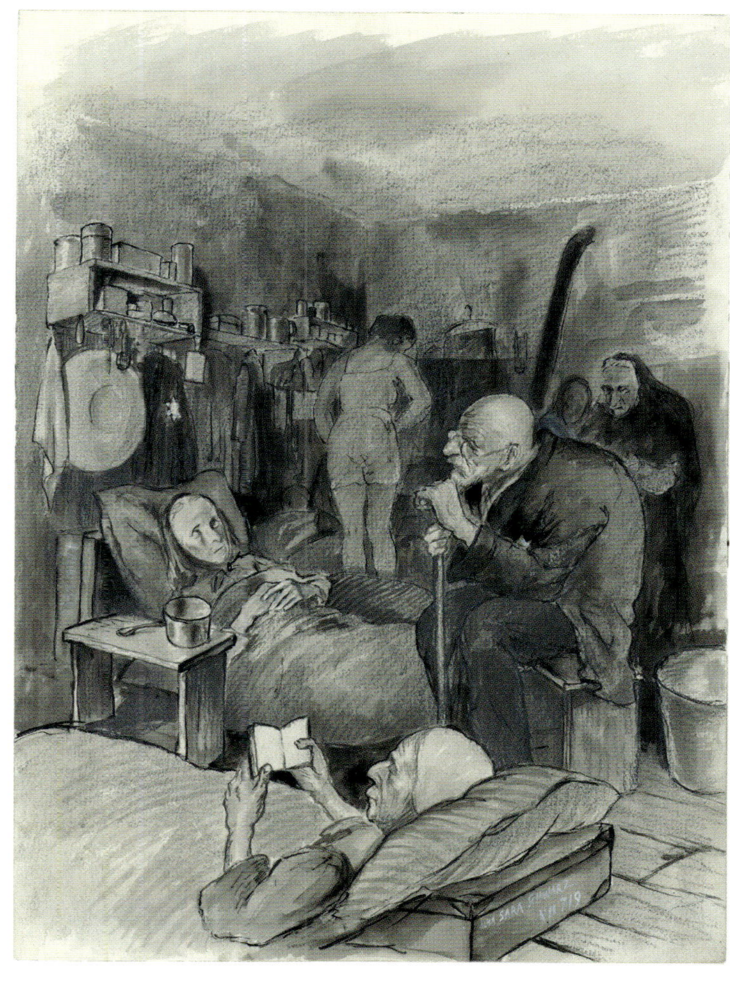

Fig. 1.1
Charlotte Burešová
Mr Scheuer Visits his Wife,
1942
india ink, gouache and pencil on paper
Collection of the Yad Vashem Art Museum, Jerusalem, gift of the artist

Children's Block in Auschwitz were an attempt to hold on to the innocence of childhood for her and the children she looked after; as a child she had loved the drawings of Walt Disney, particularly those of Mickey Mouse, who had made his screen debut in 1928. The plants and animals she painted formed a virtual window to a child's wonderland, countering the reality of Auschwitz. Marianne's art was about creating as happy and supportive an environment for the children as possible within the constraints of the camp and distancing them from trauma and pain. This was hard when the children's barrack was directly opposite the infirmary, with a clear view of not only the railway platform with its daily arrival of transports and people lining up for selection, but also of the crematoria chimneys that belched out black smoke. Yet Marianne's artworks are full of colour and hope.

Some artists worked in black and white, probably due to the scarcity of materials, but also powerfully conveying anguish and desolation. Marianne retained colour in her drawings throughout her journey through the camps – despair did not have a place. The hope that Marianne continued to feel throughout her life is expressed in the post-war act of adding spring buds and leaves to one of her Theresienstadt drawings (cat. 15).

Art materials

Marianne had brought a sketchbook, watercolours, pencils and crayons with her to Theresienstadt, where she was taken with her mother on 28 April 1942, aged 20. Personal belongings were restricted by weight to 50kg, so Marianne must have sacrificed other essentials in her small suitcase so that she would have the means to draw. She was fortunate to have held on to her art materials, as many had more innocuous personal belongings confiscated. The first picture Marianne made in Theresienstadt, *Inside the Bodenbacher Barrack* (cat. 5), was a watercolour on a page torn from the spiral bound sketchbook that she had brought with her.

Marianne probably obtained further art supplies by trading on the black market and appropriating materials intended for official purposes. Second in command of the youth garden, she was responsible for keeping a record of the produce that went to market in a ledger, which she sometimes illustrated with colourful vegetables (see fig. 2.8, p. 57). Her drawings of old German and Austrian people and musicians in the mock cafe at Theresienstadt were made on paper torn from what appears to be a book or ledger, perhaps from the youth garden. She also had the opportunity to smuggle sub-standard vegetables which she could barter for art materials.

Despite the panic Marianne must have felt when her mother was selected for transport to the east in December 1943, and her hurried decision to join her, a priority had been to make sure that her drawings were safe. Her friend Petr Erben was entrusted to look after them. When he himself faced transportation, he gave Marianne's drawings to a friend who took them back to Prague, ensuring their survival. This had been a shrewd move on Marianne's part, as all her personal belongings were confiscated on arrival at Auschwitz.

In the camps most artists had to improvise materials. Brushes were created from items such as twigs, hair, feathers and dried grass, with colours extracted from food scraps, clothing and rusted metal. Crude pencils were fashioned from charred splinters of wood. *Youth Room* (cat. 7) was painted with a fragment of wood. Images were made on scraps of paper, walls and floors.[6] Personal artwork was forbidden, so these were largely produced in secret, hidden and often destroyed to avoid punishment, even death. However, in Auschwitz Marianne was actually given art supplies by her captors. One Slovak guard asked her to create fairy tale books for his children for Christmas and to draw a beautiful Roma woman in the 'Gypsy Camp', giving her the materials she needed for this. The notorious SS doctor Josef Mengele (1911–1979), who had a particular interest in identical twins and people of restricted growth, ordered Marianne to draw twin girls with unusual skin markings and the ancestral tree of a Hungarian dwarf family, for which she was given the use of exquisite architectural drawing tools and beautiful thick paper. She and Dina Babbitt (née Gottliebová; 1923–2009) were also given supplies to paint colourful murals on the walls of the Children's Block.

In Neugraben Concentration Camp Marianne continued to find her artistic skills in demand in official quarters and was given paints and pens to decorate the walls of the officers' dining hall with cheerful culinary imagery. Marianne also used these art materials for her own private drawings, taking them with her to Bergen-Belsen in April 1945, where she created some of her most harrowing images. All official camp organization had broken down by this time, as the Allies were approaching, so she no longer had to fear reprisals for her drawings, but paper was still hard to come by. It is not surprising that some of these works are in poor condition, with soiling, stains, tears and creases; *British army arriving* (cat. 37) is not only torn but covered in Belsen mud. These drawings constitute the most authentic and powerful record of atrocity and liberation. Once the British arrived, Marianne had a supply of paper from the office job to which she was appointed, and she found herself commissioned by individual British soldiers as a kind of unofficial war artist to document the horror of the camp, for which she would have undoubtedly been given materials.

Artistic community

By the time Bergen-Belsen was liberated, most Jewish interned artists had perished. However, at Theresienstadt Marianne had been one of a large number of artists. The Nazis imprisoned more creative individuals there than at any other camp, part of an intricately constructed deception to the world of a Jewish 'spa town' whose inhabitants enjoyed an ongoing cultural life. Her drawings from this time include studies of musicians, artists, writers and actors that she met. Many artists naturally chose to work in the *Technische Abteilung* (Technical Drawing Department) of the Jewish ghetto administration, where they were engaged in producing graphs, illustrations for official reports, maps, camp signage and propaganda posters. The workshop was headed by Czech artist Bedřich Fritta (professional pseudonym Fritz Taussig; 1906–1944), shown standing third from the right in a drawing by Leo Haas (1901–1983; fig. 1.2). Positions were largely, although not exclusively, filled by men, including Czech artists Ferdinand ('Felix') Bloch (1898–1944), Haas, František Petr Kien (1919–1944) and Otto Ungar (1901–1945).[7] Other artists worked at the *Lautscher Werkstätte* (Lautsch Company Workshops) producing decorative objects, paintings and copies of Old Masters works to decorate the homes and clubhouse of the SS, or to sell outside the camp. More women worked in this workshop, including the Czech artists Charlotta Burešová, Hilda Lohsing Zadiková (1890–1974) and Greta Weinberger, the mother of Marianne's friend Gerhard (Gert) Weinberger (later Vallen), with whom Marianne sketched and painted in her spare time.[8]

One might have expected Marianne to choose to work in one of these departments, where artists experienced less harsh working conditions and had access to precious art

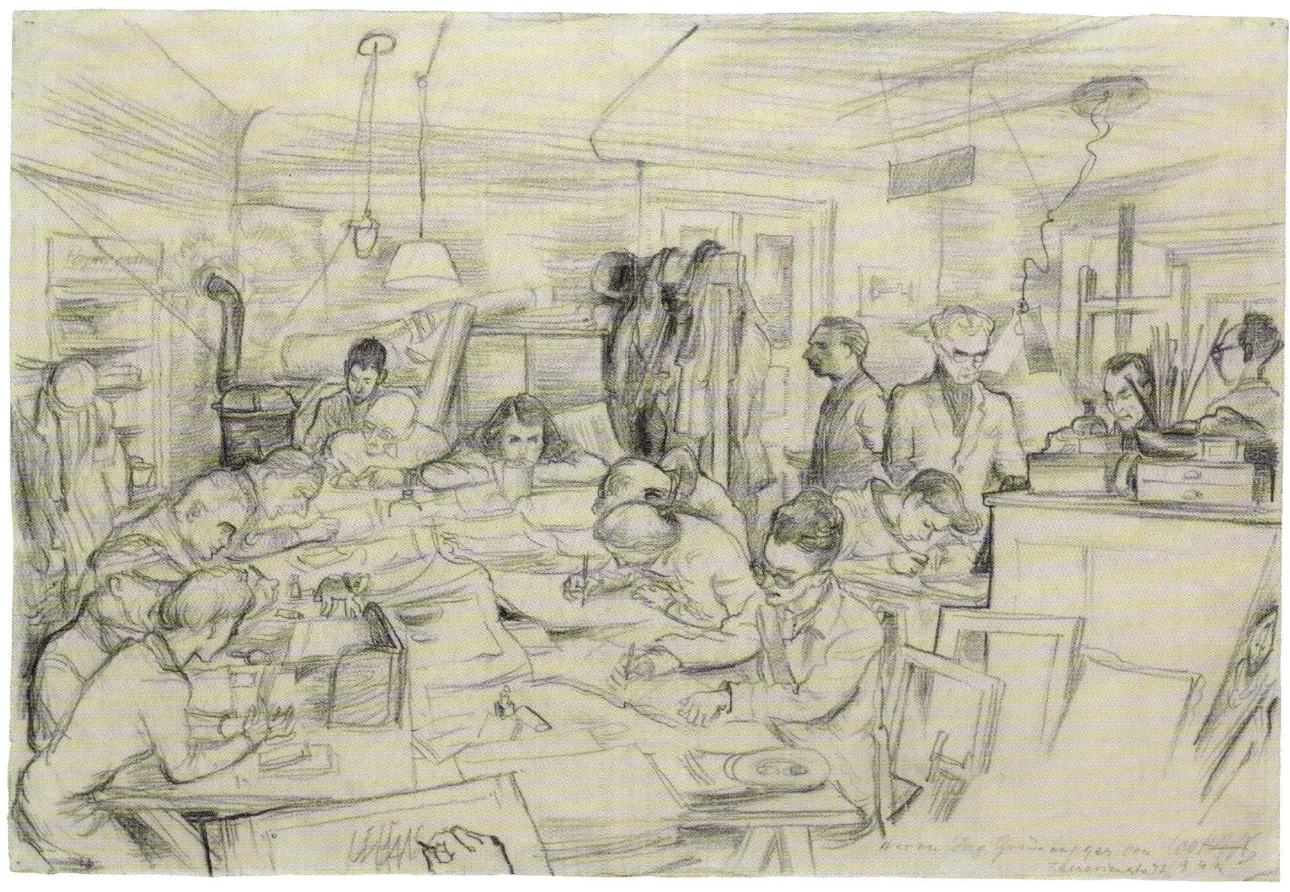

Fig. 1.2
Leo Haas
Drafting Room, Terezin, 1943
pencil and black chalk on paper
© David Haas, Daniel Haas, Ronny Haas, Michael Haas Foell
Collection of Terezin Memorial, PT1541

materials. Gert and another of her friends, František Lukáš (Lustig) (1911–1996; cat. 13), both worked in the Technical Department. However, women artists more often chose to work in another of the camp's small industries, keeping their artistic activities private. The Bauhaus designer Friedl Dicker-Brandeis (1898–1944), whose example may have been inspirational for Marianne later in the Children's Block in Auschwitz, chose to work in education and gave children lessons in art. One of her students, Helga Pollak-Kinsky (1930–2020), recalled: 'Each child could draw freely according to its imagination and wishes. This was extraordinary. It gave us a different life, another atmosphere. […] She somehow managed to awaken in us a positive attitude about our situation, about living in Theresienstadt'.[9]

Marianne simply stated: 'I chose to work in agriculture as I was told it was more lucrative'. However, the situation was more complex than this implies. Her experience with the Zionist El Al group as a teenager (see pp. 49–56) was a significant factor in her choice, and the relative freedom and health benefits that agricultural work provided must also have been attractive. Those involved in agricultural labour had fresh air, exercise and better access to food. They were also in the privileged position of being allowed outside the ghetto walls. Agricultural work proved lifesaving for many girls and young women who were protected from being transported to Auschwitz because their labour was necessary for food production. Marianne also enjoyed working with children, so the role of a youth garden leader was well suited to her.

It is remarkable that Marianne found the strength to draw after a physically demanding 12-hour shift, a day which started with Hebrew lessons at 5a.m. However, her art gave her focus and purpose and throughout it she strengthened friendships and brought a little joy to those around her. She recalled: 'I made little fancy booklets, cards etc. if it was one of my friends' birthday'. For many in the camps friendship, support and small acts of kindness were key to survival. Most of Marianne's art modestly captured daily life around her. In a diaristic way she drew bed linen being aired, the corner she made a home, children playing, Shabbat get-togethers, parental visits to the youth dormitory and views of the barracks. Importantly she also drew simple portrait heads of the elderly, whom she also helped practically, restoring lost dignity and respect, safeguarding their memory on paper. This is typical of women artists in the camps who tended to ignore atrocity and abuse in their art, instead focusing on acts of domesticity, cleanliness and care, in works that showed compassion and stressed solidarity.[10]

Art as resistance

For some artists, picture making was a form of resistance. Marianne did not use her art to directly criticize the regime, unlike others in Theresienstadt such as Bloch, Haas, Fritta, Ungar and the dermatologist artist Dr Karel Fleischmann (1897–1944). Fritta's *Quarters of the Aged* (fig. 1.3) with its skeletal figures lying prone on wooden bunks in the dark, behind bars, like corpses in a mortuary, is a direct challenge to the lies being propagated by the Germans to the world about the nature of this supposed Jewish cultural town. Neither did Marianne participate in the underground movement which operated from within the Children's Block at Auschwitz, although she was aware of plans for revolt after those on the September transport from Theresienstadt were gassed.[11] It all carried too much risk in an environment where people were hanged for minor infringements. In the summer of 1944 after the Red Cross visit to Theresienstadt, many artists were accused of producing *Greuelpropaganda* (atrocity propaganda) and taken with their families to the *Kleine Festung* (Small Fortress) where they were interrogated and tortured. The fingers of Ungar's right hand were brutally crushed and mutilated in a symbolic act by the SS. Fritta and Bloch died as the result of their beatings.[12]

However, there is a sinister suggestion of surveillance and threat in works like Marianne's *Courtyard of Bodenbacher Barrack* (cat. 4), in which a sturdy military figure is seen watching people in the courtyard below. And in her drawing of the ghetto police she caricatures black market activity going on behind the back of the Jewish council authorities (cat. 19). Further, it is tempting to see the *Hansel and Gretel* and *Little Red Riding Hood* storybooks that Marianne created for a Slovak guard in Auschwitz as a form of covert criticism, like the concerts and theatre productions held in Theresienstadt, which constituted a thinly veiled commentary on the injustice and plight of their situation. In the opera *Brundibár*, first staged in Theresienstadt

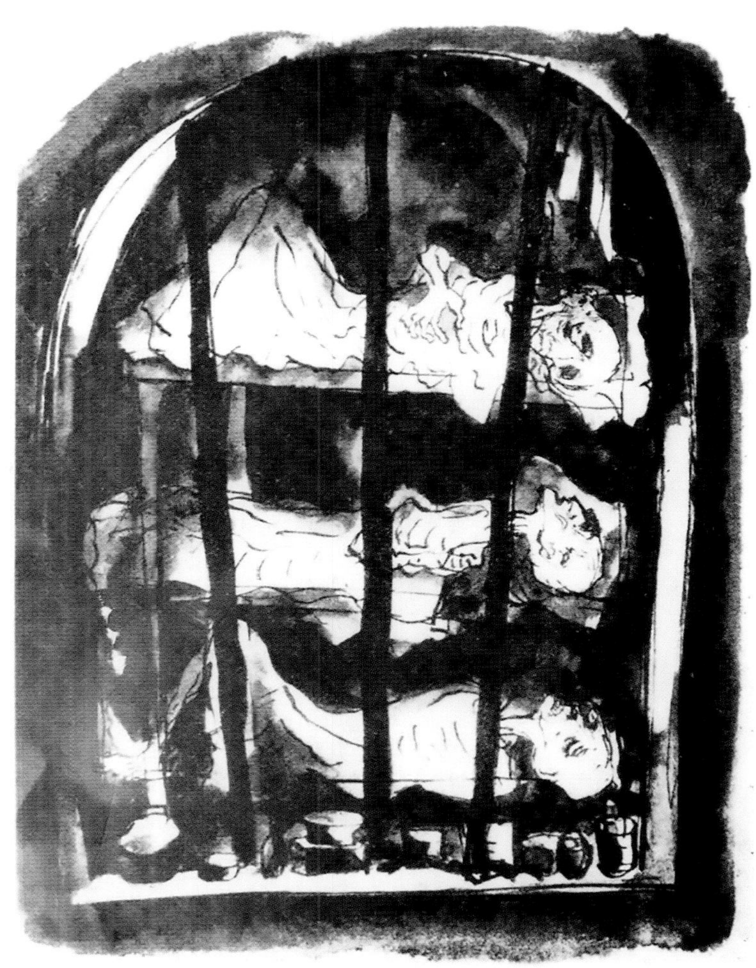

Fig. 1.3
Bedřich Fritta
Quarters of the Aged,
1943–44
pen, brush and ink wash
Thomas Fritta Haas
collection, acc. No. 21247
Public domain via
Wikimedia Commons

in September 1943, an evil organ grinder, who wouldn't let the children sing in the market square, is eventually defeated. Made in sight of Auschwitz's crematoria chimneys, Marianne's *Hansel and Gretel* picture book, in which a witch tries to force children into an oven but is pushed into the oven herself, carries unspeakable weight and significance; before 8 March 1944, when those on the September transit from Theresienstadt were murdered en masse, the gas chambers were only a rumour, but Marianne had smelt 'the stench of burning hair and flesh'.[13] She had also made an earlier version in Theresienstadt when Nazi genocide was as yet unknown. Nonetheless, in that faked-up model ghetto, the story of a cottage made of gingerbread and sugar that hides a dark secret also has extreme poignancy and cannot have been chosen unwittingly.

Similarly, Dina and Marianne's drawings on the wall of the Children's Block in Auschwitz may constitute a deeper comment on the situation in which they found themselves. Depicting children of the world in all their ethnic plurality, was Marianne subtly countering the dark racial cleansing programme of the Nazis, educating about diversity and difference? If so, these were incredibly daring acts. The Children's Block was supervised by Mengele, and everyone knew that if they put a foot wrong they would pay with their life. Marianne was brave. She secretly taught languages and nature study, when supervisors weren't officially allowed to teach. However, her criticisms during imprisonment were understandably furtive. Marianne had to survive for her mother for whom she felt immense responsibility and filial duty, particularly since the death of her father in April 1938.

Art as survival

Marianne's courage allied with a pragmatic and resourceful side is evident throughout her story. In Prague in the autumn of 1941, when there was a clamp down on educational and cultural activities, she taught teenage Jewish girls fashion design in her home, had clandestine lessons from a Czech sculptor who let her work in his studio, and learned how to repair antique china and sew lingerie in the back of a shop, at some risk to the Czech owner. In all this she was trying to gain as much professional and practical expertise as possible, recognizing that this was intrinsic to survival.

In Auschwitz, building on her experience working with the youth garden at Theresienstadt, Marianne volunteered to join a select team of 20 young counsellor-educators headed by the charismatic, gay Zionist youth movement leader Fredy Hirsch (1916–1944), looking after around 600 youngsters in the Children's Block. This brought many advantages, including better food rations, heated barracks, no punishing physical labour and a roll call that did not involve standing in the cold for hours (for the others a typical day began about 4.30a.m. with roll call that lasted two to three hours irrespective of the weather, with repeated counting, endless waiting, during which time those who fell were punished). Unlike the rest of the camp, where violence and theft were rife, the Children's Block cultivated an environment of friendship, trust and mutual support, where the SS did not abuse children or counsellors.

In Bergen-Belsen, after liberation by the British, Marianne became an interpreter for the British army because she spoke fluent Czech, German and English, as well as some French and Yiddish. She also worked in the office, distributing cigarettes. She found that the British officers were prepared to pay for her drawings: 'I had absolutely nothing and I was offered a pound each which was wonderful.' Through this Marianne was able to reclaim control of her situation and of her identity. Marianne wrote to Petr in 18 October 1945: 'even in concentration camps, I haven't changed. But I gained some business spirit, it is a miracle.' Reflecting on her survival, Marianne noted that she had been protected because her skills had been needed. She learnt the trick of making herself indispensable; in many instances her art was key to this.

Marianne showed tremendous strength of mind particularly in her drawings at Bergen-Belsen, in which she bore witness to scenes of extreme trauma, cruelty and horror. When Marianne arrived on 5 April 1945, she was shocked to see the condition of its inmates, dying from typhoid, hunger and exhaustion, barely distinguishable from the thousands of unburied corpses filling the huts and lying in piles on the ground. Marianne recalled that they looked 'Barely human. They were absolutely horrific'. Her instinct was to paint everything she saw. 'I started to paint like crazy. I had nothing to do. There was no work to do, no cooking to do, no nothing to do, so […] I painted the dead bodies.'[14] In these harrowing images of emaciation, brokenness and suffering, Marianne was able to retain an astonishing aesthetic detachment that one might expect from an experienced war artist.

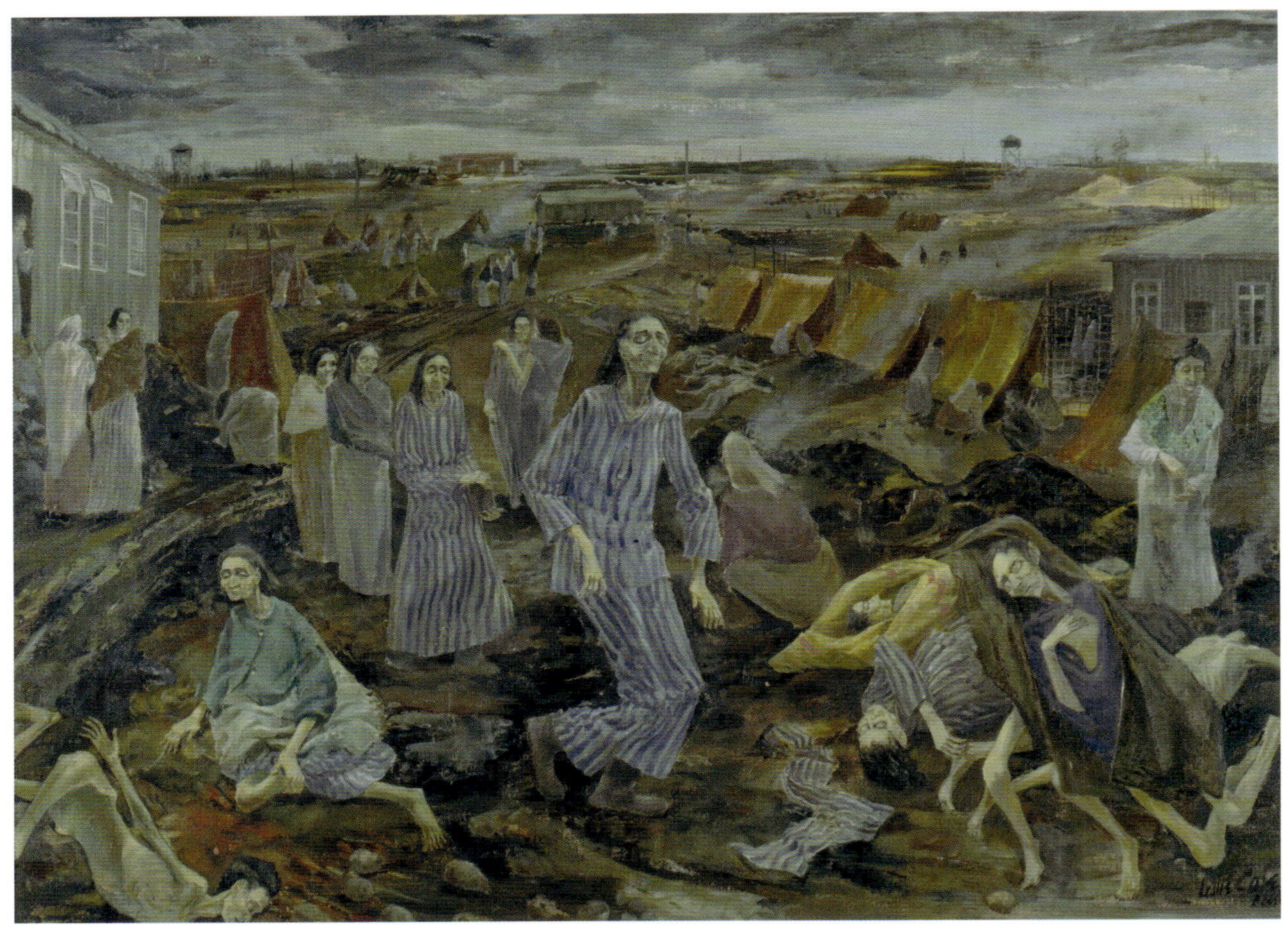

Fig. 1.4
Leslie Cole
Belsen Camp: The Compound for Women, 1945
oil on canvas
© IWM (ART LD 5104)

Four British war artists visited Bergen-Belsen after its liberation: Leslie Cole (1910–76), Mary Kessell (1914–1977), Sgt Eric Taylor (1909–1999) and Doris Zinkeisen (1898–1991). The artworks they produced are among the most graphic and distressing of the entire war. Zinkeisen was at Belsen because of her work with the Red Cross and Taylor as one of the camp's liberators. Neither was a salaried war artist, but sold their drawings to the War Artists' Advisory Committee, which was established to commission and purchase artworks documenting the war. Kessell did not actually arrive until August and so was not a direct witness to the immediate horror at liberation. Cole, a full-time war artist, had already

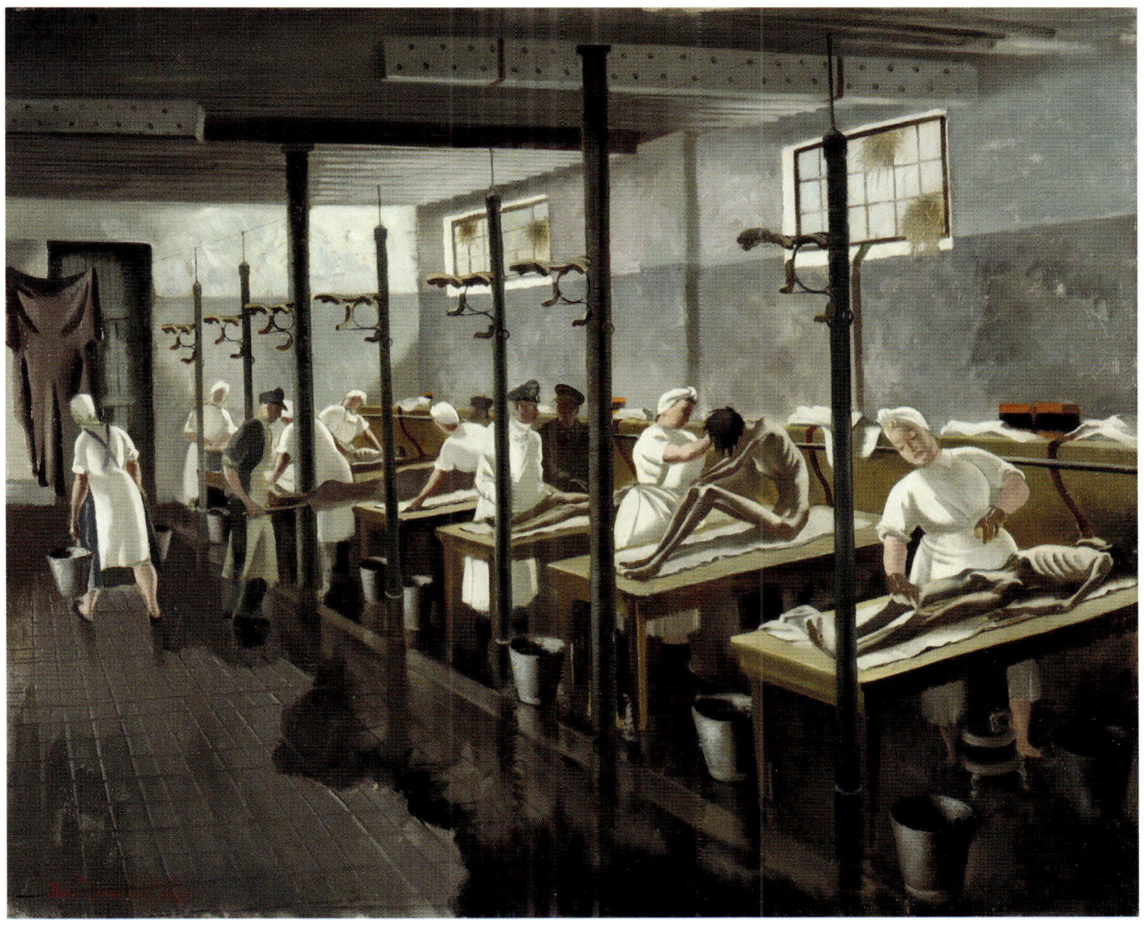

experienced atrocities, having previously been in Malta documenting the failed attempt by the Germans to take the island in 1943 and the brutality of the Greek Communist ELAS group after German withdrawal. His *Belsen Camp: The Compound for Women* (fig. 1.4) shows half-dead women navigating the camp in an almost surreal dream-state. In Zinkeisen's *Human Laundry: Belsen, April 1945* (fig. 1.5) extremely emaciated figures are decontaminated in production-line fashion, an eloquent visual comment on the dehumanization of Holocaust victims. However, both are stagey, lacking the raw immediacy of Marianne's drawings.

Fig. 1.5
Doris Zinkeisen
Human Laundry: Belsen, April 1945, 1945
oil on canvas
© IWM (ART LD 5468)

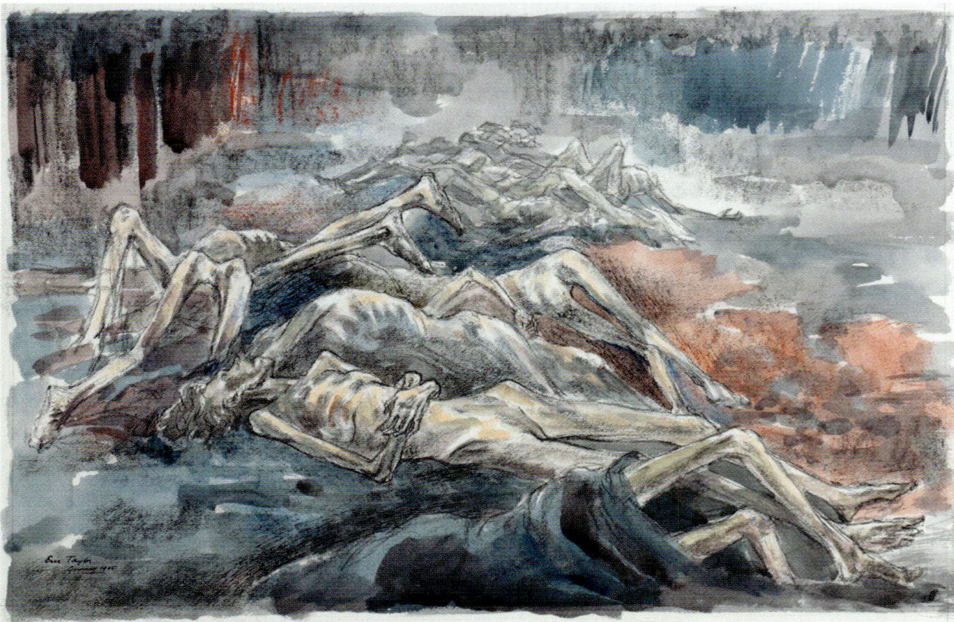

Fig. 1.6
Eric Taylor
Human Wreckage at Belsen Concentration Camp, 1945, 1945
watercolour on paper
© IWM (ART LD5588)

Unlike Taylor's *Human Wreckage at Belsen Concentration Camp, 1945* (fig. 1.6) with its confusion of bodies and disintegration of form, Marianne largely focused on identifiable, often single figures. Women, living and dead, retain their identities and defining features. In this way she asserts them as individuals, affirming beauty, restoring dignity. She was particularly haunted by the figure of a red-haired young woman, 'she was young and she was lying there naked on the ground and it was already spring and the birches had little leaves, and that was the beauty of it' (cat. 31).[15] This was an important reaction against the anonymity of the camps where clothes and personal belongings were seized, hair was often shorn and internees became the number tattooed on their arm (one of the first things Marianne did on liberation was to have her tattoo removed). When her Bergen-Belsen watercolours were exhibited by the Public Association of Art and Culture in Gothenburg, Sweden, in November–December 1945, a local reviewer noted: 'they are scenes of experienced horror registered by a trained eye and sensitive hand. But Marianne has been an artist long enough to also give a touch of grandeur and beauty to the emaciated bodies, left to meet their fate naked.'[16]

Marianne's paintings and drawings are the testimony of a survivor, a link between the living and the dead.[17] The power of her work was recognized by a member of the United Nations Relief and Rehabilitation Administration in Lübeck, probably the Chicago-based Fred Hoehler (1893–1969), Director of the Division on Displaced Persons, who talked to her about the possibility of organizing an exhibition of her oil paintings in New York. The significance of her work was also acknowledged by Margaret Emmeline Montgomery (née Drennan) (1901–1993), the sister-in-law of Field Marshal Montgomery (1887–1976), who was working with the British Red Cross in Belsen and recommended Marianne's work to the Home Office.[18] Yet none of her remarkable artwork was acquired for the nation.

However, for Marianne her art was less about reportage or remembrance for future generations, and more a source of personal hope and strength in the darkest of times. Her artistic skills proved key to her survival, bringing extra provisions, strengthening friendships and creating community. The unique art collection, purchased from her by Glasgow Museums in 2004, is a witness statement, a memorial to those who perished, but more importantly, it is a document of survival.

Notes

1   Marianne to Petr Erben, 21 October 1945. Family archive.

2   *Marianne's Story*, interview by Rex Bloomstein, Nucleus Production for Glasgow Museums, 2002, tape 6. Marianne Grant Collection Archive, Glasgow Museums, GMA.2021.1.

3   Bloomstein, 2002, tape 1. Marianne Grant Collection Archive, Glasgow Museums, GMA.2021.1.

4   Ruth Klüger, *Weiter leben: Eine Jugend*, Göttingen, 1992, pp. 85–87, quoted in Anne D. Dutlinger (ed.), *Art, Music and Education as Strategies for Survival: Theresienstadt 1941–45*, Herodias, New York & London, 2000, p. 33.

5   Marianne to Petr Erben, 2 November 1945. Family archive.

6   Monica Bohm-Duchen, *Art and the Second World War*, Lund Humphries, Farnham, 2013, p. 193.

7   Johanna Branson, 'Seeing through "paradise": art and propaganda in Terézin', in *Seeing Through 'paradise': Artists and the Terézin Concentration Camp*, exh. cat., Massachusetts College of Art, 6 March – 4 May 1991, Boston, 1991, p. 40.

8   Dutlinger, p. 38.

9   Dutlinger, p. 76.

10 Bohm-Duchen, p. 197.

11 *It Didn't Have to be Me*, interview by Deborah Haase, Glasgow Museums, 2001, Marianne Grant Collection Archive, Glasgow Museums, GMA.2021.1.

12 Gerald Green, *The Artists of Terezin*, Hawthorn, New York, pp. 111–22.

13 Bloomstein, 2002, tape 4. Marianne Grant Collection Archive, Glasgow Museums, GMA.2021.1.

14 Excerpt from *Marianne's Story*, interview by Rex Bloomstein, Nucleus Production, 2002, tape 5, Marianne Grant Collection Archive, Glasgow Museums, GMA.2021.1.

15 Bloomstein, 2002, tape 5. Marianne Grant Collection Archive, Glasgow Museums, GMA.2021.1.

16 Sten Karing, 'Nya konstintryck', review of Public Association of Art and Culture and Arbetarnas Bildningsförbund (ABF) exhibition, Gothenburg, Sweden, 7 December 1945. Translation Victoria Rudebark. Family archive.

17 Glenn Sujo, *Legacies of Silence: The Visual Arts and Holocaust Memory*, Philip Wilson and Imperial War Museum, London, 2001, p. 10.

18 Marianne to Petr Erben, 1 October 1945. Family archive.

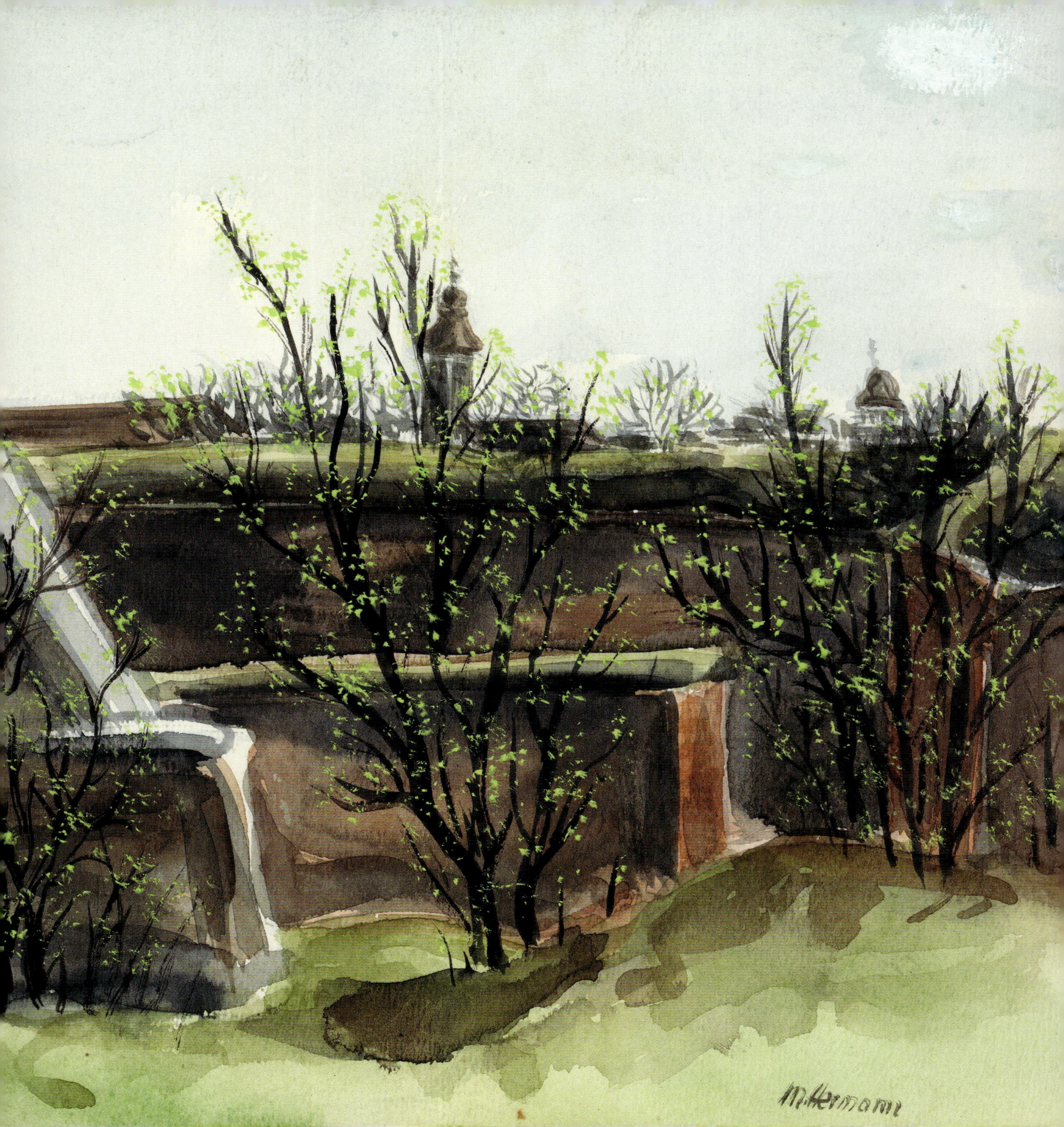

M. Hermann

Stars in Place of Butterflies
Marianne and the Zionist Movement

Peter Tuka

The Butterfly
by Pavel Friedmann (1921–1944)

the last the very last
so richly bitterly dazzlingly yellow
      as if the Sun's tears twinkled against the white stone
such such a yellow
it floated lightly and went up high
it went surely surely aimed to kiss my world goodbye

for seven weeks I've lived in here
ghettoized
my people have found me
the dandelions call to me
and so do white branches of chestnut tree
      here I haven't seen a butterfly

that one then was the last
butterflies don't live here   in the ghetto.

THE BUTTERFLY is a famous poem written by Pavel Friedmann (1921–1944) in Theresienstadt ghetto on 4 June 1942.[1] In this poem, a butterfly, the ultimate symbol of freedom, floats away until it disappears forever. Throughout, the bright and vivid colour yellow sharply alternates with dull and deathly white. The sun, the symbol of life, is crying. The vital energy of its warm yellow glare meets the coldness of the white stone. Later, the vibrant yellow of blooming dandelions turns into the lifeless white of a drying chestnut tree. The yellow butterfly vanishes into the unreachable heights. Seven weeks in Theresienstadt ghetto were enough for Pavel Friedmann to understand the reality of this place – a place where freedom ends and where life met death. His journey through the inferno of the Holocaust started on 28 April 1942, on the very same transport from Prague to Theresienstadt as his friend Marianne. Out of 999 people on this transport, only 72 survived until liberation by the Allies; 927 were murdered.[2] Marianne was among the lucky ones: Pavel, like countless other talented young Jews, was murdered in Auschwitz.

The loss of freedom, so aptly expressed in Pavel's poem, did not suddenly happen overnight with deportation. Confinement behind the ghetto walls was a further escalation of the ongoing policy of extermination which the Nazis called 'The Final Solution to the Jewish Question'. With the German invasion of Czechoslovakia, and the establishment of the Protectorate of Bohemia and Moravia on 15 March 1939, the process of systematic discrimination and exclusion that had pushed the local Jewish minority to the margins of society intensified sharply. The principles of the 1935 Nuremberg Race Laws were quickly implemented, and the number of discriminatory measures was growing rapidly, affecting all spheres of everyday life. For example, Jews were denied access to public places such as town squares and parks. In Prague, the first to which entry was prohibited was Stromovka, the vast park near which Marianne's family lived before the war. These prohibitions quickly extended across all public areas including theatres, libraries, sports facilities and restaurants. Jews were only allowed to use specially allocated sections on public transport, they could only do their shopping between 3p.m. and 5p.m. by which time most of the goods had already been sold, and a curfew of 8p.m. was enforced. Jewish professionals such as lawyers, doctors, managers, but also musicians, actors and many others, were forbidden to practise their professions. Beginning in the school year 1939/40, Jewish children were expelled from schools.[3] Jewish properties were systematically confiscated; in Prague, many Jews were

p. 46:
Youth Garden, 1942/43
(cat.15, detail)

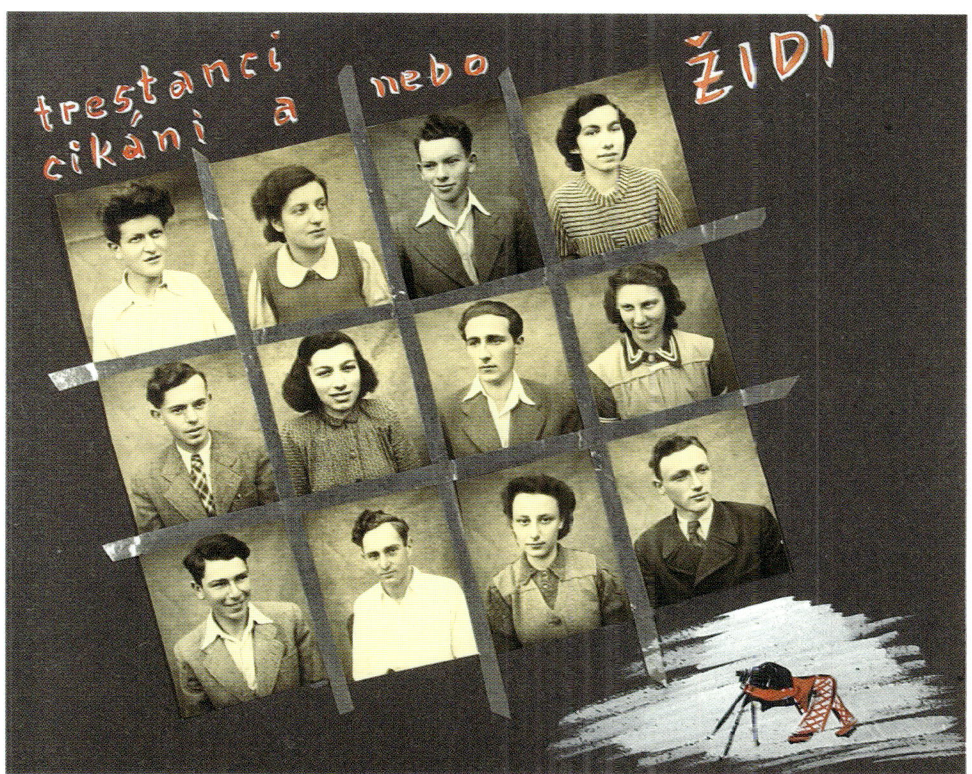

Fig. 2.1 'Convicts, Gypsies or JEWS', Summer 1941, a group of young Zionists, all members of El Al, on Hachshara near the village of Pátek u Louny. Marianne is far right, middle row, Pavel Friedmann is far left, top row. The identities of the others are unconfirmed. Page from Marianne's photograph album, family archive

forcibly rehoused from their desirable, spacious homes to shared apartments with one room per family, and the inconvenience of a shared kitchen and bathroom. This is when Marianne and her mother were forced to leave their flat in Prague-Holešovice, a modern neighbourhood where Jews were now no longer permitted to live. These are only a handful of examples of the many antisemitic laws put into practice by the occupying Nazis. The ultimate aim of these prohibitions was the gradual isolation of Jews from the rest of Czech and German society (at the time there was a large German-speaking population living in Prague and other parts of the country, mainly in the region bordering with Germany and Austria). Thus, even prior to the start of the mass deportations from the Protectorate in October 1941, Jews found themselves entrapped in this 'ghetto without walls' – excluded from society and deprived of their rights.

Quite telling of this situation is Marianne's photographic collage of summer 1941 (fig. 2.1) inscribed 'trestanci, cikáni a nebo ŽIDI' which translates into English as 'convicts, gypsies or JEWS'. Ironically, not realizing how predictive of the near future this would actually be, she symbolically placed the portraits of herself, Pavel and 10 other friends behind bars. Beside the negative themes of persecution, confinement and loss of freedom, Pavel's poem and Marianne's collage have another important element in common – the motif of friendship. In Pavel's poem, his traumatic experience of ghettoization is immediately counterbalanced with the presence of 'my people'. Similarly, in Marianne's collage, her enforced identity as a convict is eased by the presence of her closest friends. Both Marianne and Pavel were members of a tight-knit collective of young Zionists, who remained well organized even after their deportation to Theresienstadt. This is very important, because the strong bonds and friendships Marianne created in the early years of the war helped her not only to get through the years of humiliation and elimination of personal rights and freedoms, but ultimately had a great impact on her survival of the horrors of the Nazi concentration camps, particularly in Theresienstadt and Auschwitz. These bonds were little lights in the darkness of the Holocaust, in a world full of yellow stars but no butterflies.

This photographic collage is a page from Marianne's Hachshara photo album. Hachshara was agricultural training undertaken by members of Zionist movements in preparation for their future aliyah[4] to Pre-State Israel, where they would lead a life of collective agriculture in a kibbutz, a workers' settlement. Although the Zionist programme of actual emigration was thwarted soon after the Nazi occupation, in the new reality that confronted the Jews of Czechoslovakia, membership of Zionist movements and Hachshara training created a rare and much-needed environment for self-realization. Marianne belonged to El Al, an association of Jewish youth. A fellow member, Eva Adorian (1926–2019), recalled: 'we were meeting during the occupation and that was a huge support for ourselves. Because everything was closed for us – socially and ideologically. We got everything we needed in this small group, also friendship. […] The only thing we were left with was this group, and here we could develop as people and also build social relations.'[5] El Al was one of a number of Jewish Zionist youth movements, but the only one to use Czech as its official language. It was formed in 1937 in Prague with the aim of bringing Czech-speaking Jewish youth towards Zionism, to teach them Hebrew, and to lead discussions about Jewish culture and traditions. In the beginning, El Al had only some 50 members in Prague, but numbers

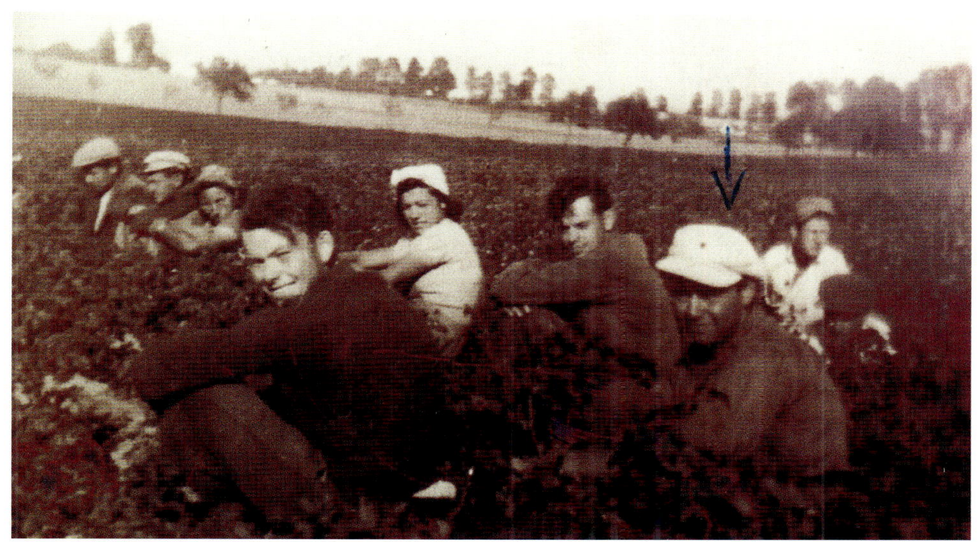

Fig. 2.2 At Hachshara in 1940 or 1941. The arrow points to Otto Kraus. Pavel Friedmann and Marianne were there too – Marianne may be third from left. Photograph © Dita Kraus, reproduced by kind permission

began to grow swiftly with the rising tide of ant semitism, and in the early days of German occupation over 250 young people were organized in more than 20 branches around the Protectorate.[6] Otto Kraus (1921–2000; fig. 2.2) Marianne's friend and El Al member, most aptly identified the pressing troubles of many of the Czech Jewish youth that led them to join the ranks of Zionists – the identity crisis.[7] Many of them grew up in families with Czech traditions and customs, and with an awareness of Czech nationalism. With the occupation, Nazism not only took their homeland, but by diminishing them, by making them lesser and unwanted members of society, also took away their sense of belonging. Suddenly, these Jewish youngsters found themselves surrounded by a society in which there was no place for them. Rachel Har-Tsvi (1922–2010) remembered: 'all my world grew dark. I cannot describe the crisis of losing one's identity and the agony of alienation. The only anchor left, the last resort, was to join the Zionist youth movement […].'[8] Here, in a close group of equals, young Jewish people could embrace their collective identity, gain a new sense of direction, and, at least temporarily, chase away fears about the future. Being involved in Hachshara and in agricultural work was particularly effective in all these aspects. Due to the war, the summers of 1940 and 1941 saw a great shortage of agricultural workers, which gave an opportunity for

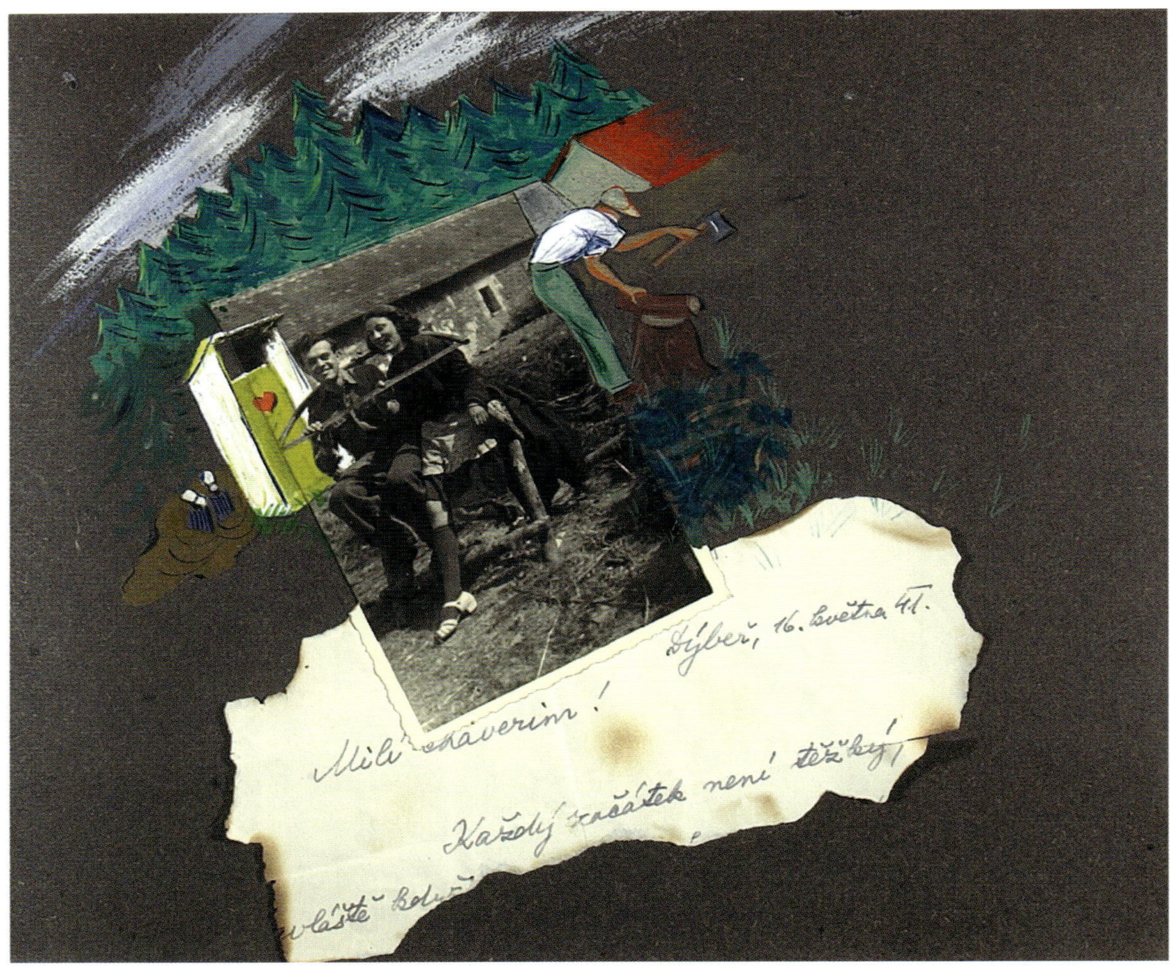

Fig. 2.3 Dýbeř, 16. Května 41. Milí chaverim! Každý začátek není těžký, zvlášte když… (Dýbeř, 16 May 1941. 'Dear comrades! Not every beginning is difficult, especially when…') Family archive

Hechalutz (an umbrella organization under which numerous youth movements joined their efforts) to send dozens of Hachshara groups to farms all over the Protectorate. These groups of 10 to 12 people worked hard, often 12 hours a day, for food and a place to sleep, occasionally for a minimal amount of money.[9] Few of them were used to hard physical labour, but despite it all, Marianne's best friend Ruth Bondy (1923–2017; see cat. 22) remembers it as 'the most wonderful time in our lives', adding that 'at the end of the week we met with friends from the youth movement El Al, we went hiking, we danced

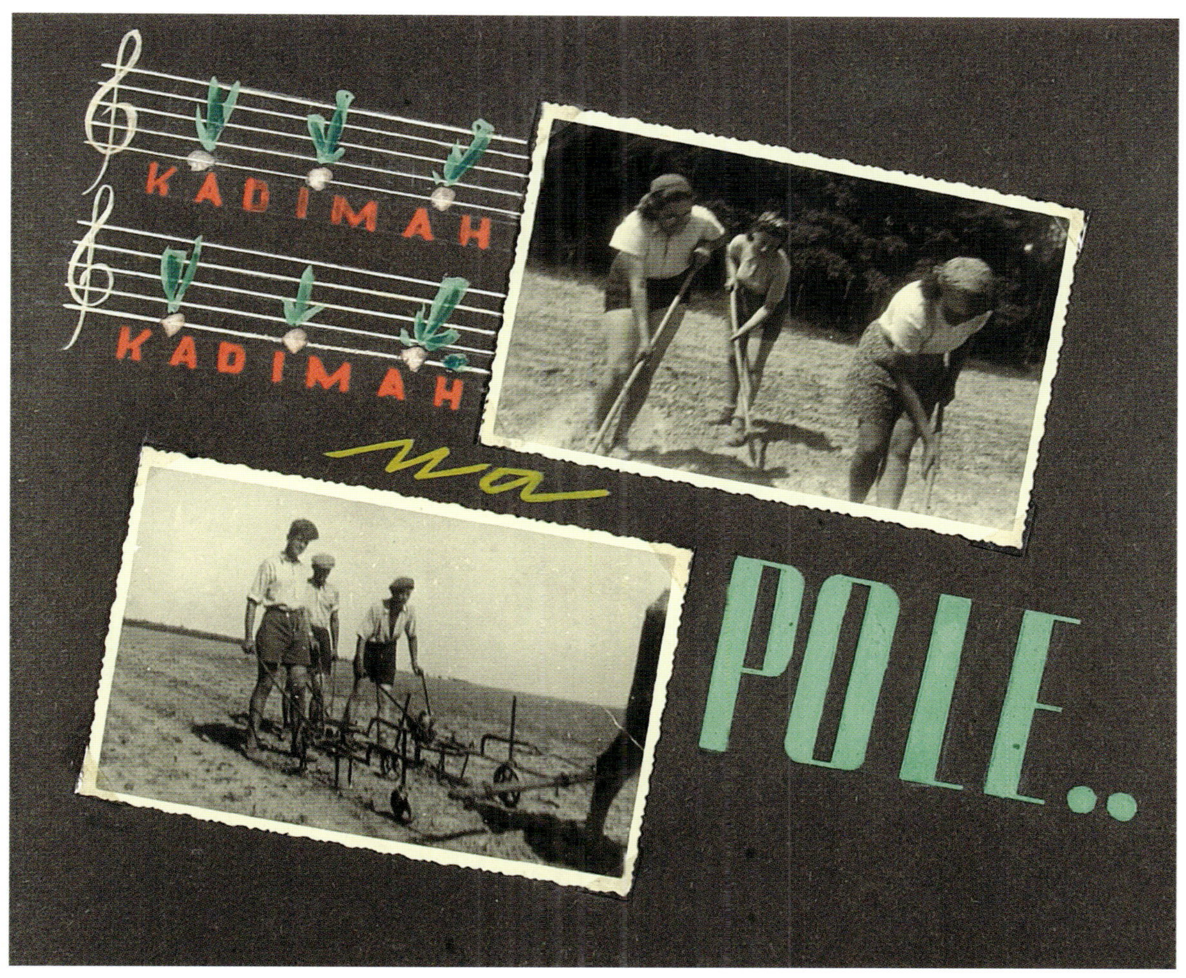

Hora, and we always found something to laugh about.'[10] The photographs in Marianne's Hachshara album (figs. 2.1, 2.3–2.6) communicate exactly the same message; they are full of positive energy and humour, despite the fact that during the summer of 1941 Jewish persecution in the Protectorate was slowly reaching its climax. The Nazis stopped all official activities of the Zionist movements and in September all Jews were forced to wear the yellow Star of David as a visual mark of their segregation (see cat. 12). It was the end of the agricultural season 1941 and Marianne was saying farewell to the farmers in

Fig. 2.4 'Kadimah' translates as 'forwards, advance, let's go' and also 'in the direction of the east/Zion; 'na pole' means 'to the fields'. Top: Marianne may be the middle figure. Bottom: Pavel Friedmann is far left. Family archive

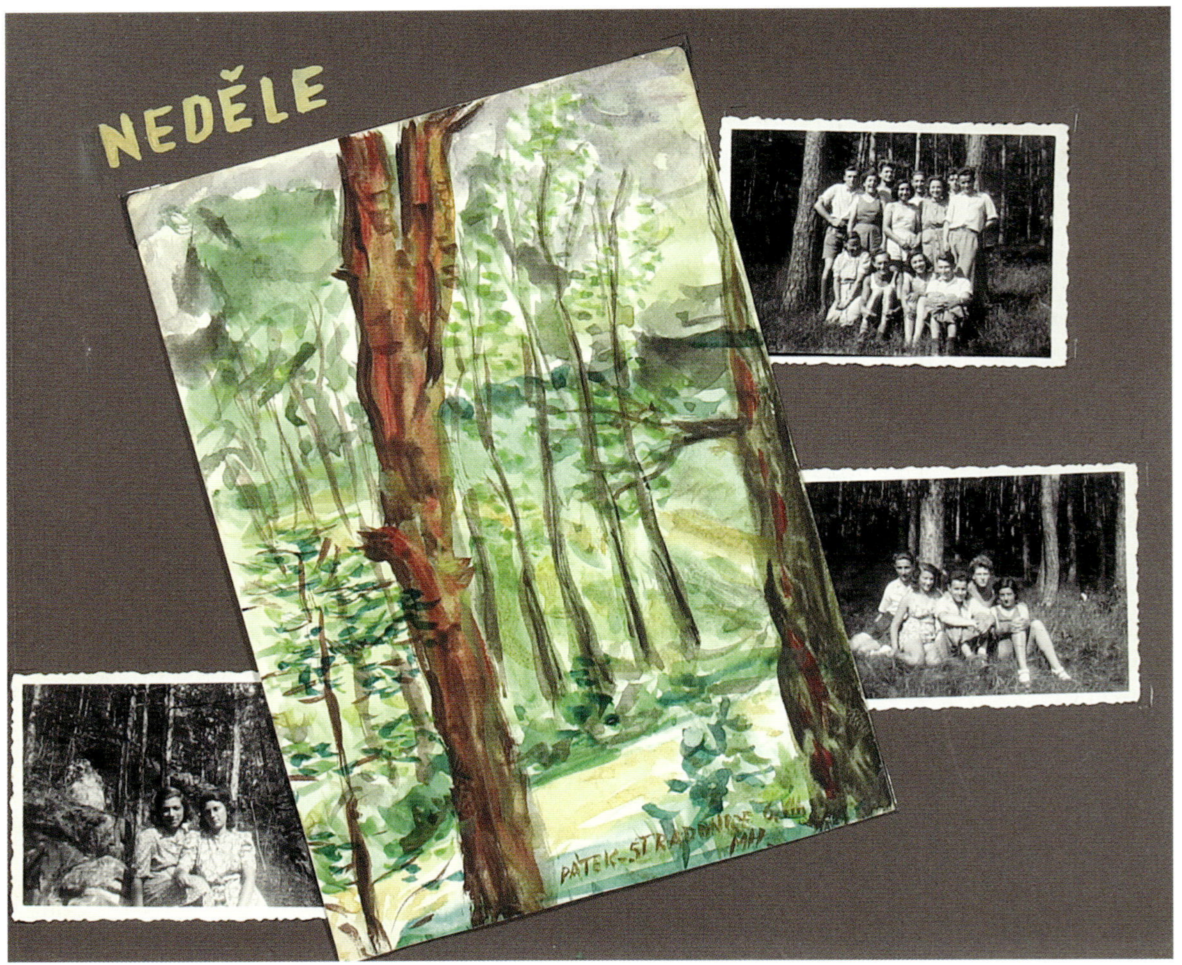

Fig. 2.5 'Neděle' (Sunday) near Pátek u Louny, painting dated 6 July 1941. The photograph top right shows the group from the fig. 2.1 collage. Family archive

Moravia (see fig. 2.7) before returning home to Prague. She already had the yellow star attached to her clothes. Not yet knowing where it would all lead, she remembers being proud to display her Jewish faith, saying that she and her friends were 'proud, young and always optimistic'. She further explains that 'optimism is a wonderful thing, because you are always hopeful, and you never give up. […] If you haven't got optimism you get depressed. […] In every situation, even later on, depression did not do any good. You had to be cheerful and optimistic.'[11] Indeed, Marianne's positive thinking, the collective

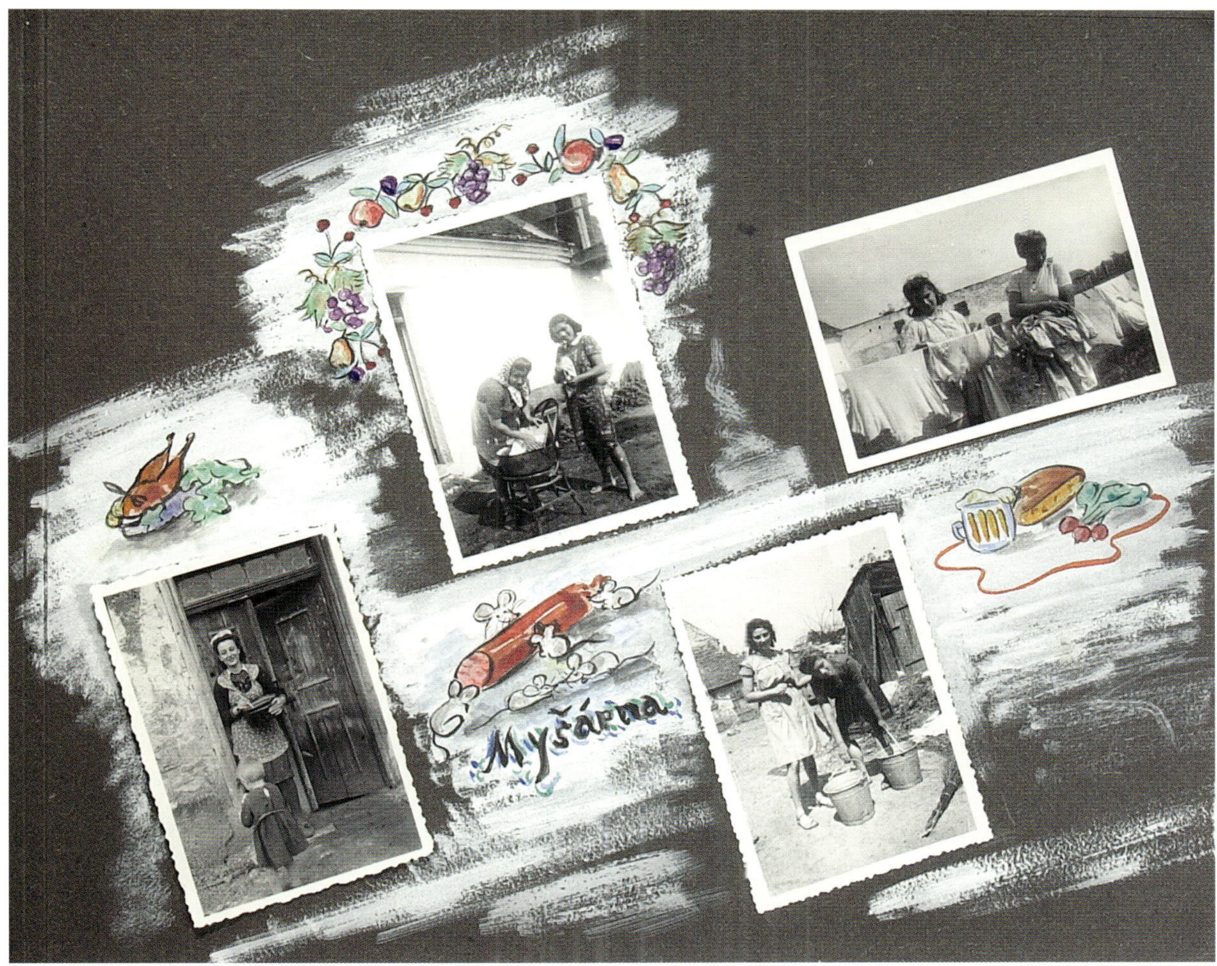

Fig. 2.6 Marianne and her friends carrying out farm chores, 1941. 'Myšárna' under the illustration of mice eating a sausage refers to a place full of mice. Marianne was known as 'Mausi' (little mouse) to friends and family. Family archive

spirit, her experience of productive labour, and the Zionist movement were to become important assets after her deportation to Theresienstadt the following spring.

According to Czech Zionist leader Jacob Edelstein (1903–1944), the responsibility of an active Zionist was not only to be a labourer, but within the inhuman conditions of the ghetto 'also to carry the burden of personal fulfilment, to extract the positive even from the negative, and to create new sources of life for the community [...]'.[12] Marianne's paintings are a vivid testimony of her life in the ghetto and concentration camps, and

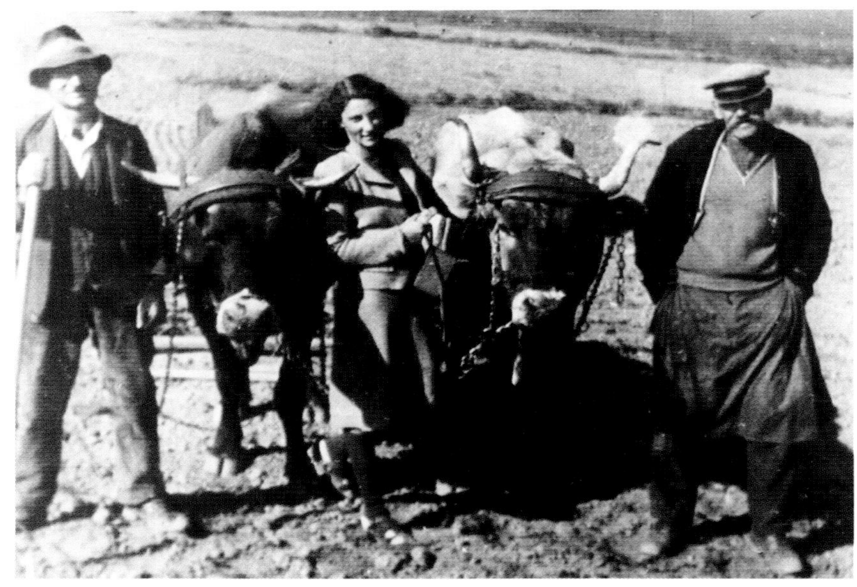

Fig. 2.7 Marianne saying farewell to the farmers in Moravia, probably autumn 1941. Family archive

when read together with her memories, they illustrate how well she actively participated in the fulfilment of this vision.

Edelstein was appointed first Elder of Theresienstadt's Jewish Council, which was in charge of all the ghetto's internal affairs. In this way, everyday life in the ghetto, as well as its key industries, was 'under strong Zionist influence'.[13] Zionists formed a tight-knit and ordered community, and from the beginning organized the ghetto around the model of a kibbutz where people were involved in collective labour, shared resources[14] and where many children grew up in communal homes rather than with their parents (see cats. 6–11). Otto Kraus remembers that no matter how ludicrous it sounds to compare the unspeakable conditions of Theresienstadt with a kibbutz, the El Al members and the Zionists in general 'didn't consider the ghetto as a threat, but rather as an opportunity for their Hachshara, their preparation for kibbutz life.'[15] Thus, they tried to make the best of the terrible conditions.

Zionist leaders made great efforts to ensure the survival of, and secretly educate, young people and children as they meant the future of the Jewish nation. It was also in their interest to involve as many of their young members as possible in productive labour and other ghetto essential services, as they would be protected from the transports to the 'East' for as long as possible. One of these areas was agriculture, where Marianne was offered a place shortly after her arrival. More experienced members of the movement were appointed to leadership roles within the Youth Care Department working in the children's homes, in the youth theatre productions (see cat. 23), as educators, or in working groups. As an already experienced worker, Marianne, along with Meda Becková, was put in charge of the ghetto's youth garden (see cats. 15–18, and fig. 2.8). While being an active member of the Zionist collective in Theresienstadt meant having a great deal of responsibility for others, at the same time members of the group could expect some advantages, such as better work assignments, or accommodation in houses with other *chaverim* (comrades) with shared ideas and cultural values.[16] Having good contacts among the ghetto's Zionist leadership could even mean the opportunity of having somebody's name removed from the horrifying transport to the 'East'. With the help of her friend František Lukáš (see cat. 13), Marianne managed to remove her mother's name three times,[17] although eventually in December 1943 they both found themselves on the transport to Auschwitz.

Even there, in Auschwitz-Birkenau, in the unspeakable conditions of the death camp, members of the Zionist youth movements did not lose their spirit and continued to secretly

Fig. 2.8　Marianne's garden book, in which she kept a record of the produce from the Youth Garden. The coat of arms on the title page reads 'Eisernes Tor' (Iron Gate), the Garden of the Iron Gate which Marianne mentions (see cat. 15). Collection of Beit Terezin, Israel

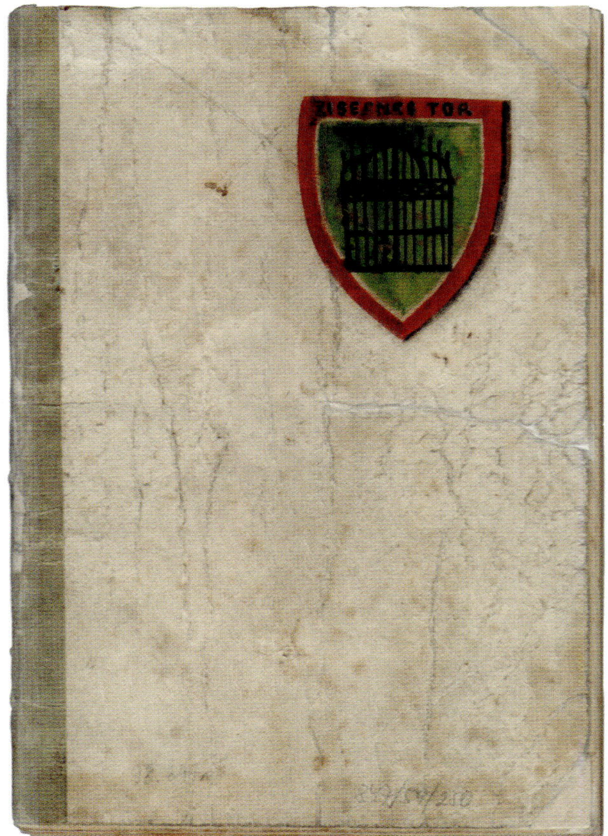

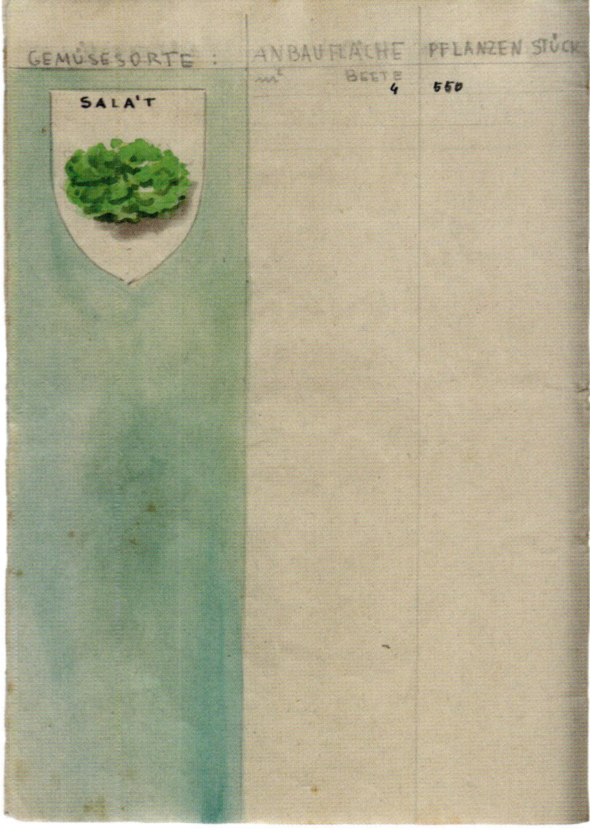

educate children. Youth leader Fredy Hirsch managed to persuade the notorious Dr Josef Mengele to allow them to use Block 31 of the Czech Family Camp as an activity space for children. Although education was not officially allowed by the Germans, under Hirsch's guidance and in impossible conditions, a small number of devoted youth counsellors took the risk and looked after around 600 children aged 8 to 14, maintaining their physical and mental health through a range of educational games and activities.[18] Marianne herself was very active, teaching children nature sciences, drawing, and, depending on their age, languages.[19] Together with Dina Babbitt (née Gottliebová; 1923–2009) she painted the windowless walls of the barrack with cheerful images to brighten up the space, but also to be used for the children's education (fig. 4.15, p.110).

Holocaust historian Shimon Adler described the activities and environment at the Children's Block 31 as 'an island of stability in the sea of constant changes and traumas the children had to endure', adding that 'the children and the staff there were able to live for the moment, distancing themselves from the pain and terror reigning outside.'[20] Indeed, the main idea behind the block's existence was to divert the children's attention from the horrors happening all around them, to create a positive little world, detached from a reality filled with hunger, suffering and death. However, this small island was still surrounded by the death machinery of Auschwitz and despite all the efforts, almost all of the children and their families who arrived from Theresienstadt in September 1943, just three months before Marianne, were murdered on 8 March 1944.[21] In early July 1944, Marianne passed the selection for slave labour in Germany. After her transport left Auschwitz, the Family Camp was liquidated and everyone who remained there was gassed. About one third of the counsellors in the Children's Block of the Family Camp were Marianne's comrades from the youth movement El Al; Otto Kraus described their activities as 'one last flowering of El Al in the abysses of the Final Solution', adding that only five of its former members survived the Holocaust.[22] Marianne was among the few who lived to share this story through her memory and artworks, so that new generations would learn from the mistakes of the past, and make sure these atrocities are not repeated ever again.

Notes

1   The poem, typed in Czech by Pavel Friedmann, was discovered after the ghetto was liberated, and it is now in the collection of the Jewish Museum in Prague: ID: DOCUMENT.JMP.SHOAH/T/2/A/10j/326/017/003 http://collections.jewishmuseum.cz/index.php/Detail/Object/Show/object_id/2131 (last accessed 8/10/2021). Translated from the Czech by Peter Tuka.

2   Miroslav Kárný *et.al.*, *Terezínská Pamětní Kniha*, vol.1, Melantrich, Prague, 1995, pp. 507–521.

3   Miroslav Kárný, *'Konečné Řešení' Genocida Českých Židů v Německé Protektorátní Politice* [*'Final Solution' Genocide of Czech Jews in German Protectorate Politics*], Academia, Prague, 1991, pp.50–51.

4   Aliyah, meaning 'ascent', refers to the immigration of the Diaspora Jews to the land of Israel.

5   Eva Adorian interview recorded for the project 'Memory of Nations: Stories of 20th Century', 24.11.2013. https://www.memoryofnations.eu/en/adorian-eva-1926 from the Post Bellum collection [last accessed 19.10.2021]. Translated from the Czech by Peter Tuka.

6   Otto B. Kraus, 'The El Al Divertimento' in *Rhapsody to Tchelet Lavan in Czechoslovakia*, Amos Sinai, Gershorn Amir and Nanne Margol eds., The Association for the History of Tchelet Lavan – El Al in Czechoslovakia, Israel, 1996, pp. 256–58.

7   *Ibid.*, p. 256.

8   Rachel Har-Tsvi (Růža Porgesová), 'I was a Member of El Al' in *Rhapsody to Tchelet Lavan in Czechoslovakia*, Amos Sinai, Gershorn Amir and Nanne Margol eds., The Association for the History of Tchelet Lavan – El Al in Czechoslovakia, Israel, 1996, p. 263.

9   Hanka Fischl-Hofmann and Lisa Kummermann-Gidron, 'The Movement During the Nazi occupation' in *Rhapsody to Tchelet Lavan in Czechoslovakia*, Amos Sinai, Gershorn Amir and Nanne Margol eds., The Association for the History of Tchelet Lavan – El Al in Czechoslovakia, Israel, 1996, p. 287.

10   Ruth Bondy, *Víc Štěstí Než Rozumu*, translated from the Hebrew original into Czech by Jindřiška Zajíčková, Argo, Prague, 2005, p. 124. Quote translated by Peter Tuka.

11   Marianne Grant, 'Personal Touch – Marianne Grant', interview for BBC Radio 3, originally broadcast 26 January 2003, https://www.bbc.co.uk/archive/personal-touch--marianne-grant/zb7xkmn (last accessed 21/10/2021).

12   Yaakov Edelstein, 'Theresienstadt – One Year On (from a letter)' in *Rhapsody to Tchelet Lavan in Czechoslovakia*, Amos Sinai, Gershorn Amir and Nanne Margol eds., The Association for the History of Tchelet Lavan – El Al in Czechoslovakia, Israel, 1996, p. 297.

13   Anna Hájková, 'To Terezín and Back Again: Czech Jews and their Bonds of Belonging from Deportations to the Postwar' in *Dapim: Studies on the Holocaust*, 2014, 28:1, p. 43.

14   The resources were not shared equally. One of the hardest moral decisions the Jewish Council had to make was adopting the strategy of 'survival through labour'. This meant that children and people involved in physical labour were favoured before the weak and old, and were given extra food rations. In practice the difference was often just a slice of bread a day, but in the conditions in the ghetto this difference was huge. For more on this topic see: Ruth Bondy, 'The Theresienstadt Ghetto: Its Characteristics and Perspective' in Yisrael Gutman and Avital Saf eds., *The Nazi Concentration Camps*, Yad Vashem, Israel, 1984, pp. 303–14.

15   Otto B. Kraus, 'The El Al Divertimento' in *Rhapsody to Tchelet Lavan in Czechoslovakia*, Amos Sinai, Gershorn Amir and Nanne Margol eds., The Association for the History of Tchelet Lavan – El Al in Czechoslovakia, Israel, 1996, p. 256. See also: Hájková, *To Terezín and Back Again*.

16   Hájková, p.42. Marianne was living with girls from the Zionist youth movement, as illustrated in her paintings of the Youth Room.

17   *Marianne's Story*, interview by Rex Bloomstein, Nucleus Production for Glasgow Museums, 2002, tape 6. Marianne Grant Collection Archive, Glasgow Museums, GMA.2021.1.

18   For a more detailed account of the activities in the Children's Barrack see Ruth Bondy, 'Games in the Shadow of the Crematoria, The children's barracks in the Birkenau family camp (September 1943–July 1944)' in Ruth Bondy, *Trapped, Essays on the History of Czech Jews, 1939–1943*, Yad Vashem, Jerusalem, 2008, pp.152–76.

19   *Marianne's Story*, interview by Rex Bloomstein, Nucleus Production for Glasgow Museums, 2002, tape 6. Marianne Grant Collection Archive, Glasgow Museums, GMA.2021.1.

20   Shimon Adler, 'Block 31: The Children's Block in the Family Camp at Birkenau' in *Yad Vashem Studies* XXIV, Aharon Weiss ed., Yad Vashem, Jerusalem, 1994, pp. 291–92, 314–15.

21   Marianne managed to save one of the children – Hana Káňová (née Heit erová) – see p. 109.

22   Otto B. Kraus, 'The El Al Divertimento' in *Rhapsody to Tchelet Lavan in Czechoslovakia*, Amos Sinai, Gershorn Amir and Nanne Margol eds., The Association for the History of Tchelet Lavan – El Al in Czechoslovakia, Israel, 1996, pp. 259–260.

Marianne's Legacy

Paula Cowan

SINCE THE PUBLICATION of *I Knew I Was Painting For My Life* in 2002, Holocaust educators around the world have conscientiously engaged with preserving the legacy of the Holocaust. The art and testimony of the late Marianne Grant, and the new edition of this book, contribute to the body of this work. Marianne's art and testimony were more than a legacy; they were her way of remembering and honouring people, some of whom were very young, who did not survive the Holocaust – her friends, family members and fellow inmates. This contributes to our general understanding of the experiences and suffering of Jewish people during the Holocaust and provides us with an insight into the experiences of individuals.

Marianne was born in Prague, one of the oldest Jewish communities in Europe. There is clear evidence of a Jewish community living there as far back as 1091, and it is thought that Jews may have even lived there in Roman times. Persecution of Jews in Prague was not exclusive to the Holocaust. At the end of the eleventh century Bohemian Jews were required to wear 'special' clothes, Jews in Prague lived in the ghetto (then called the Jewish Quarter), and the only occupation that Jews were allowed to adopt was moneylending. Further, attempts were made at the beginning of the sixteenth century to expel Jews from Prague. An order issued in 1744 led to Jews being expelled from Bohemia and Moravia, resulting in Prague Jews being banished, although they were later allowed to return on the condition that they paid high taxes.

Immediately prior to World War II, Prague had become a safe home for Jewish people. At the end of the nineteenth century its largest university, the oldest in Central Europe, the Charles University, was divided into Czech and German institutions. Its famous alumni included the Prague-born writer Franz Kafka (1883–1924) who was then a law student (and also, incidentally, related through marriage to Marianne – his sister Gabriele (Elli) was married to Marianne's paternal uncle Karl Hermann), and between 1911 and 1912 it employed Albert Einstein (1879–1955) as Professor of Physics.

Following the 1935 Nuremberg Laws, Jews in Germany and Austria became 'subjects' of the state and lost their rights to citizenship. By 1938, refugees from Germany, then Austria and the German-speaking occupied parts of Czechoslovakia, started to arrive in Prague. In November 1938 *Kristallnacht* (meaning 'Night of Broken Glass'), also referred to as the 'November pogrom', took place. This was 24 hours of street violence across Germany and Austria, when Jewish shops, schools, synagogues and other Jewish establishments, including cemeteries and homes, were set alight. Tens of thousands of Jews were terrorized, about 30,000 Jews were taken to concentration camps, more than 260 synagogues were destroyed, and over 90 people killed. One month later, British stockbroker Nicholas Winton (1909–2015) visited Prague, met Doreen Warriner (1904–1972), a representative of the British Refugee Committee of Czechoslovakia, and became committed to organizing a rescue operation for children in Czechoslovakia. Known as the *Kindertransport*, this operation brought 10,000 unaccompanied Jewish children from Germany, Austria and Czechoslovakia to safety in the UK.

Warriner's essay on the 1938 winter in Prague tells of the desperation of 100,000 refugees from the Sudetenland (a historical name for the northern, southern, and western areas of former Czechoslovakia) who could neither return to their home nor stay in Czechoslovakia. She telegrammed to the UK, 'Thousands starving children pouring into Prague, urgent appeal necessary',[1] and when the Nazis invaded and occupied the Czech provinces of Bohemia and Moravia in March 1939, wrote of Prague, about the 'fresh shock: the great guns at the bridgeheads, the swastika flying from the Castle'.[2] This was the world in which Marianne Grant and her mother, Anna, found themselves.

Following the Nazi invasion and occupation of Czechoslovakia, resistance by the Czech regime to the Nazis and anti-Jewish restrictions that excluded Jews from economic and social life was short-lived. In 1941 the appointment of Reinhard Heydrich, one of the architects of the 'Final Solution', as Acting Reich Protector of the Protectorate of Bohemia and Moravia was accompanied by new restrictions for Jews and the adoption of the Nuremberg Laws.

What followed could never have been predicted or imagined. Marianne and her mother journeyed from Prague to Theresienstadt (also known as Terezín) in Czechoslovakia to Auschwitz-Birkenau in Poland, to Neuengamme, near Hamburg in Northern Germany, to Bergen-Belsen, near Celle, also in Northern Germany, where they were liberated.

Theresienstadt was the fortress that in 1941 became a concentration camp and ghetto for Jews. Prague Jews had initially thought that their move to Theresienstadt would be permanent, and that living in this self-supporting city would provide them with safety. This was not so, as Nazi antisemitic policy did not stop with segregating Jews from society. When the 'Final Solution' was announced in 1942 it became evident that the Nazis' intention was the destruction and mass murder of Jews in Europe. Although Theresienstadt masqueraded as a model camp to the outside world, to show the world that the Nazis were treating Jews well, tens of thousands of Jews were deported from there to the East, and this included Marianne's mother. Such was Marianne's love for, and sense of duty to, her mother that in 1943, when her mother was deported, Marianne followed her on the cattle wagons, which unknown to her, were headed for Auschwitz (Oświęcim). This camp has become the ultimate symbol of the horror and cruelty of the Holocaust and remains the largest Jewish burial ground in the world.

Built in 1938, Neuengamme was a satellite or sub-camp of Sachenhausen concentration camp, where primarily Soviet nationals and Jews were deployed as forced labour in camp construction, or in the brickworks factory. Originally built as a prisoner-of-war camp in 1943, Bergen-Belsen became a complex of camps which included a concentration camp. By the time Marianne and her mother arrived at Bergen-Belsen in 1945 thousands of people, mainly Jews, were prisoners of this already overcrowded camp; between December 1944 and April 1945 its population had swelled from 15,000 to 60,000 prisoners. When the British forces liberated Bergen-Belsen on 15 April 1945, they found 10,000 unburied dead, and thousands of prisoners requiring medical care due to malnourishment and starvation, no running water or sanitation, and typhus, typhoid and tuberculosis epidemics had broken out.

The significance of the Holocaust is sometimes forgotten as there is a tendency to remember it alongside other genocides, rather than on its own. *Every* genocide is a human tragedy that demonstrates 'man's inhumanity to man', so what makes the Holocaust any different? For Jews the Holocaust has a special meaning as the unspeakable and unforeseen depths of cruelty and scale of Nazi antisemitism denied so many of their family, friends and colleagues, a community and home. For Jewish children of Holocaust survivors, those friends of their parents who survived often became their immediate family. The Nazi intent to destroy Jews and Jewish life in the Holocaust is a constant reminder of antisemitism at its most extreme.

Historian and Holocaust survivor Yehuda Bauer identifies three key elements that help us further understand the difference between the genocide of the Jews in the Holocaust and other genocides, such as Rwanda and Darfur.[3] Firstly, the basic motivation was rooted in an antisemitic murderous ideology whose basis was ill-founded on myths and illusions such as the international Jewish conspiracy to control the world, and Jews having too much power in a country where Jews actually had neither military nor political power. Secondly, its geographical reach; persecution of Jews began in Germany, spreading across Europe to countries, like Czechoslovakia, that were under German occupation. But the Nazi intention to murder Jews did not stop with Europe. The Nazi plan was to extend the persecution and murder of Jews across the world; this is why Jews living under Italian-controlled Libya or French colonial rule in Morocco, Algeria and Tunisia were sent to labour and concentration camps in their respective countries, with some Libyan Jews being sent to camps in Europe. Thirdly, the totality of its intent. There was to be no exemption for any individual whom the Nazis defined a Jew. It is, Bauer claims, the extremeness of these three elements that makes the Holocaust unprecedented.

Marianne painted for the children in the Children's Block at Auschwitz-Birkenau and often spoke about the importance of the Nazis viewing her as someone who could be useful to them. Marianne considered this to have been essential to her survival. Her usefulness was largely due to her aptitude for languages, as she spoke German, Czech, Polish, English and a little French, her knowledge of agriculture, and her artistic talent. In Auschwitz-Birkenau, Marianne made storybooks for Christmas for the family of a Slovak guard, and was assigned several artistic duties by SS physician Josef Mengele, who conducted inhumane medical experiments on inmates at Auschwitz. Known as the 'Angel of Death', Mengele's particular interest was in twins and people of restricted growth; he hoped to discover ways in which German women could bear more than one foetus in every pregnancy, and to discover the causes of dwarfism to prevent its occurrence among German children. This was in accordance with Nazi ideology which promoted the development of the 'Aryan', or 'pure', race, and the belief that the human race could be improved by limiting the reproduction of people they considered to be inferior. Such racial 'purity' was required for the superiority of the 'Germanic race'.

This ideology was first put into practice in 1933, when German physicians were allowed to perform forced sterilizations, and operations that prevented their victims from having children. Roma, and disabled individuals, including those with mental illness and people born deaf and blind, were initially targeted. This racist ideology was antisemitic in that it regarded Jews as 'impure', a poisonous race who wished to destroy 'Aryan' life. Under Nazi legislation, irrespective of one's level of observance of Judaism or identity with Jewish culture, anyone with three or four Jewish grandparents was Jewish. This explains the dehumanization, alienation and segregation of Jews that followed in Germany and German-occupied countries.

It is also important to remember that the Holocaust led to the adoption of the term 'genocide' and the subsequent United Nations (UN) declaration of genocide as a crime under international law, the indictment of the term 'crimes against humanity', the UN Declaration of Human Rights that led to the implementation of the UN Convention relating to the status of refugees, and the UN Convention of the Rights of the Child.

As we learn more about the Holocaust, we realize that categorizing people as perpetrators, bystanders, upstanders or victims is problematic. For example, Marianne's children later learned that while in Auschwitz-Birkenau, Marianne saved a young girl's life. On hearing that all those on the transport previous to hers were going to be taken and killed, Marianne had gone to the Children's Block and insisted that one girl, Hana Káňová (née Heitlerová; b.1930), whom she had grown fond of, be taken to the sick bay or hospital immediately. Hana's name was then taken off the list for selection, and as a result Marianne became an upstander and saved Hana's life. Hana later verified Marianne's actions in her survivor testimony.[4]

We also have to remember that the experiences of European Jews varied according to their age, physical and emotional health, skills and 'usefulness' to the Nazis, country of origin and year of German occupation, and duration of incarceration. Although Marianne enjoyed a childhood free from antisemitism in Prague, by 1941, as a result of the Nuremberg Laws, one of Marianne's Jewish friends was arrested for breaking the rules by going to the cinema and Marianne and her mother had had to move out of their apartment. As Jews living in the Reich and the Protectorate, Marianne and her mother were also required to sew a yellow Star of David with the word *Jude* (Jew), printed in black letters on their outer clothes on the left side of their chests, so as to be clearly identifiable in public.

While there have been many positive developments in teaching and learning about the Holocaust in the last 20 years, new challenges have emerged. One of these is the instant and wide range of information available on the internet and social media that has led, and continues to lead, to a distortion of the facts and evidence of the Holocaust. In response to this, the International Holocaust Remembrance Alliance (HRA) have adopted a working definition of Holocaust Denial and Distortion (2013). As 'virtually' anyone can write anything about the Holocaust, incorrect and sometimes offensive material, lies and misinformation about the Holocaust are freely accessible. These perpetuate misconceptions and myths about the Holocaust and about Jewish people that are difficult to unlearn. We all therefore require to be vigilant and responsive to those who deny the existence of the Holocaust, and/or distort its facts.

In his keynote address at the First International Conference of Children of Holocaust survivors in 1984, Nobel Peace Prize Laureate author and Holocaust survivor Elie Wiesel (1928–2016) said that since the Holocaust 'Human beings were still inhuman, society still cruel, Jews still hated, others jailed, victimized'.[5] Antisemitism did not disappear with the Holocaust; unfortunately, in Europe antisemitic incidents still regularly occur, with one in two Europeans considering antisemitism a problem (EU, 2021).[6] Here in Scotland, the Jewish community continues to shrink, yet antisemitism impacts on Jewish people on our streets and university campuses, necessitating additional security when entering synagogues and Jewish communal events. Disappointingly, contemporary expressions of antisemitism are often accompanied with imagery and language that is associated with the Holocaust. The emergence of new expressions of antisemitism presents further challenges to Holocaust remembrance and education.

One positive development is the adoption of the IHRA's working definition of antisemitism by the UK (2016) and Scottish (2017) Governments. Another is the recognition by international organizations UNESCO and the Organization for Security and Co-operation in Europe (UNESCO/OSCE, 2018) that antisemitism should be addressed through education in schools.[7] In response to this, *Vision Schools Scotland*, a national programme that identifies schools that demonstrate innovation and good practice in teaching the Holocaust, produced a teaching resource for secondary schools (2021), based on Marianne's testimony (figs. 3.1 and 3.2). This resource is freely available to registered Scottish teachers on the General Teaching Council for Scotland's website.

In 2003 Marianne Grant was made a Freeman (a person who has been given special rights in a city or area, as an honour) of East Renfrewshire, where she lived the greater part of her adult life and raised three children. This meant a great deal to Marianne, who had lost her citizenship in her home country of Czechoslovakia, and who had been alienated in, and segregated from, her home city of Prague. This book reminds us that the tragedy of the Holocaust includes the loss of talents and skills of those murdered, as well as those of future generations. Had the Nazis succeeded with their implementation of the 'Final Solution', they would have dismantled the death camps by ploughing the land or planting trees. There was to be no trace of the human destruction and cruelty that had occurred there, and if Jews *were* to be remembered it would have been on the Nazis' terms.[8] It is our responsibility to remember this as well as the nature of the treatment and fate of millions of innocent people.

Children, grandchildren, and great-grand-children of Holocaust survivors are guardians of Holocaust legacy. As you read this book, I invite you to join Marianne's family in becoming a guardian of this legacy.

The Holocaust
a resource for secondary schools
Second Edition
Paula Cowan
Reader in Education
University of the West of Scotland
Lynn Nisbet
Lecturer in Education
University of the West of Scotland
SUPPORTING HOLOCAUST EDUCATION
VISION SCHOOLS SCOTLAND
UNIVERSITY OF THE WEST of SCOTLAND
UWS

Fig. 3.1 Cover of the teaching resource produced by *Vision Schools Scotland* showing Marianne

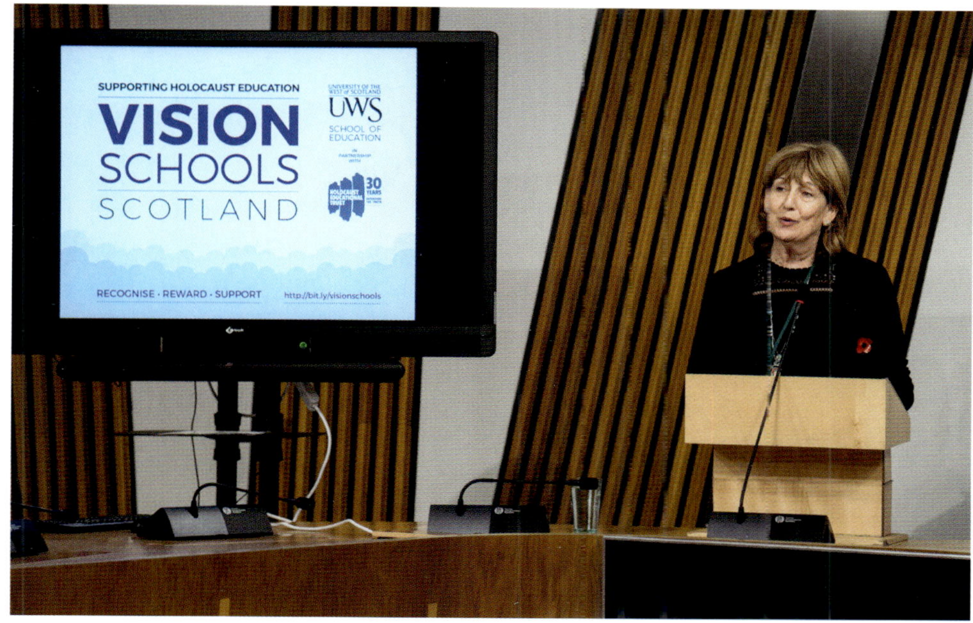

Fig. 3.2 Paula Cowan speaking at the *Vision Schools Scotland* Awards Event at the Scottish Parliament, November 2019

overleaf:
KZ Osvědčím, 1952
(cat. 29, detail)

Further Reading

IHRA (2013) Working definition of Holocaust Denial and Distortion:
https://www.holocaustremembrance.com/resources/working-definitions-charters/working-definition-holocaust-denial-and-distortion (last accessed 21/10/2021).
IHRA (2016) Working definition of Antisemitism:
https://www.holocaustremembrance.com/working-definition-antisemitism (accessed 21/10/2021).

Notes

1   D. Warriner, 'Winter in Prague', *Slavonic and East European Review*, 1984, 63:2, pp. 210.

2   *Ibid.*, p.227.

3   Y. Bauer, *Rethinking the Holocaust*, Yale University Press: New Haven and London, 2002, pp. 48–50.

4   Hana Káňová interview recorded for the project 'Memory of Nations: Stories of 20th Century', https://www.memoryofnations.eu/en/kanova-hana-1930 (last accessed 21/10/2021).

5   E. Wiesel, 'Prologue: To Our Children', in M. Z Rosensaft (ed.), *God, Faith and Identity from the Ashes: Reflections of Children and Grandchildren of Holocaust Survivors*, Vermont: Jewish Lights Publishing, 1984, p.xvi.

6   EU Strategy on Combating Antisemitism and Fostering Jewish Life (2021–2030), Strasbourg, 2021https://ec.europa.eu/info/files/eu-strategy-combating-antisemitism-and-fostering-jewish-life-2021-2030_en (last accessed 5/11/2021).

7   UNESCO/OSCE. *Addressing Anti-Semitism Through Education: Guidelines for Policymakers*, Paris and Warsaw: UNESCO/OSCE, 2018, https://www.osce.org/odihr/383089?download=true (last accessed 21/10/2021).

8   I. Wollaston, *War Against Memory: The Future of Holocaust Remembrance*, London: SPCK, 1996.

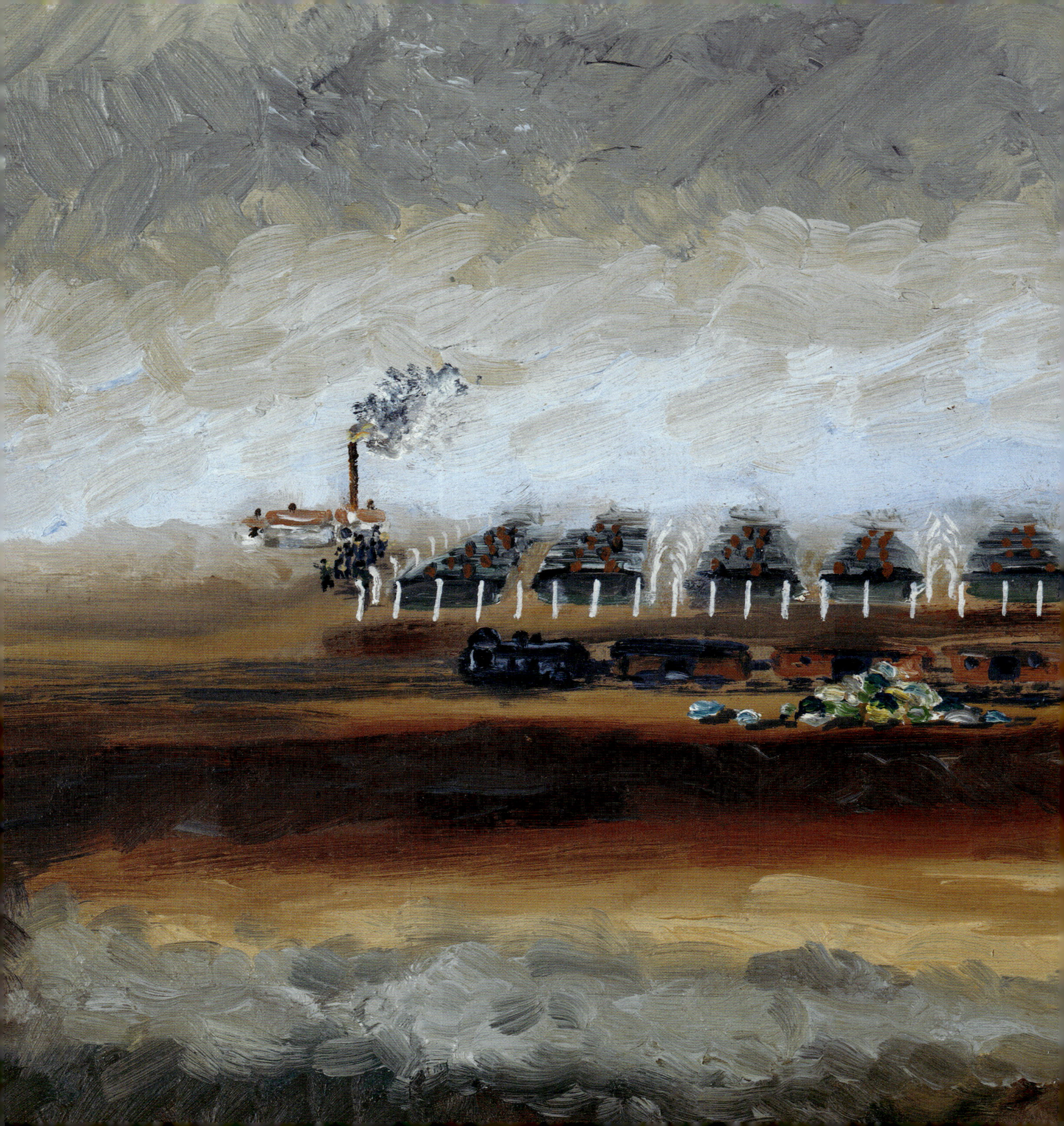

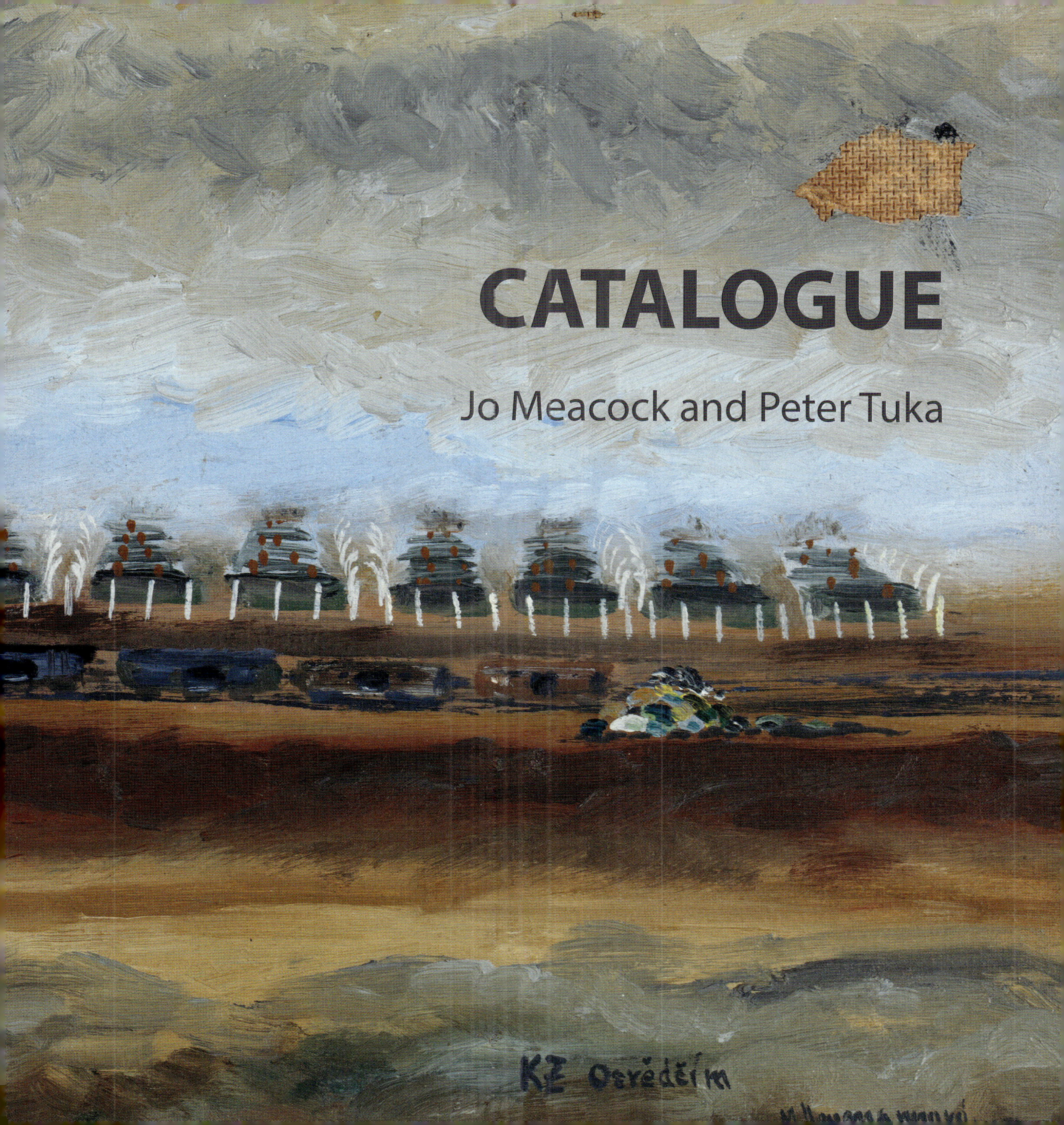

CATALOGUE

Jo Meacock and Peter Tuka

Art in Prague: 1937–1942

PRAGUE, THE CAPITAL CITY of the Czech Republic, is celebrated for its rich artistic, architectural and cultural heritage. Its historic buildings and monuments include the medieval stone Karlův most (Charles Bridge) which crosses the Vltava (Moldau) river, connecting the Old Town with the Castle of Hradčany (Prague Castle) and the Gothic St Vitus Cathedral on the left bank. The Art Nouveau Industrial Palace Výstaviště Praha (Prague Exhibition Centre) and summer palace Lapidarium with its medieval sculptures and monuments, are located near the large Stromovka Park in the fashionable district of Holešovice, where Marianne and her family lived in the 1930s; little would they have guessed that in 1942 the exhibition grounds would be used to corral Jews being transported to Theresienstadt.

The city's principal art collection was held in the Picture Gallery of the Society of Patriotic Friends of the Arts, nationalized in 1936, with nineteenth- and twentieth-century art on display in the Modern Gallery of the Kingdom of Bohemia. In these museums Marianne could have seen works by renowned international artists such as Albrecht Dürer, El Greco, Rembrandt, Eugène Delacroix, Paul Cézanne and Pablo Picasso. From 1887, the city had been home to the notable Mánes Association of Fine Artists which played an important role in the development of Czech Cubism, and amongst whose members were artists such as Zdenka Braunerová (1858–1934), the first woman artist member; Josef Čapek (1887–1945); Emil Filla (1882–1953); and Max Švabinský (1873–1962). Devětsil, an association of Czech avant-garde artists, was active in Prague between 1920 and 1930; it brought together artists from all genres, including fine arts, music, theatre, poetry and architecture. Among the most notable members were leading representatives of European Surrealism Jindřich Štyrský (1899–1942) and Toyen (1902–1980), as well as

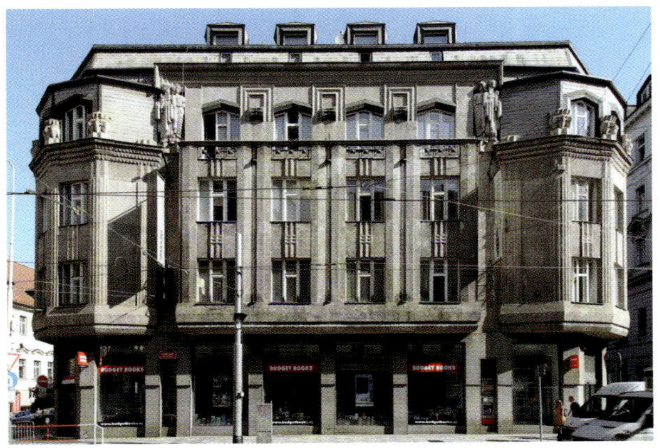

Fig. 4.1 The Diamant Palace in Prague, built between 1912 and 1913 by architect Emil Králíček, is a prime example of Czech Cubist architecture. It is home to the Mánes Association of Fine Artists. Photo by VitVit, used under a Creative Commons 4.0 International Licence

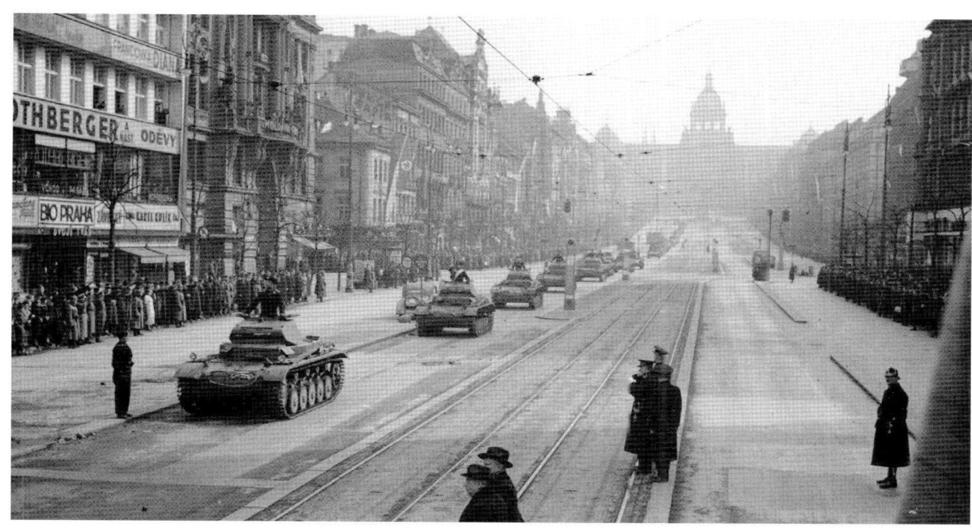

Fig. 4.2 The German army of occupation in Wenceslas Square, Prague, 17 March 1939 © Czech News Agency – Photo 2021

Marianne's favourite actors Jiří Voskovec (1905–1981) and Jan Werich (1905–1980). Prague boasts one of the oldest universities in Europe and its art school, the Academy of Fine Arts, was awarded university status in 1925. At the age of 16, Marianne began to attend the stylish Studio Rotter.

Studio Rotter was a graphic design workshop established in Prague in 1928 by the Czech painter and designer Vilém Rotter (1903–1978), and situated on Vodičkova 32, next to the Palace Lucerna and near the famous fashion salon of Hana Podolská (1880–1971). In 1934 Rotter opened a school which soon gained an international reputation for the quality of its modernist design. However, the design studio and school were forced to close after the German occupation of Czechoslovakia in 1939, and Marianne had to leave without graduating. Rotter fled, first to France, where he joined the Czechoslovak Army in exile, and then to Britain, where he served briefly with the RAF before being discharged in 1940. Marianne's mother paid for her enrolment on a two-year course at Bezalel Academy of Art and Design in Jerusalem, but Marianne, who would not be parted from her mother, turned the opportunity down.

The enactment of the Nuremberg Race Laws in the newly formed Protectorate of Bohemia and Moravia meant that Marianne had to continue her art education in Prague in secret, first with a local sculptor, and then, purposefully, skilling herself in applied crafts, such as ceramic restoration and needlework, in preparation for the work camps to which the Jewish community in Prague expected to be sent. She also passed on her skills to others, teaching fashion design to young Jewish girls.

Before her deportation to Theresienstadt, Marianne left her student artworks with neighbours and relatives in Prague, together with other valuables such as money, porcelain, fur coats and evening dresses, which she could not take with her and which she wanted to save from confiscation by the Nazis.

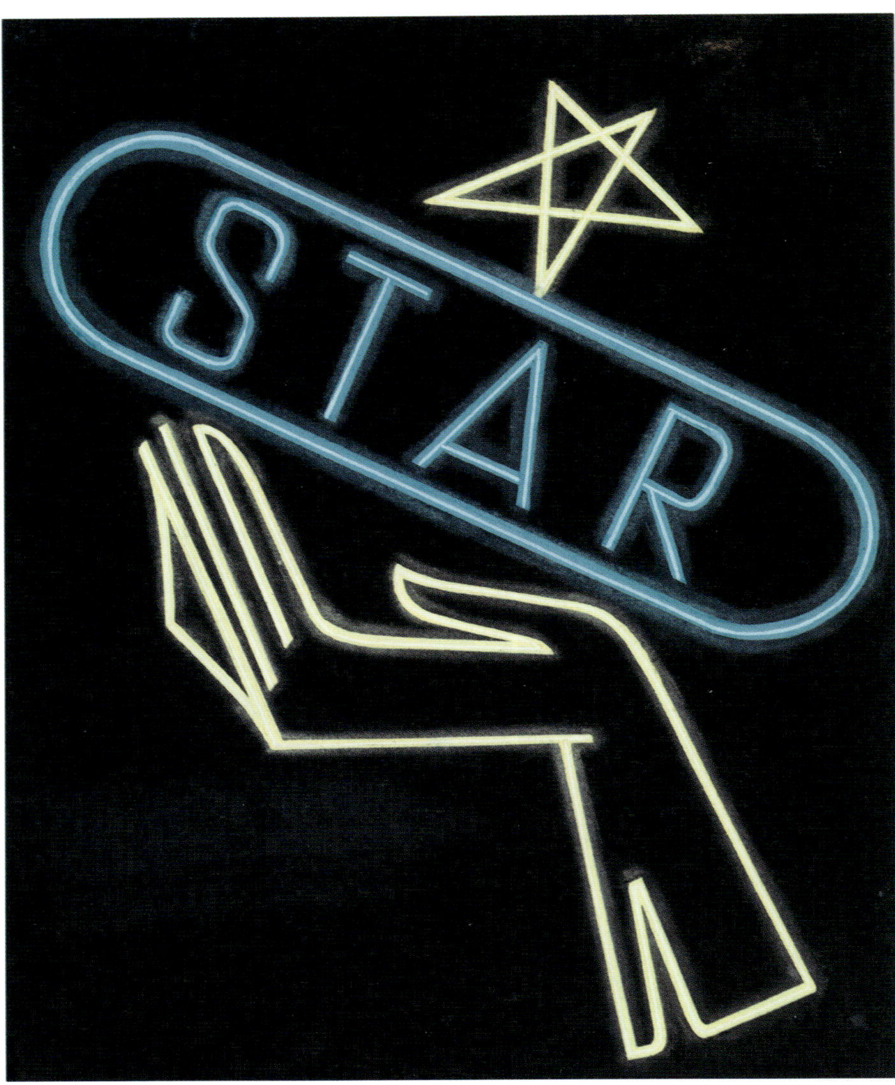

1

Star, about 1937–38
Advertisement design
Inscribed on reverse
'Hermannová/16/112'
PP.2005.38.46

Courses at the Studio Rotter were not cheap but, persuaded by Marianne's mother and three paternal aunts, Marianne's father gave her permission to enrol. Students were provided with a comprehensive understanding of, and training within, the applied arts. Besides the basics in drawing and painting, the curriculum included advertisement and poster design, fashion design and calligraphy.

This elegant and stylized design, possibly for a neon sign for a shop or theatre, is an example of Marianne's early work at the Rotter School, made when she was 16 to one of their design briefs. She signed her artwork 'Hermannová' at this time, using her birth name Mariana Hermannová. Later, she would anglicize this to 'Marianne Hermann'.

2

New York Světová Výstava
(New York World's Fair), 1939
Poster design
Inscribed on reverse
'Hermannová/17'
PP.2005.38.45

The New York World's Fair, an international event, which took place in Flushing Meadows in Queens, New York City in 1939–40, occasioned this geometric and modernist poster design by Marianne, demonstrating her developing skill as a graphic designer. The theme of the exhibition was the future, with the header 'Dawn of a New Day'.

A number of significant Czech artists and designers, such as Adriena Šimotová (1926–2014) and František Bělský (1921–2000), studied at Studio Rotter. Their impressive Art Deco-inspired advertisement posters were highly acclaimed for their artistic quality and are among the best examples of Czech avant-garde design.

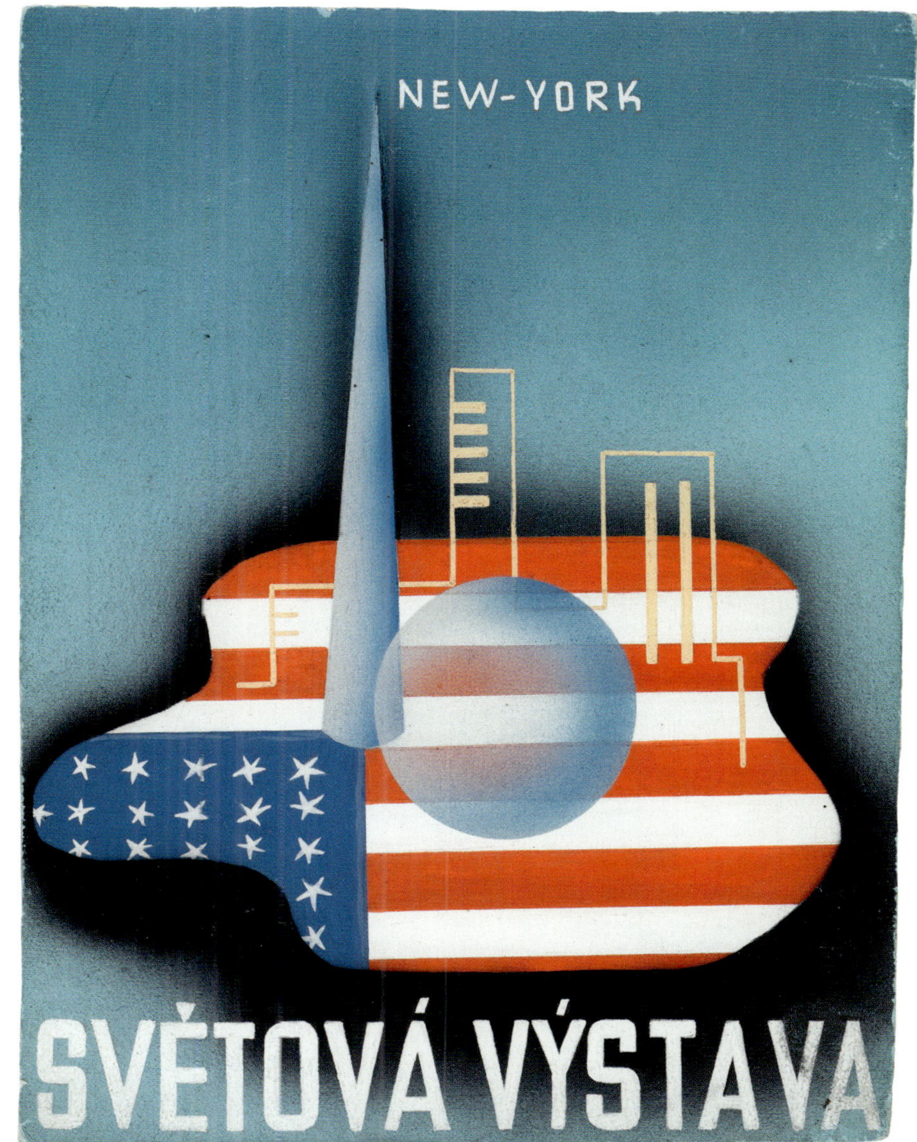

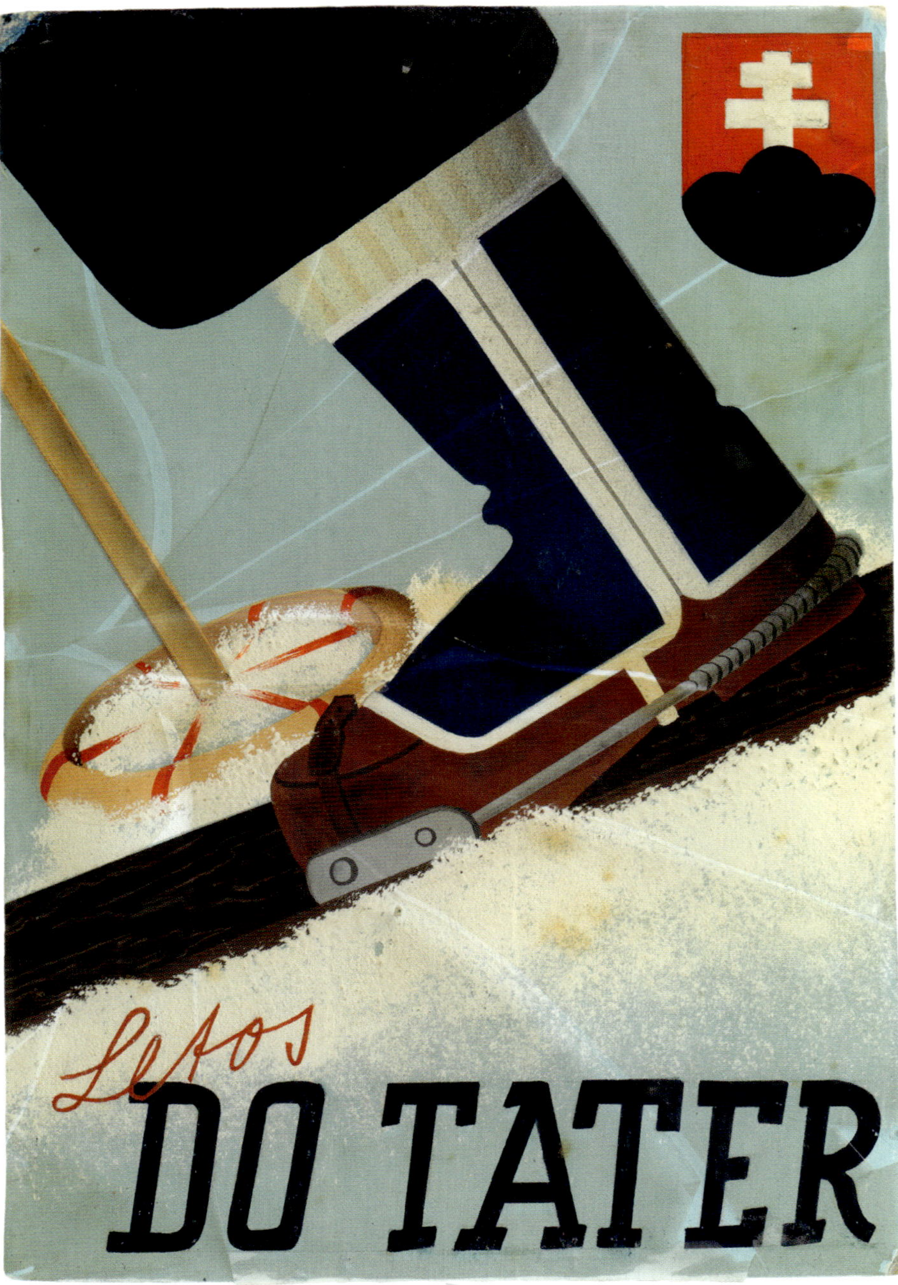

3

Letos Do Tater (This year to the
Tatras), about 1938–39
Advertising poster design
Inscribed on reverse '1112.
Hermannová/17/Titelseite für
ein Prospekt "Heuer in die Tatra"'
(Title page for a leaflet "This year
to the Tatras")
PP.2005.38.49

This is a design for a poster
promoting winter holidays in
the popular skiing resort of the
Tatra Mountains on the border
between former Czechoslovakia
and Poland. Perhaps an exercise
suggested for the local tourist
board, the Slovak coat of arms
can be seen in the upper right
corner. This simple design,
comprised of one booted
foot, a ski and a pole with the
suggestion of snow underfoot is
bold and effective.

   A 1945 letter from Marianne
to her friend Petr Erben showed
that she liked to ski in the winter.
However, on 20 December 1941
the Nazis forced the Jewish
population in Prague to hand
over all ski equipment as part
of increasing restrictions on
Jewish life.

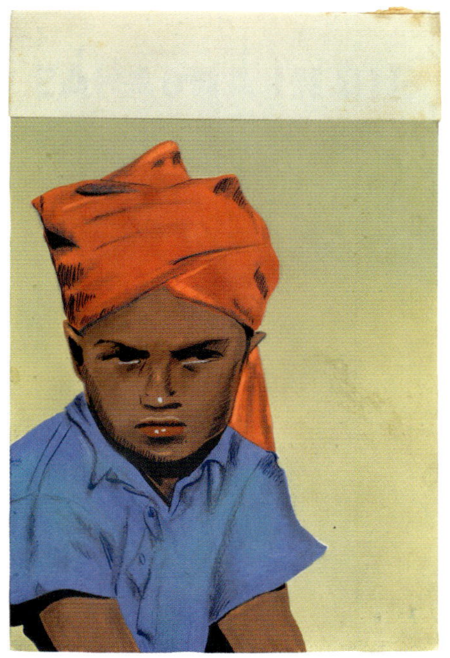

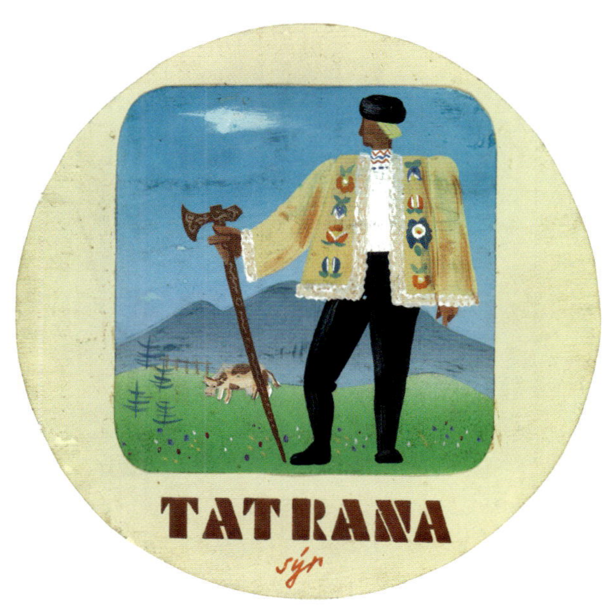

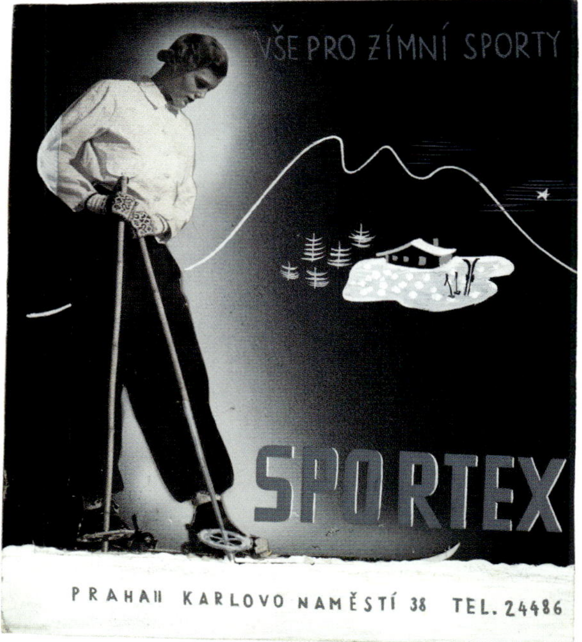

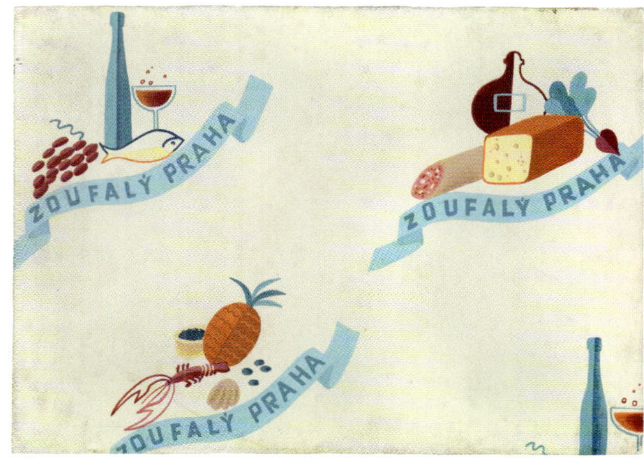

Fig. 4.3 Further examples of Marianne's student artworks include exercises in designs for product packaging, book covers, wrapping papers and business adverts
PP.2005.38.47, .48, .54, .56

Theresienstadt: 28 April 1942 –18 December 1943

Transport designation Ao, 28 April 1942 from Prague to Theresienstadt, 927 people murdered, 72 survived

THERESIENSTADT (IN CZECH, TEREZÍN), neither strictly a ghetto nor a concentration camp but something between the two, was established by the Nazis in a walled fortress town about 39 miles north of Prague as a place to hold wealthy and high-profile, mainly Czech, Jews. The first transport of people arrived on 24 November 1941. Promoted as a model camp, it was used in Nazi propaganda to conceal the truth about

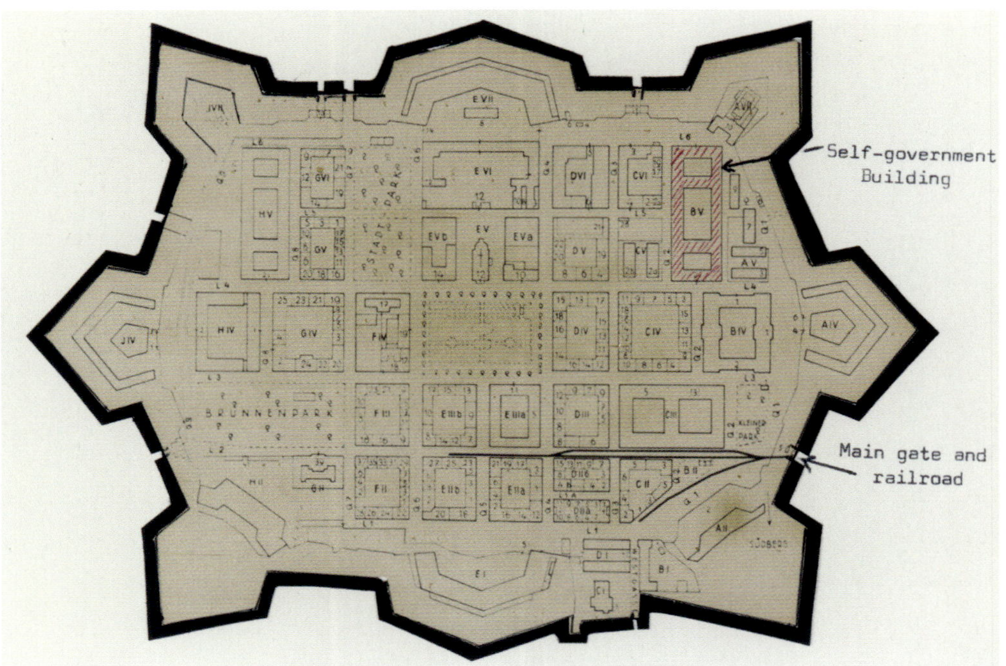

Fig. 4.4 Map of the Theresienstadt ghetto, from an original document (1942–1945), mounted in an album assembled by a survivor. Collection of the US Holocaust Memorial Museum, courtesy of Henry Kahn

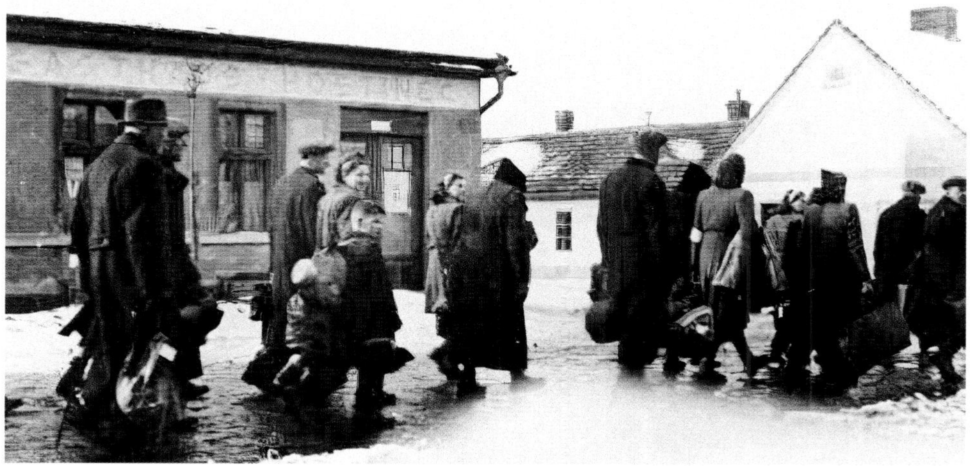

Fig. 4.5 Jewish transportees walking to Theresienstadt from the railway station in Bohušovice nad Ohří, before tracks were built directly to the ghetto in 1943.
The Jewish Museum in Prague

Jewish deportations. In an elaborate ruse to deceive an international Red Cross inspection of living conditions on 23 June 1944, the town was beautified, flowers planted, buildings painted, and fake coffee houses set up. The impression of a well-run resort for Jews was further presented in a film, *The Führer gives the Jews a Town*, and in an album of picture postcard views by Dutch artist Joseph Spier (1900–1978). Joseph Goebbels (1897–1945), Minister of Propaganda for the German Third Reich, claimed, 'While the Jews in Theresienstadt sit in cafes, drinking coffee, eating cake and dancing, our soldiers bear all the weight of a horrible war'.

In reality, Theresienstadt was only a temporary stop on the way to concentration, labour and extermination camps. Of the approximately 155,000 Jews who passed through its gates before its closure on 8 May 1945, nearly 90,000 were taken further east to almost certain death. Poor hygiene and malnutrition killed over 35,000 in Theresienstadt itself, and this too was deliberate. However, despite the terrible conditions and constant threat of deportation, a vibrant cultural life developed in Theresienstadt, reflecting the many talented artists, writers, musicians, actors and intellectuals imprisoned there and the inmates' strong will to survive. Against the odds they put on theatre performances and concerts and ran a clandestine school and lending library.

Many of Marianne's artworks are stained and torn, a testament to the dangerous times in which they were made, the dark places in which they were secreted, and the arduous journeys they endured. When Marianne was transported from Theresienstadt to Auschwitz, she left her drawings with her friend Petr Erben for safe keeping. When he was deported, he in turn gave them to a trusted friend to hide. Both Petr and the pictures survived. After the war he sent them to Marianne in Sweden. She wrote to thank him on 30 November 1945: 'Thank you for your letter and for the drawings that I received today. I had forgotten them almost completely and they aroused in me the old memories from Terezín, and especially memories of people who were then so close to me and now are dead. You know Petr, never in my life will I forget and will never come to terms with what happened. It is simply going to stick with us forever like a rock on the bottom of a lake.'[1]

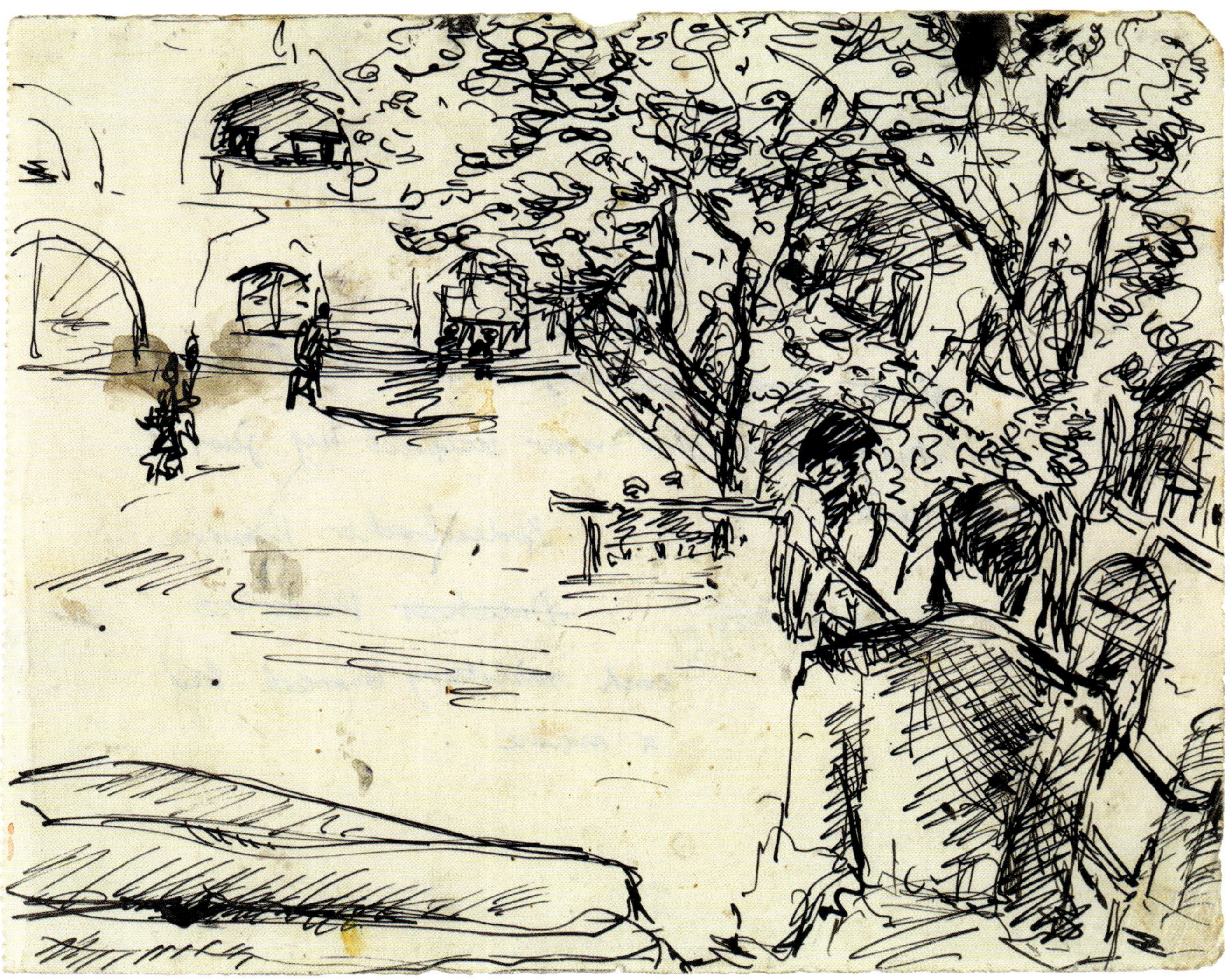

4

**Courtyard of
Bodenbacher
Barrack**, 1942–43,
Ink on paper page
from spiral bound
notebook
Unsigned
P.P.2005.38.5

*View of courtyard showing part of the military barrack, which was housing Jewish women. It was called Bodenbacher Kaserne (military barrack).**

Marianne adds an air of menace and surveillance to this quick sketch, showing the back of a uniformed male officer watching figures in the courtyard below. Families were split up in the ghetto, and living quarters for men and boys older than 12 were separate from those for women and children. Sanitary facilities were poor. In July 1943 Bodenbacher Barrack was cleared and repurposed as archival storage for the Reich's Main Security Office (*Reichssicherheitshauptamt* or RSHA), relocated from Berlin due to the threat of Allied bombardment.

* Throughout the catalogue Marianne's own words are indicated by the use of italics.

5

Inside the Bodenbacher Barrack,
1942
Watercolour on paper page from
spiral bound notebook
Signed and dated at top right 'MH 42.
BDK'.
PP.2005.38.6

*My corner which I shared with my
mother Anna Hermann in Bodenbacher
Kaserne showing all our possessions,
and also how we tried to make our
corner look beautiful, with little shelves
and wall hangings. This was the first
picture I did in Theresienstadt. The wall
hanging was a sheet to camouflage our
clothing and other meagre possessions.*

Prisoners were only allowed to bring
50kg of luggage with them, and
valuables, such as fur coats, money
and jewellery, were confiscated at
the 'Schleuse' (sluice), where newly
arrived deportees were registered
and searched. Somehow Marianne
managed to keep hold of her
watercolour paints. Forty women
were crowded into their dormitory,
each allocated only about 60 x 200
cm, just enough room to lie down.
Marianne described the corner site
they were given as a luxury, and they
had shelves made. Painting helped
Marianne maintain a positive attitude
when so much had been taken away.

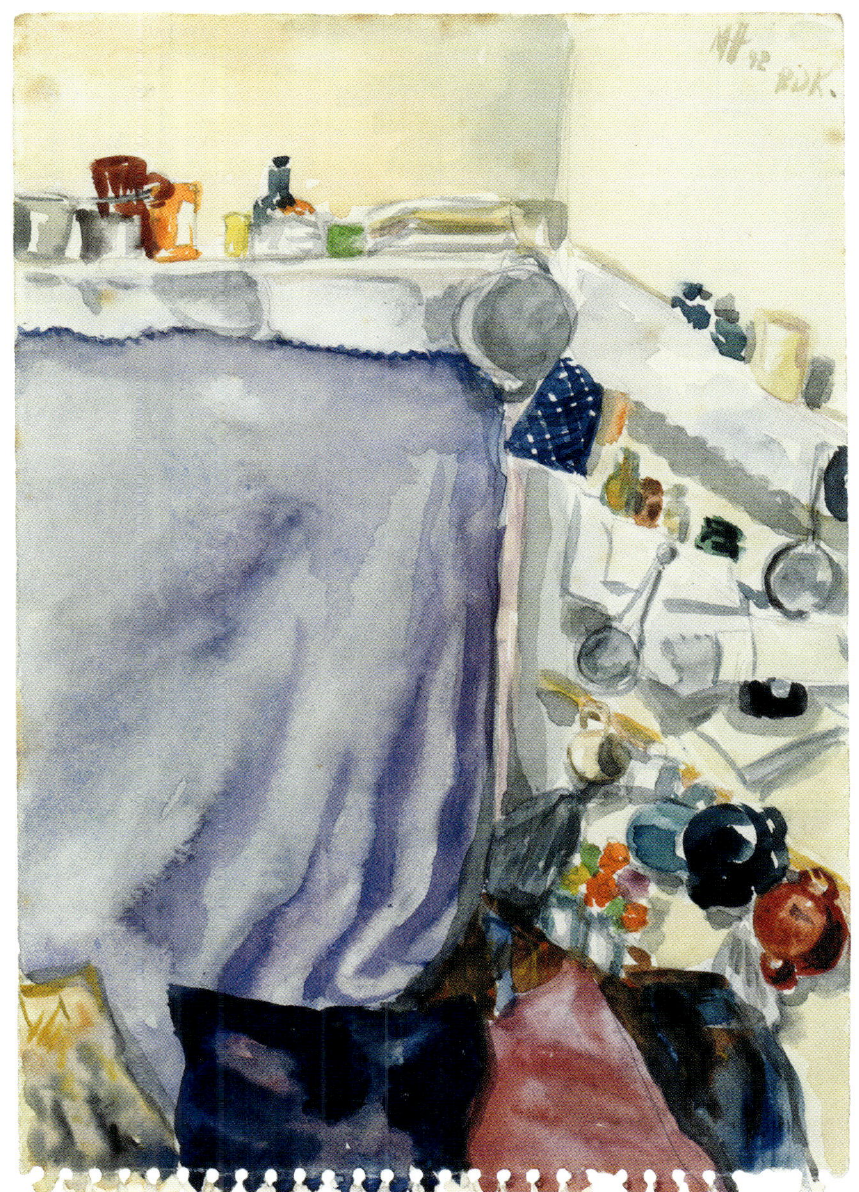

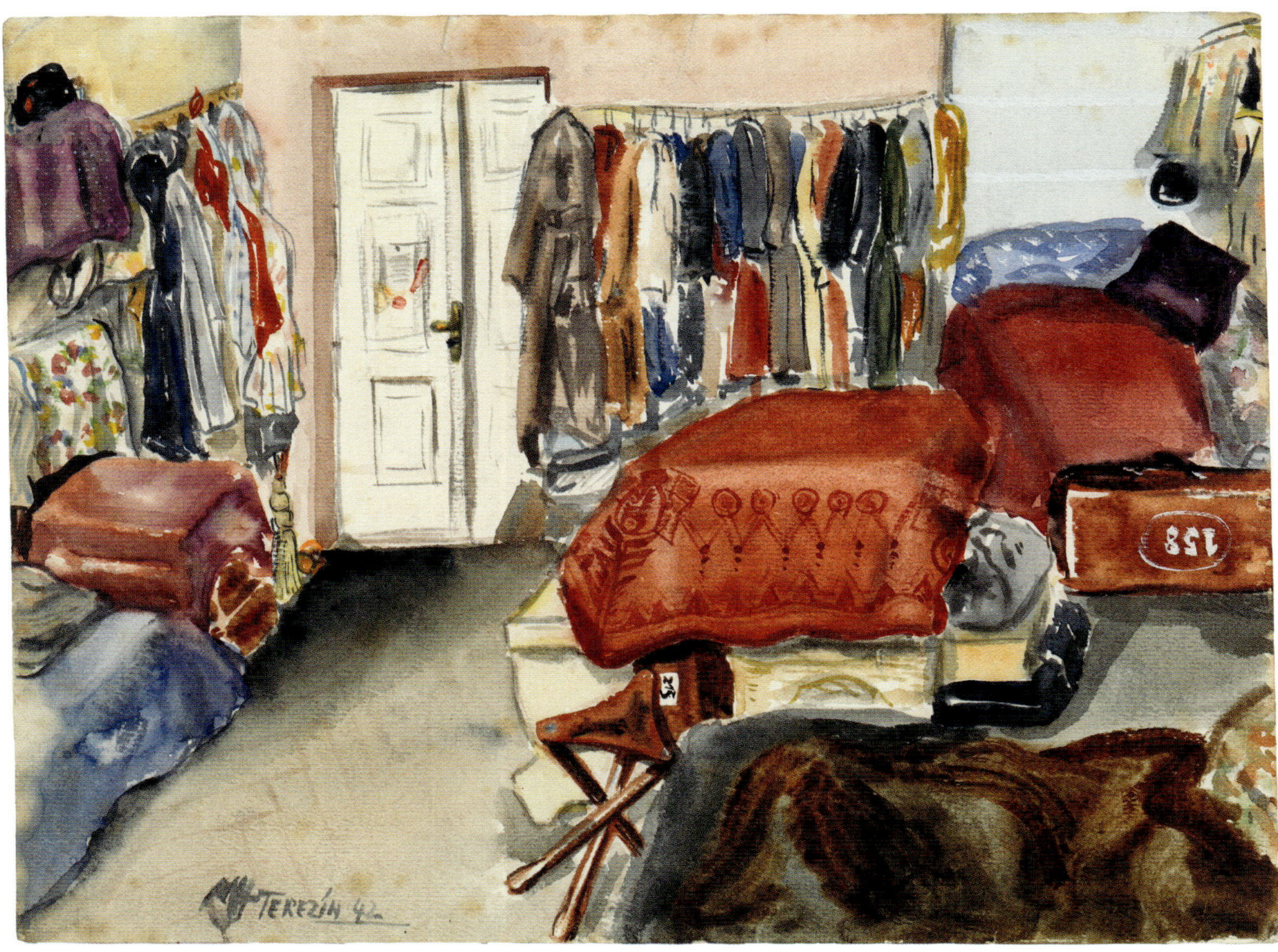

6
Youth Room, 1942
Watercolour on paper, 1942
Signed and dated at lower left
'MH Terezín 42'.
PP.2005.38.13

After the Czech population was moved out of the ghetto some of the dwelling houses were allocated to the Jewish youth. This was the room I was in. Before the bunk beds were installed, we slept on the floor and made our furniture to sit on from suitcases.

Until mid-June 1942 almost 3,000 of Theresienstadt's original residents still lived there, and Jewish prisoners were accommodated in the former military barracks. After the Czech residents were moved out of the town, 218 townhouses were made available to Jewish prisoners, Nazi officers and the ghetto administration. Marianne was moved to a special dormitory allocated to Jewish youth; she remembers this as being L49. In this watercolour you can see the beautiful parquet floor and panelled door with an ornate brass handle in what had been somebody's home.

7

Youth Room – visitor at the bunk bed of Lotte Lang,
1942/43
Black ink drawing painted with a
piece of wood on paper
Unsigned
PP.2005.38.23

The name of the girl was Lotte Lang. She survived, married and went to live in Germany.

In the youth homes set up by the Jewish council in Theresienstadt, children lived a collective life under the guidance of youth leaders rather than with their own parents. However, the council did not enforce separation, and only about half of the children in the ghetto lived in these homes. Indeed, Marianne's mother shared a bed with her in the youth dormitory. Other parents, immersed in the daily struggle for survival, felt separation was better for the children. Is the woman in this tender drawing, with headscarf and gloves, a mother visiting her daughter?

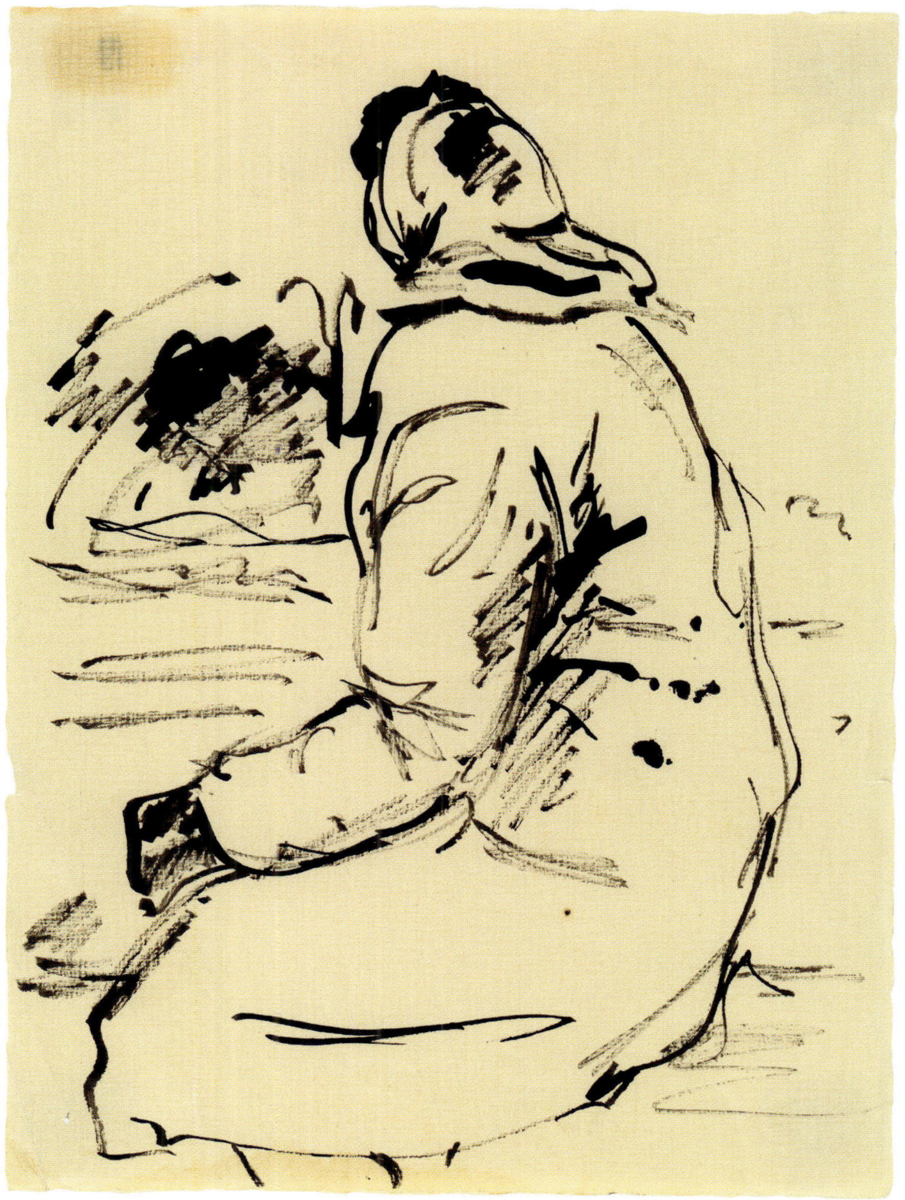

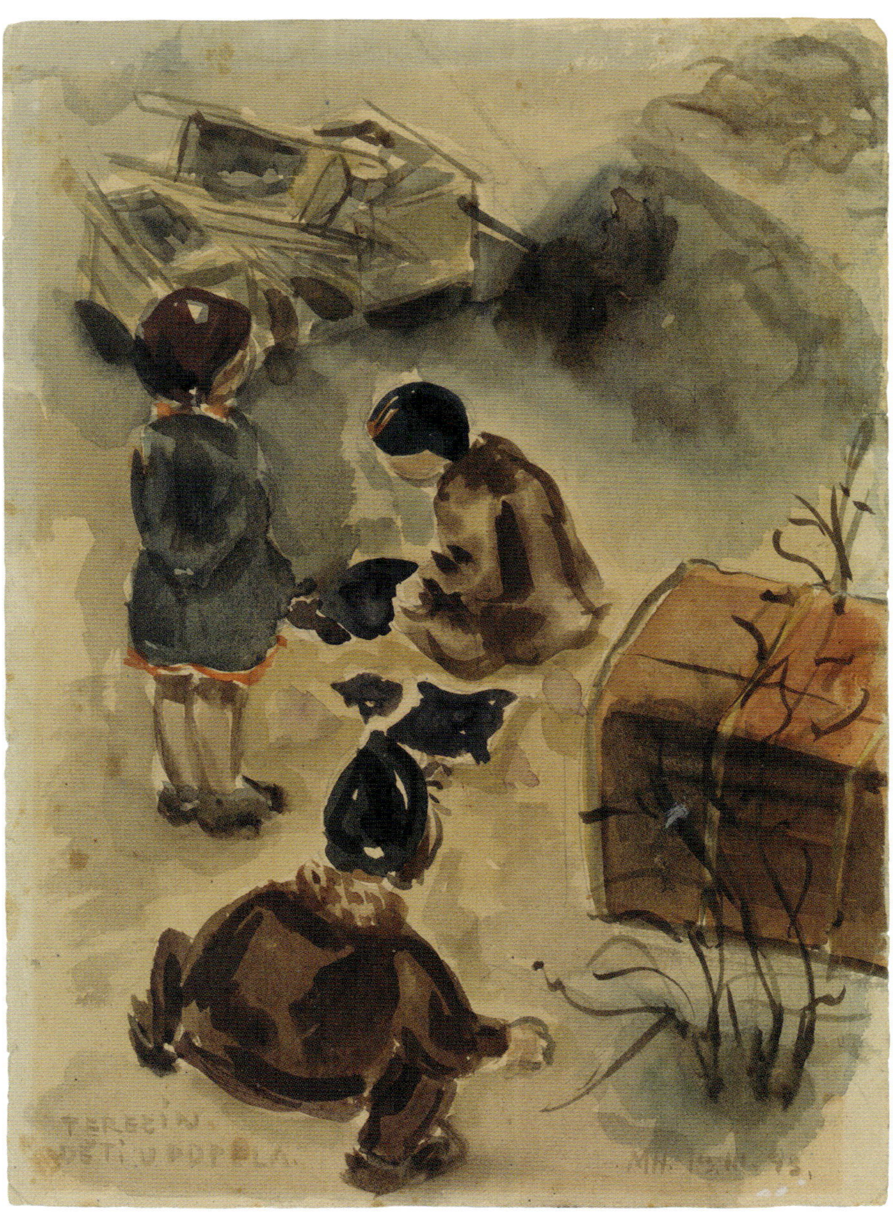

8

Děti u Popela – Children at the Ashes, 19 March 1943
Watercolour on paper
Inscribed at lower left 'TEREZIN/ DĚTI U POPELA', signed and dated at lower right 'MH. 19.III.43.'
PP.2005.38.16

Children playing in winter with hot ashes from the stoves that heated the dwellings. View is from below the balcony of L49 showing the courtyard of an original Czech house.

Children in the youth houses experienced slightly better living conditions and were less exposed to the negative influences of ghetto life. Here Marianne paints them playing with ash as if at a sandbox. Ash piles were common in societies where households had coal or wood burning fires, but have added poignancy here with the painful knowledge that Theresienstadt was just a staging post on the way to the furnaces of Auschwitz. Besides playing, children in the youth houses were also secretly educated by their leaders and in the evenings took part in cultural activities.

9

Singsong on the Shabbat in the Youth Room, 1942/43
Watercolour on paper
Unsigned
PP.2005.38.14

Sitting in twilight on furniture made of luggage in the Youth Room L49 in a dwelling house originally belonging to Czech people.

Marianne paints her friends gathering together on a Friday evening for the Shabbat. The intimacy of the group, who also secretly learned Hebrew every day at 5a.m. before work, is evident in the way they comfortably lean in together. These were among Marianne's happiest memories of Theresienstadt. While educational activities were officially forbidden by the Nazis and had to be carried out covertly, religious rites and celebrations of religious holidays were largely tolerated. Participation in these events was vital for the mental wellbeing of prisoners, creating, at least temporarily, the illusion of normal life.

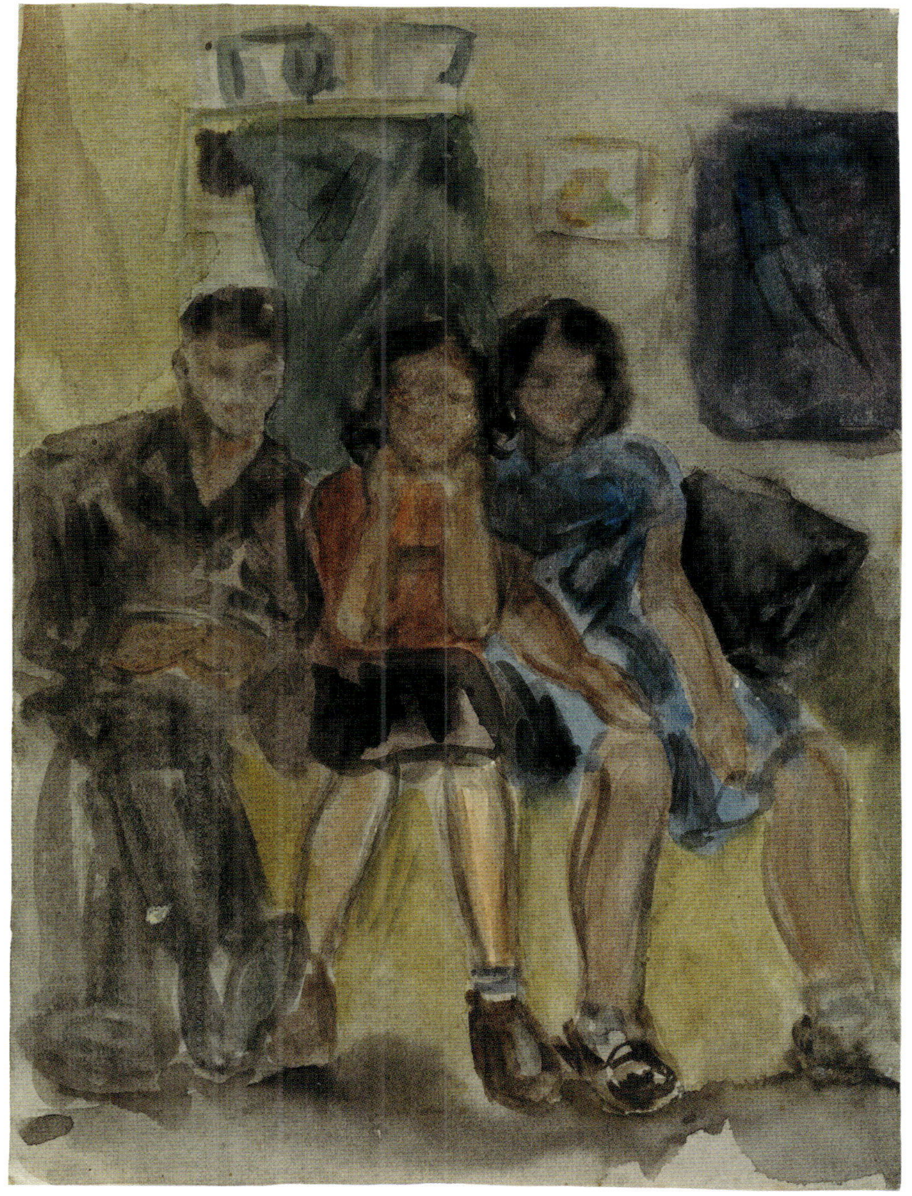

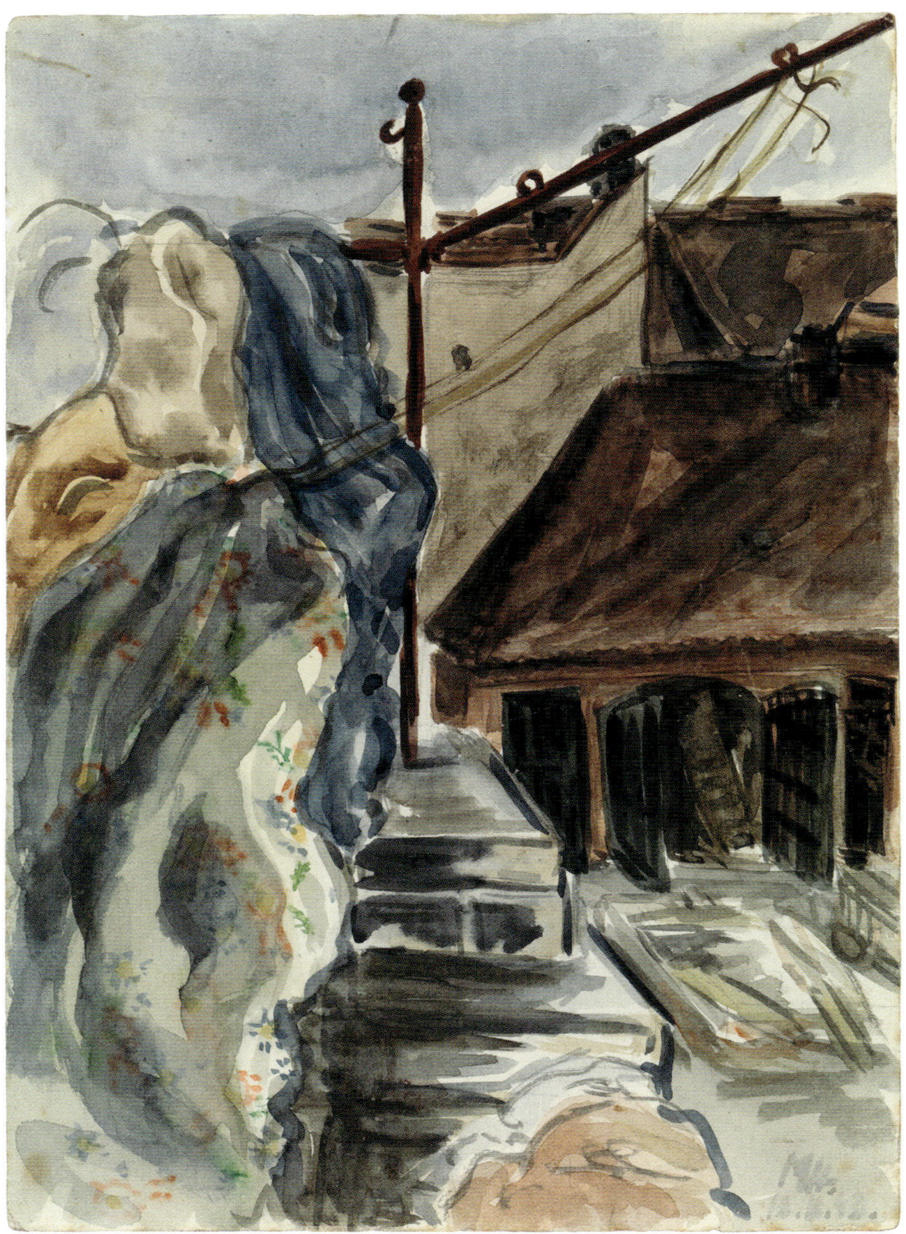

10
View onto the courtyard from Youth Home, 13 October 1943
Watercolour on paper
Signed and dated at lower right
'MH./13.10.43.'
PP.2005.38.15

Airing the bedding on the balcony. During the warm summer we aired the bedclothes on the balcony to try and get rid of the bedbugs infesting the bedding.

Marianne was probably drawn by the decorative potential of this scene, colourful bedding blowing in the breeze. However, the truth was that the ghetto was plagued by lice, fleas, flies and bedbugs as a result of overcrowding and poor hygiene. Blankets and pillows had to be aired every morning. In some cases of extreme infestation, mattresses and bedsheets had to be fumigated with Zyklon B which was originally developed as an insecticide. However, the product became infamous for its later use by the Nazis in the gas chambers of the extermination camps.

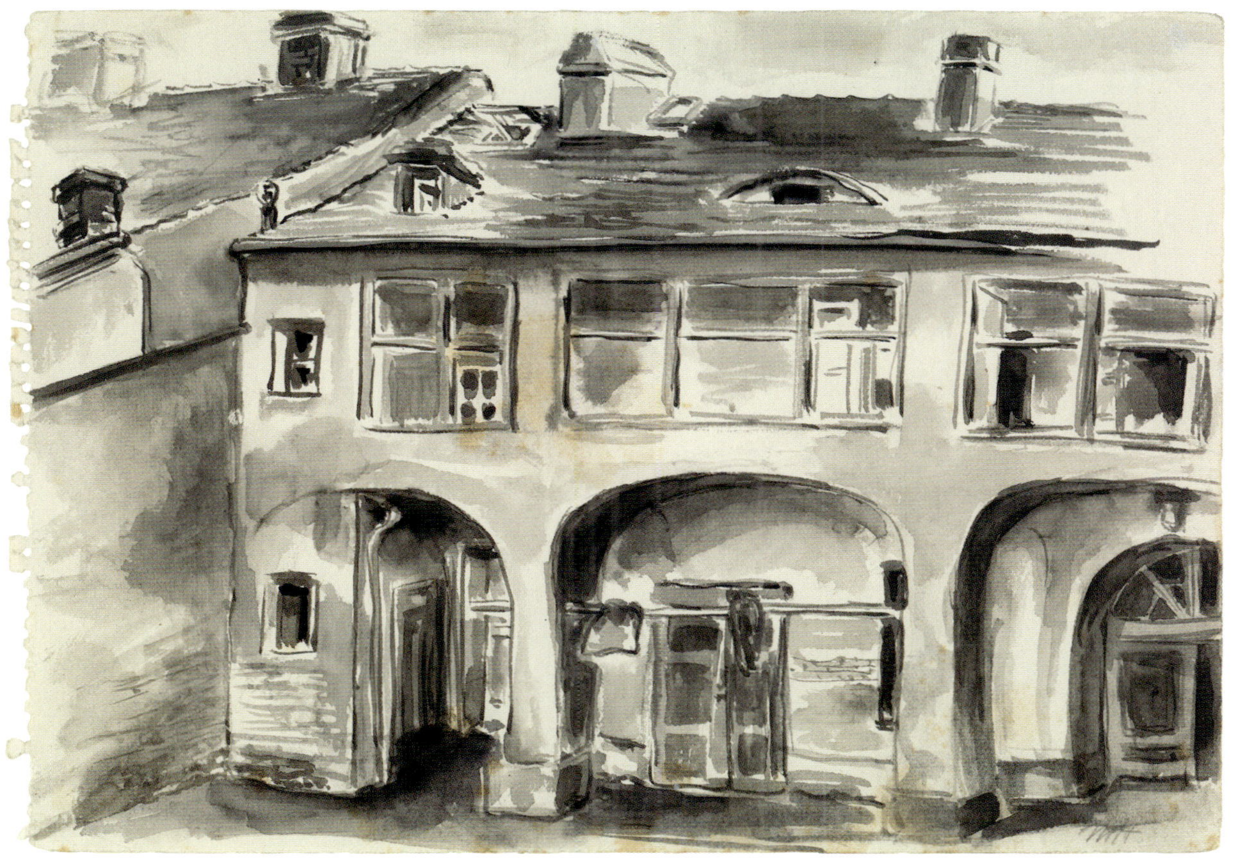

11
**Courtyard of Youth
Home L218**, 1942/43
Watercolour on paper
page from spiral bound
notebook
Signed at lower right 'MH'
PP.2005.38.4

This is the courtyard of L218, another 'Jugendheim' (Youth Home), where Marianne's dear friend Petr Erben (1921–2017) lived. It was he who ensured the survival of her Theresienstadt drawings when she was deported to Auschwitz.

Petr arrived in Theresienstadt on 30 September 1942. There he became a youth leader like Marianne. He was deported to Auschwitz on 28 September 1944 and subsequently to Mauthausen in January 1945. From there, he was sent to Gusen, a sub-camp of Mauthausen, where he was liberated on 5 May 1945. After the war he lived in Prague and kept up correspondence with Marianne, helping her to recover some of the belongings she had stored with relatives and friends before deportation. In 1948, Peter and his fiancée Eva (neé Lövidtová, b. 1930) emigrated from Czechoslovakia to Israel, where they lived in Ashkelon and were closely involved in many Holocaust awareness initiatives.

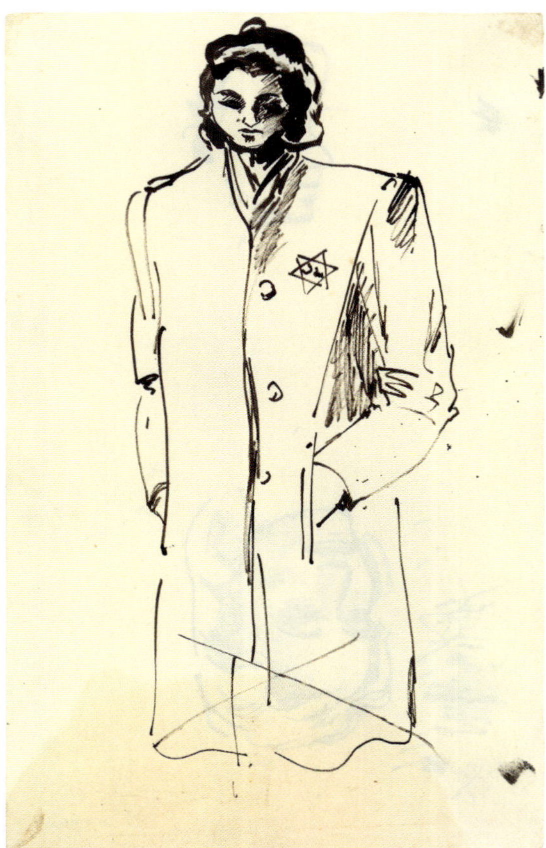
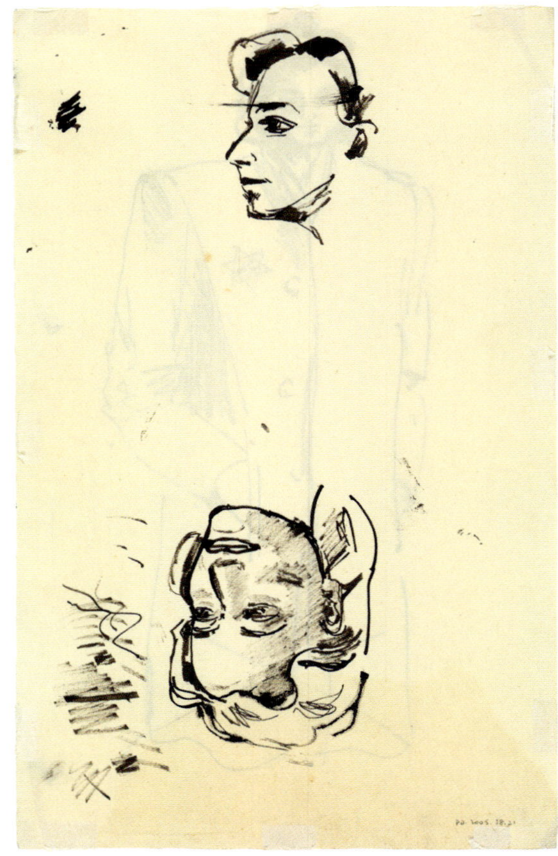

12
Girl with yellow star, 1942/43
Ink on paper, double-sided
Unsigned
PP.2005.38.21

Paper was precious and Marianne used this single sheet to make three separate head and figure studies. The head of a man bears a close resemblance to Petr Erben. The two women have not been identified but the full-length sketch is particularly notable. The cross in the lower section was probably intended to situate the figure in space. The woman stands with sorrowful, downcast eyes, hands in the pockets of a coat onto which a Star of David badge has been sewn.

Reinhard Heydrich, Chief of Reich Security and one of the principal figures behind the 'Final Solution', ordered that from 1 September 1941 all Jews over the age of six in the Protectorate of Bohemia and Moravia must wear a yellow Star of David badge with the word *Jude* on the left side of their clothing. A series of restrictions and antisemitic laws had gradually pushed Jewish citizens to the margins of society, but this was one of the most significant signs of their segregation. It was part of the Nazis' plan to humiliate and control the Jewish population and better facilitate their deportation and ultimate destruction.

13

**My artist friend at work in
Theresienstadt – František Lukáš,**
1942/43
Watercolour on paper
Signed 'MH' at lower right
PP.2005.38.19

*In the ghetto there were a number of large
cottage industries including making pictures,
photo albums, sewing and cobblers – all
different sorts of things. It was slave labour.*

In Theresienstadt, everyone aged 14 and
above was required to work. Many artists in
the ghetto were exploited by the Nazis to
create idealized images of Theresienstadt
for propaganda purposes. František Lukáš
(previously Lustig) (1911–1996) was a
good friend whom Marianne had known
from her art student days in Prague. Three
times he managed to get her mother Anna
off the transport to Auschwitz because of
contacts he had in the Jewish Council. He
was one of the professional artists working
in the printing workshop of the Technical
Drawing Department in the Magdeburg
Barracks. In Marianne's watercolour a
female figure stands to his right at an
easel. Fewer women chose to work in the
technical drawing studio but there were
some, as can be seen in Haas' drawing (fig.
1.2, p.37). Could this even be a self-portrait
of Marianne painting Lukáš' portrait? In his
free time, Lukáš drew humorous caricature
portraits of ghetto inmates.

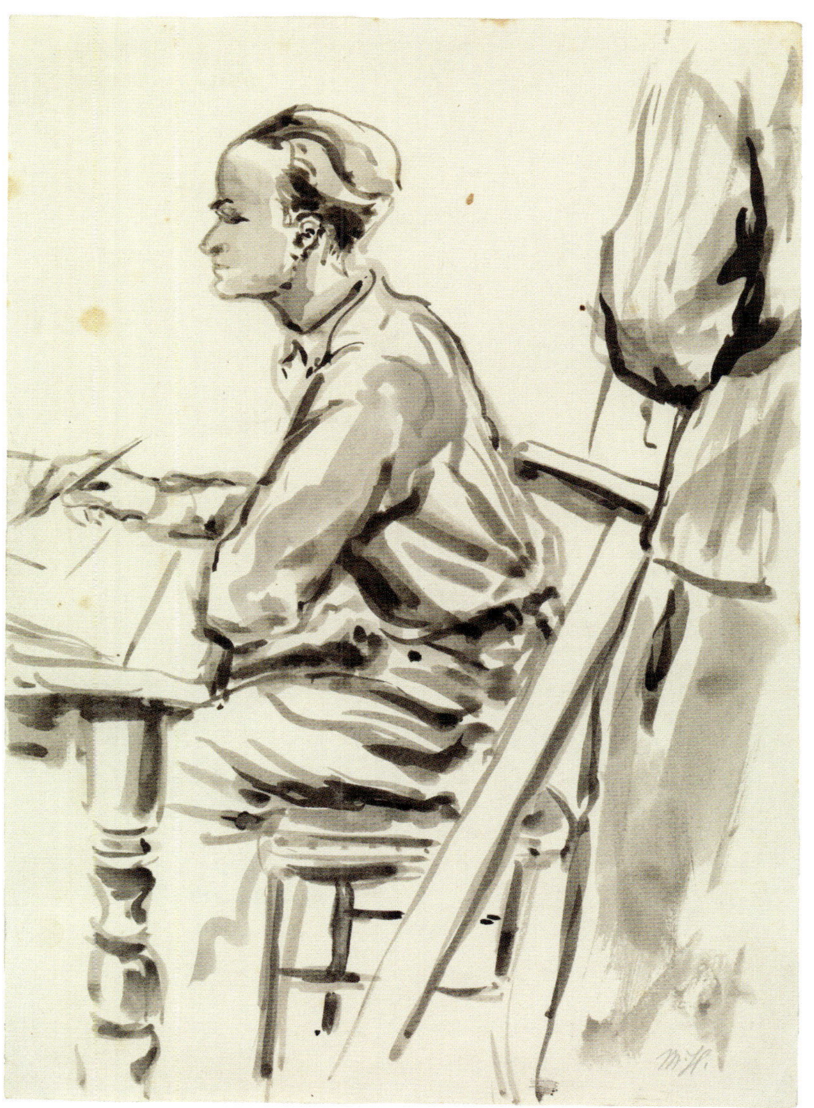

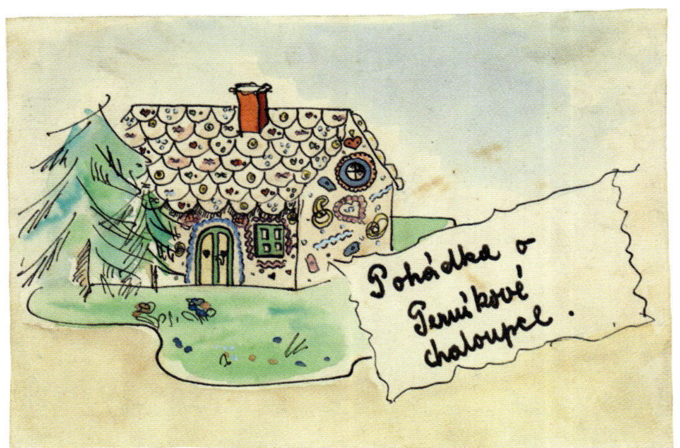

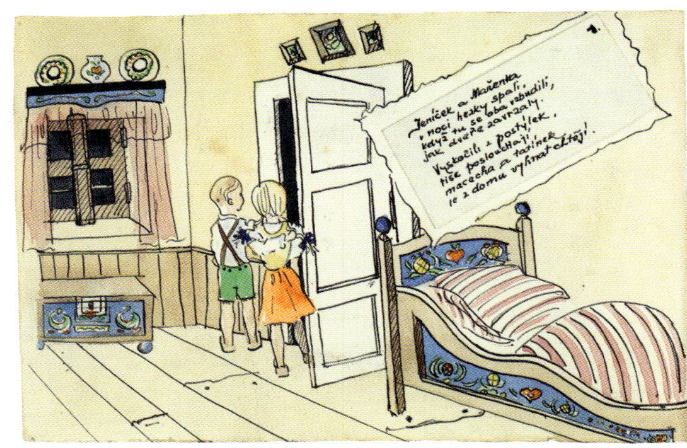

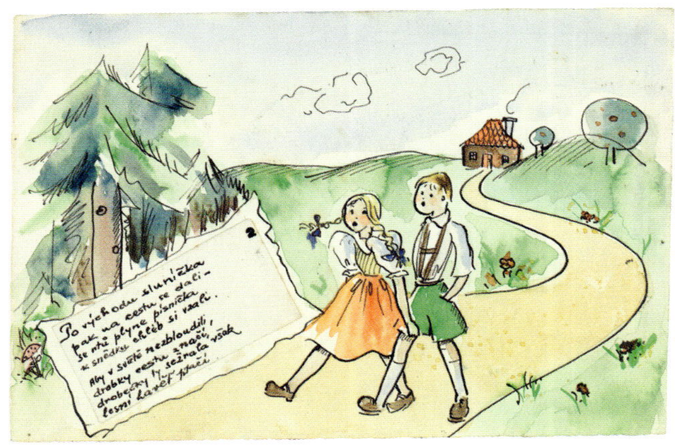

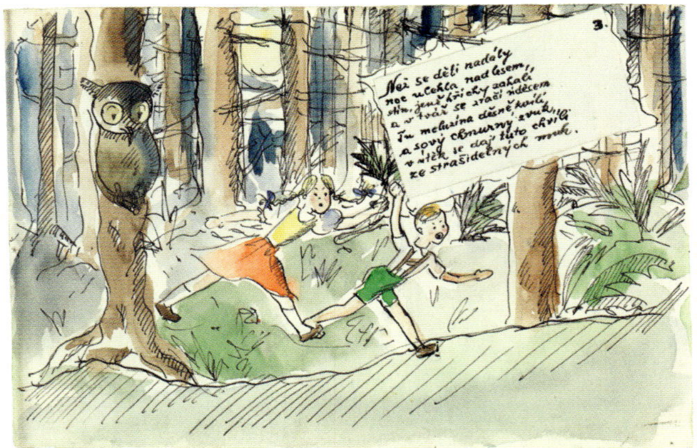

14
Pages from
Hansel and Gretel storybook, 1942/43
Watercolour and ink on paper, folded and double-sided with
written story applied
Poem signed with initials 'JP'
PP.2005.38.17

*I made different things, like this storybook, for children's
and adults' birthdays. Somebody wrote the poem. I did the
illustration and made the storybook.*

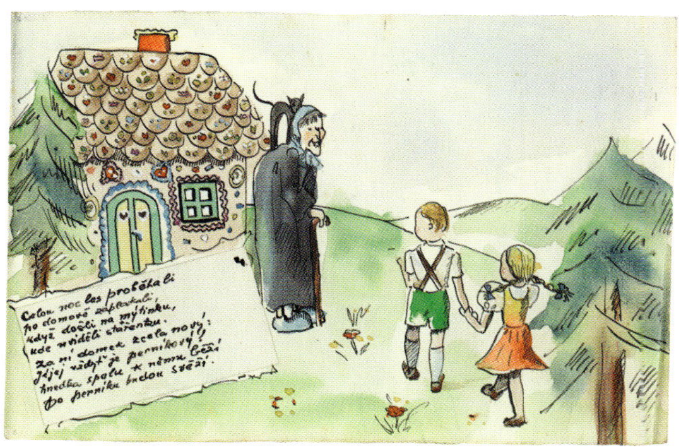

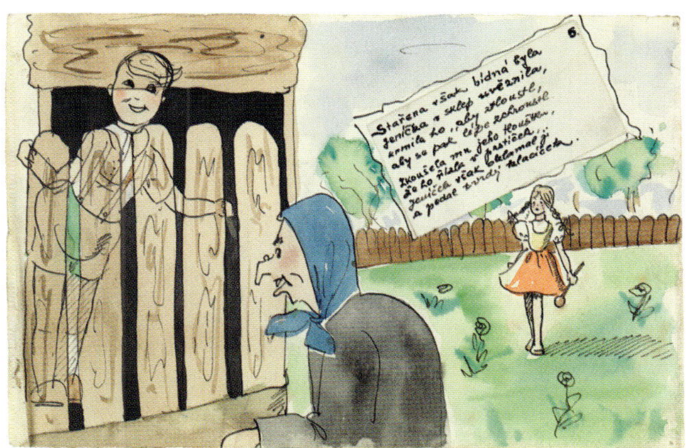

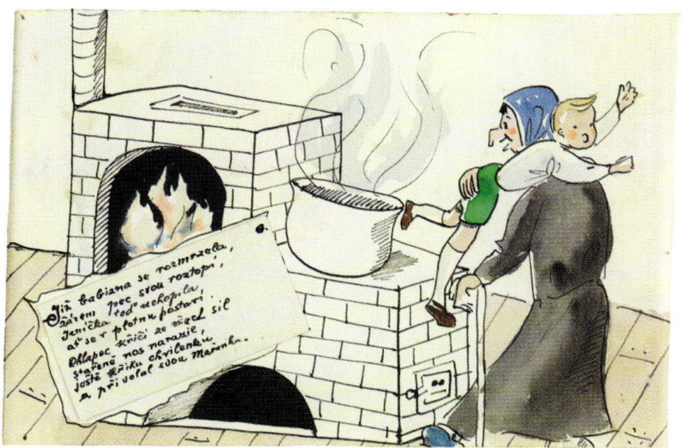

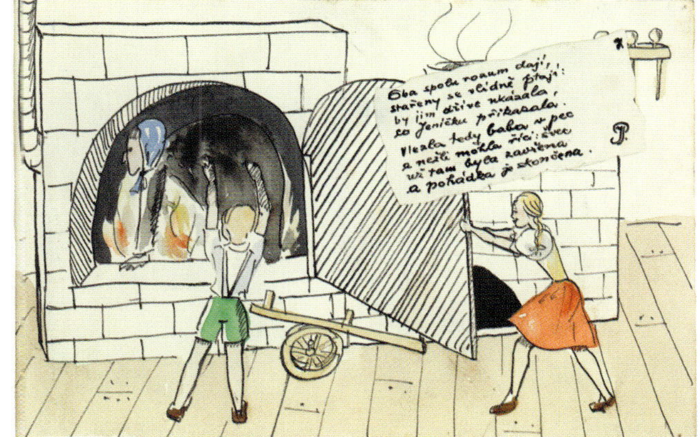

In the harsh conditions of the ghetto prisoners found joy in keeping festivals and celebrating birthdays. Resources were limited, so gifts were all the more meaningful. Acts of personal kindness and generosity were a means of spiritual revolt against the Nazi oppressors; they signalled a refusal to give up on their previous lives, a desire to remember happier times. Made before Marianne knew about the gas chambers and crematoria of Auschwitz, there is nevertheless great poignancy in this storybook retelling of the Hansel and Gretel tale. In Auschwitz, she made a further Hansel and Gretel picture book as a late Christmas present for the family of a Slovak SS guard.

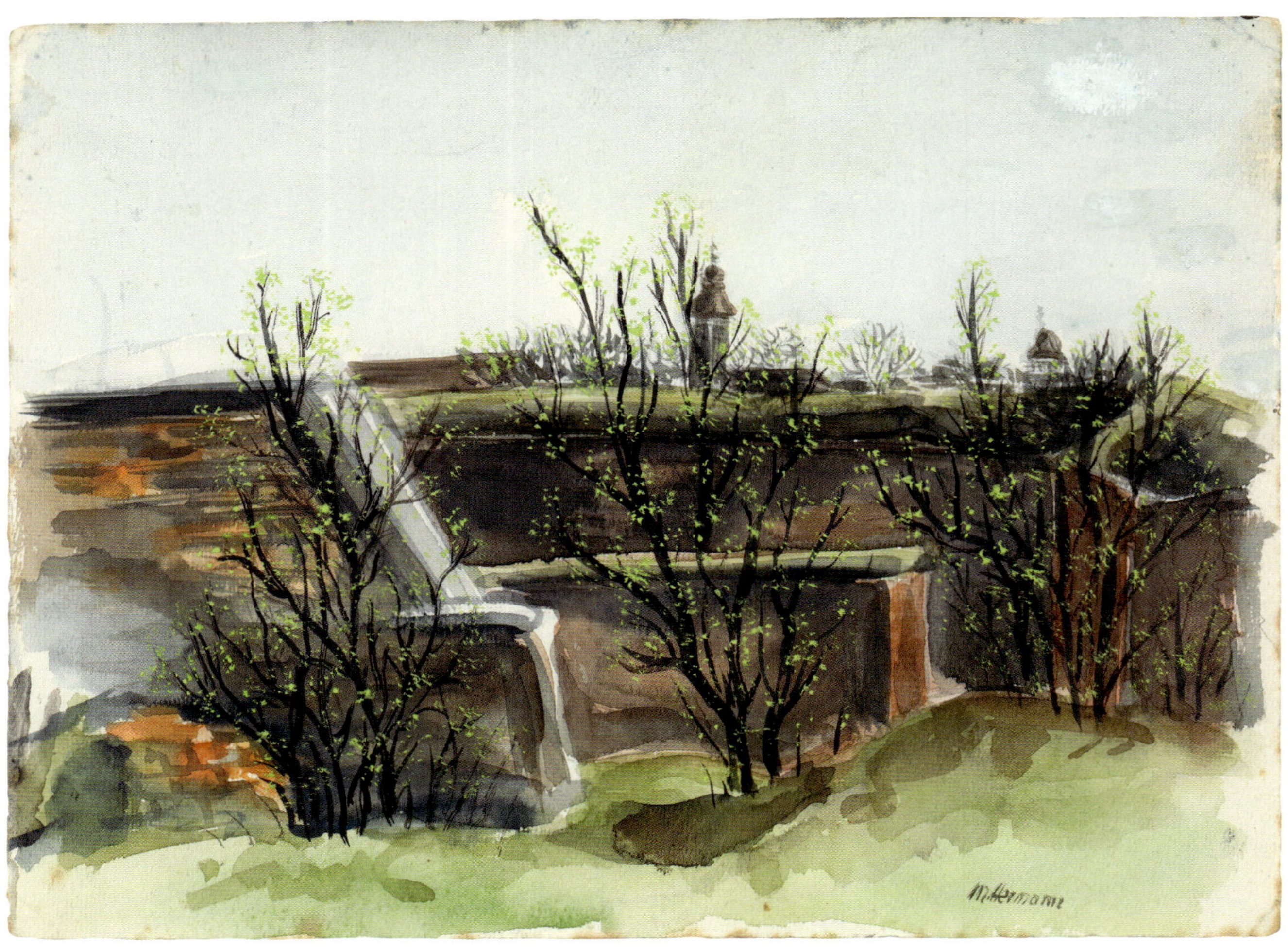

15
Youth Garden, 1942/43,
retouched about 1997–2002
Watercolour and gouache on
paper
Signed at lower right 'M.
Hermann'
PR.2005.38.24

The surrounding walls of Theresienstadt where the small youth market gardens were. We called it the 'Garden of the Iron Gate'. There was a small decorative iron gate that had been left there neglected. We cultivated on top of the walls and in between the walls. Girls from about 12 to 18 made it fertile by turning it over and growing seeds we were given. I was second in charge. I kept the record of the produce that went to market. The leader was a girl called Meda. She didn't survive.

Despite being an artist, Marianne chose to work in agriculture. Having already had experience of farming as part of her Zionist training, she became a supervisor in one of the youth gardens. Marianne added the green leaves to this painting later. She had meant to include them when it was first painted, as it was spring.

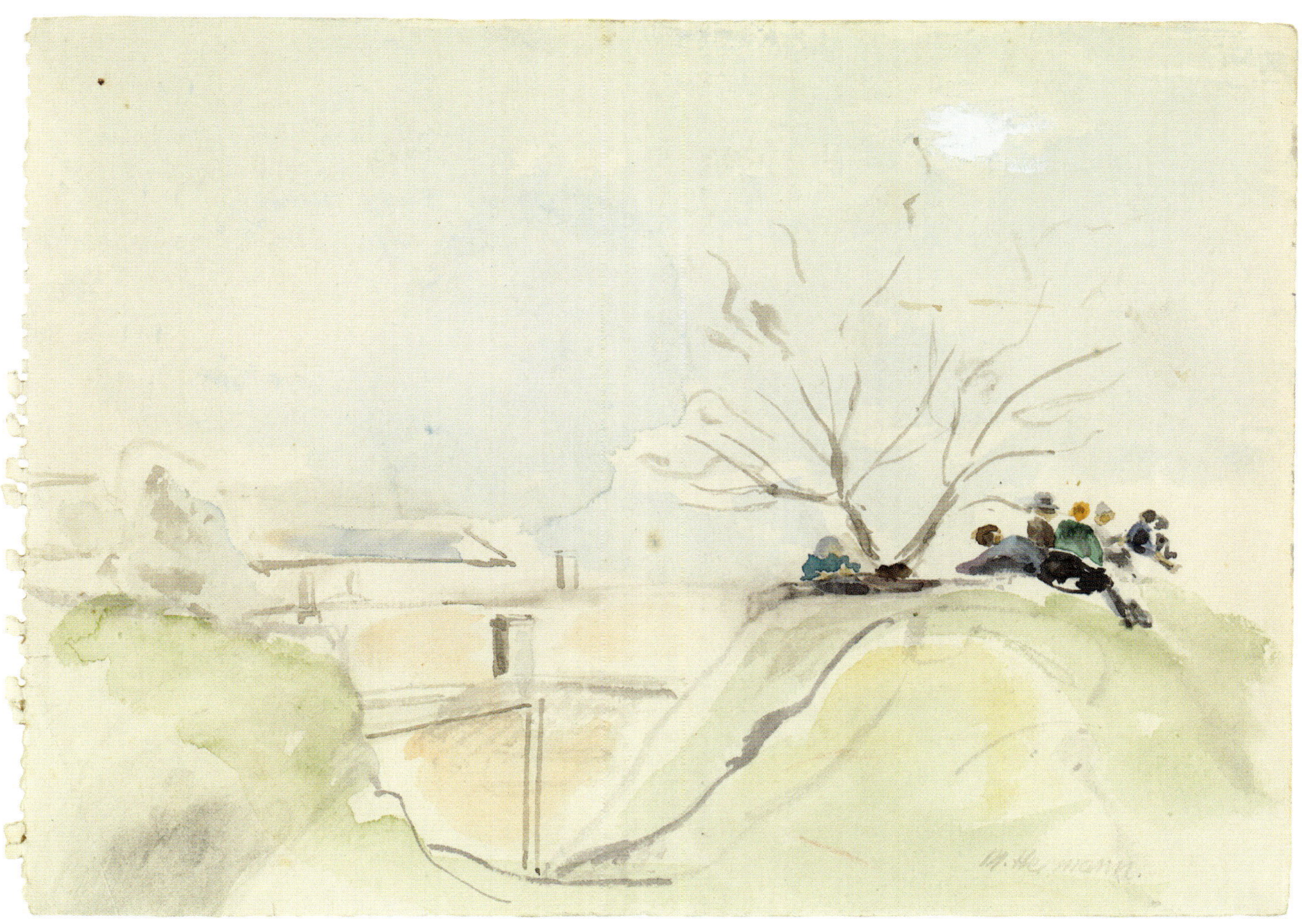

16

**Na Baště. Leisure time on
the mounds surrounding the
ghetto**, 1942/43
Watercolour on paper page from
spiral bound notebook
Signed at lower right
'M. Hermann'
PP.2005.38.12

*My leisure time was late afternoon after a long day working in agriculture in the youth
garden.*

Each working group in Theresienstadt had precisely allocated time slots for work and
'leisure'. Marianne spent much of her precious free time outside drawing and painting,
which brought brief respite and happiness. The Czech title of this work, *Na Baště*, means
'On the Bastion'. The inmates turned part of the ghetto's massive fortifications into a
green recreational area which they called 'Southern Hill', or simply 'the Bastion'. They
were not allowed on any other green areas inside the ghetto as these were fenced off
and reserved for German officers.

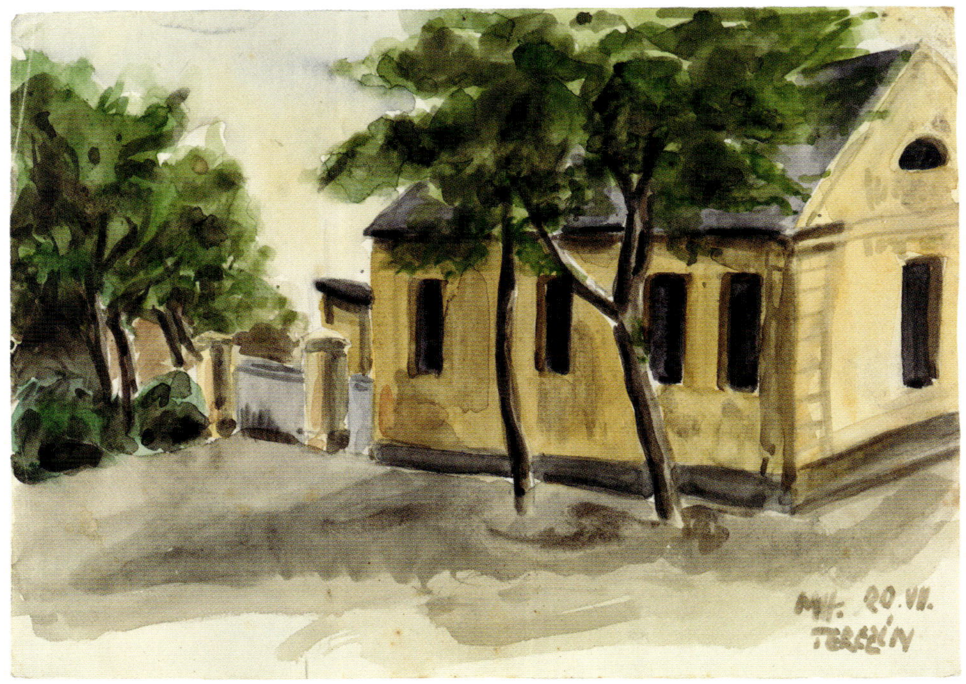

17

Military police house, border entrance, 20 July 1942/43
Watercolour on paper
Signed and dated at lower right 'MH. 20.VII./Terezín'
PP.2005.38.25

The people going to do agricultural work beyond the ghetto would pass through here and would be counted in and out by the Czech guards.

Although working as part of the agricultural team was physically demanding and the hours were long, at least it was carried out in the open air and outside the enclosed space of the ghetto. Going to the gardens located on top of, between, and beyond the walls gave the workers a much-needed temporary escape from the constrained and extremely overcrowded streets of Theresienstadt. The surrounding walls of the ghetto were guarded by Czech non-Jewish police.

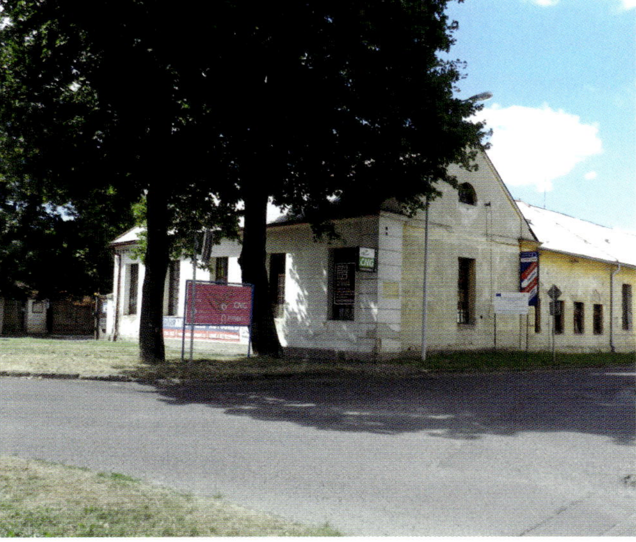

Fig. 4.6 The military police house as it looks today
© Peter Tuka

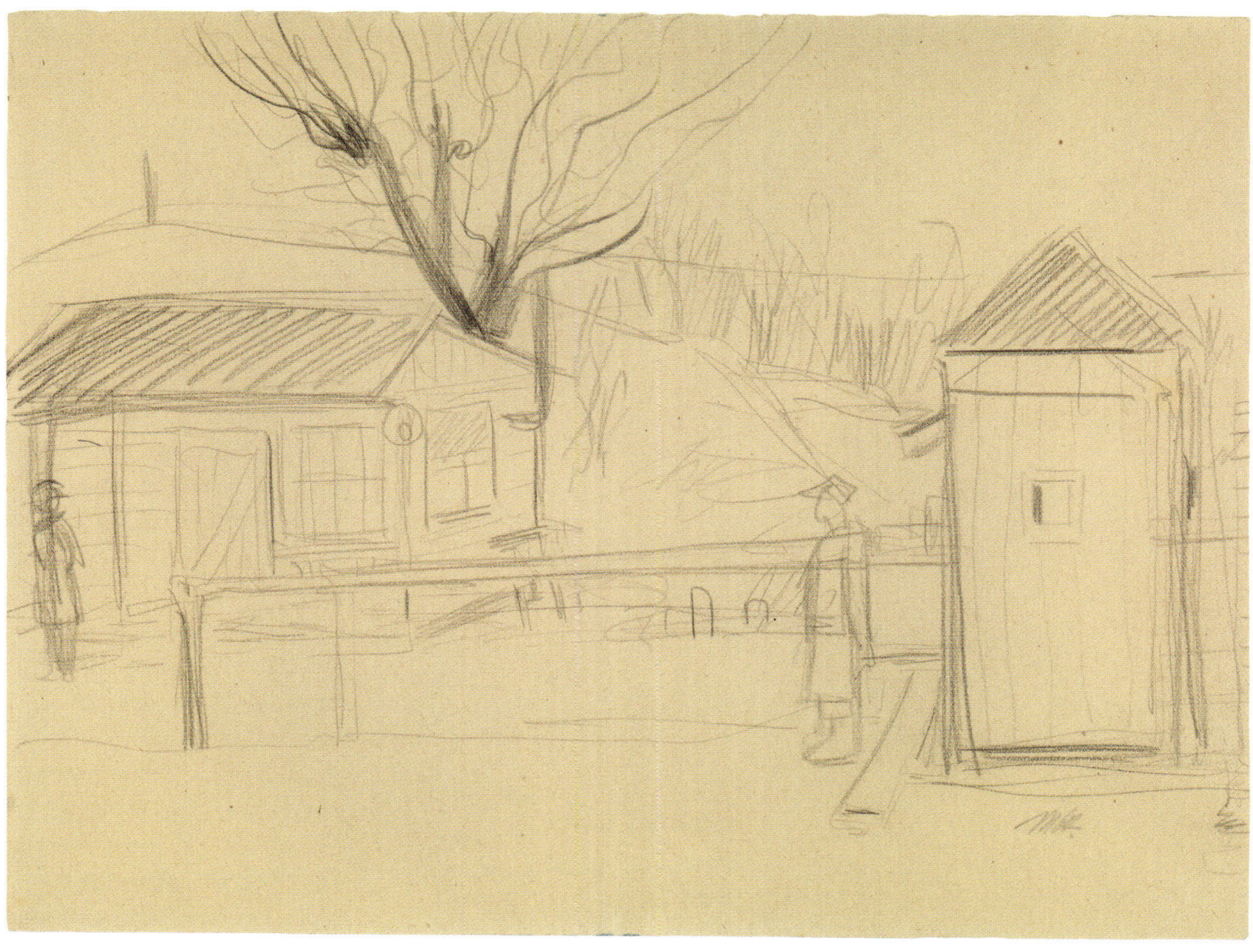

18

The sentry guardhouse entrance and exit, Theresienstadt Ghetto, 1943
Pencil on paper
Signed at lower right 'MH'
PP.2005.38.1

The hut on the left seems to be a wooden barrack. 'Western Barracks' and 'Southern Barracks' were built outside the ghetto walls in 1943 as additional accommodation to help combat overcrowding, but also for purposes such as storing agricultural tools. Produce from Theresienstadt gardens was intended entirely for the German market. However, as the diet of Jewish inmates was very poor and did not include any fruit or vegetables, agricultural workers were sometimes allowed to keep sub-standard produce. Additional items were frequently smuggled past the guards. Carrots, radishes, potatoes or lettuces hidden in clothing could be bartered among prisoners for other goods.

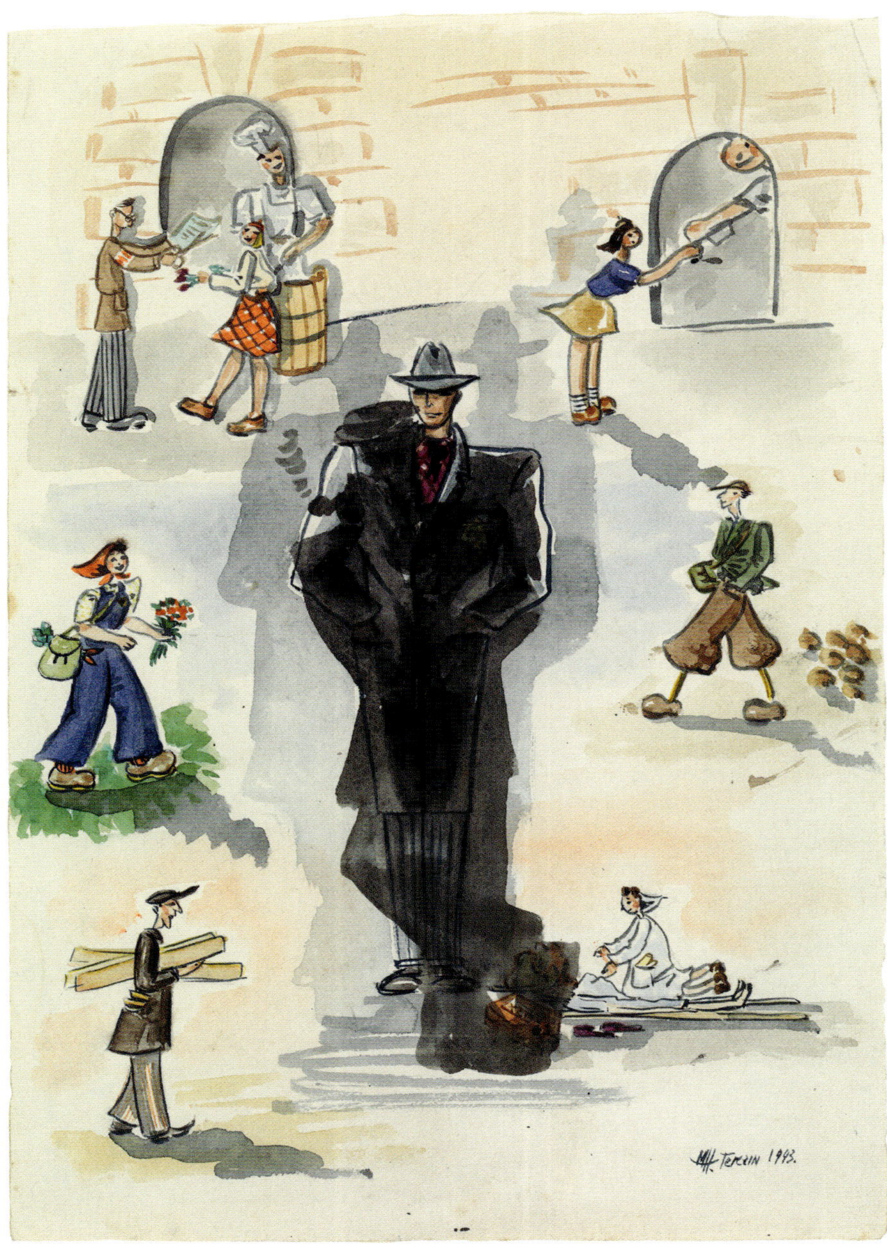

19

Die Ghetto Polizei, 1943
Watercolour on paper
Signed and dated at lower right
'MH. Terezín 1943.'
PP.2005.38.18

Caricature of Die Ghetto Polizei *(Jewish secret police). Theft and bartering were the means of survival and became part of daily life in the ghetto. Sometimes the ghetto police turned a blind eye. The Jewish secret police was created by the Jewish Council, which was obliged to manage the ghetto.*

In this watercolour Marianne shows a ghetto policeman nonchalantly smoking as all around him black market activities are taking place. The figure on the left in headscarf and dungarees may be a self-portrait of Marianne with illicit produce from the youth garden. Cigarettes bought silence. Three shadow policemen suggest the omnipresence and shadiness of these so-called law-enforcers. The Jewish police, *Ghettowache* or *Ordnenwache*, were described with irony in the magazine *Vedem* (*We Lead*), secretly published by teenage boys in Theresienstadt between 1942 and 1944.

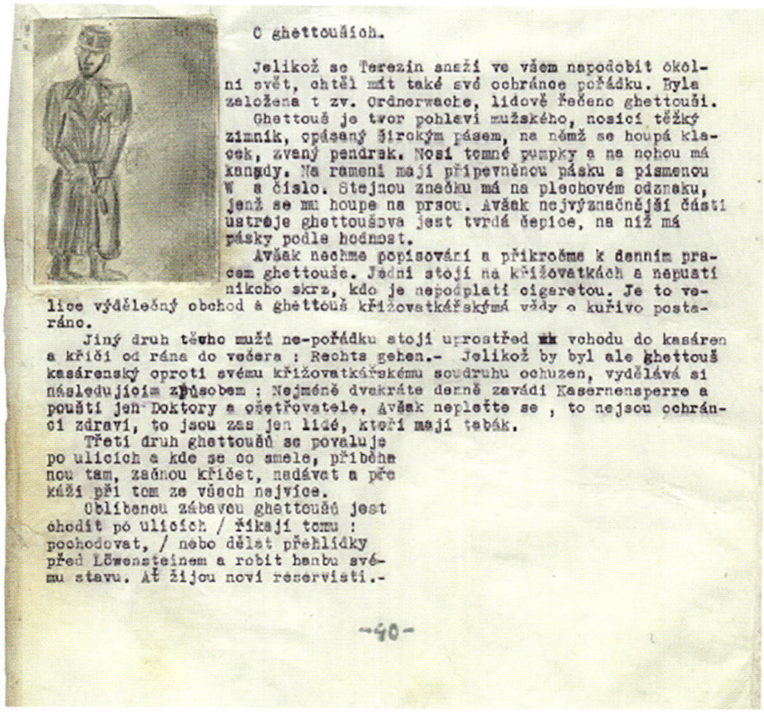

O ghettouších.

Jelikož se Terezín snaží ve všem napodobit okolní svět, chtěl mít také své ochránce pořádku. Byla založena t zv. Ordnerwache, lidově řečeno ghettouši.

Ghettouš je tvor pohleví mužského, nosící těžký zimník, opásaný širokým pásem, na němž se houpá klacek, zvaný pendrek. Nosí temné pumpky a na nohou má xangdy. Na rameni mají připevněnou pásku s písmenou W a číslo. Stejnou značku má na plechovém odznaku, jenž se mu houpe na prsou. Avšak nejvýznačnější částí ústroje ghettoušova jest tvrdá čepice, na níž má pásky podle hodnost.

Avšak nechme popisování a přikročme k denním pracem ghettouše. Jedni stojí na křižovatkách a nepustí nikoho skrz, kdo je nepodplatí cigaretou. Je to velice výdělečný obchod a ghettouš křižovatkářský má vždy o kuřivo postaráno.

Jiný druh těvho mužů ne-pořádku stojí uprostřed vchodu do kasáren a křičí od rána do večera : Rechts gehen.- Jelikož by byl ale ghettouš kasárenský oproti svému křižovatkářskému soudruhu ochuzen, vydělává si následujícím způsobem : Nejméně dvakráte denně zavádí Kasernensperre a pouští jen Doktory a ošetřovatele. Avšak nepleťte se , to nejsou ochránci zdraví, to jsou zas jen lidé, kteří mají tebák.

Třetí druh ghettoušů se povaluje po ulicích a kde se co smele, přibéhanou tam, začnou křičet, nadávat a přeckáží při tom ze všech nejvíce.

Oblíbenou zábavou ghettoušů jest chodit po ulicích / říkají tomu : pochodovat, / nebo dělat přehlídky před Löwensteinem a robit hanbu svému stavu. Ať žijou noví reservisti.-

-40-

Fig. 4.7
O ghettouších
(*About ghettouši*)

Page from the magazine *Vedem*, vol. 7, published 29 January 1943, giving an ironic description of the Jewish police. The translation is shown below.
Collection of Terezín Memorial

About ghettouši.

Since Theresienstadt is trying hard to imitate the outside world in everything, it also wanted to have its own guardians of order. Therefore, the so-called *Ordnenwache*, popularly called ghettouši, has been established.

Ghettouš is male, he wears a heavy winter coat with a wide belt, to which a swinging stick called a baton is attached. He also wears dark breeches and heavy leather boots. He has an armband with the letter 'W' and a number. He has the same symbol on a metal badge that hangs from his chest. However, the most peculiar feature of ghettouš equipment is a hard cap on which he has stripes indicating his rank.

But let's move on from descriptions and proceed to the daily duties of a ghettouš. Some of them stand at the crossroads and won't let anyone pass who doesn't bribe them with a cigarette. This is a very prosperous business and a traffic ghettouš has always enough to smoke.

A different kind of these men of dis-order stands by the entrance to the barracks and shouts: 'Rechts gehen!' [Walk to the right!]. Barracks ghettouš, not wanting to be disadvantaged compared to his comrade traffic ghettouš, earns his living in the following way: At least twice daily he introduces 'Kasernensperre' [enforced curfew of a barrack] and lets only doctors and paramedics in. However, don't be misled, this is not to improve our health, it is simply because these are the people who have tobacco.

The third kind of ghettouš can be found kicking about the streets, and whenever something happens, he rushes in, starts to shout and swear and gets more in the way than anyone else.

A favourite amusement of ghettouš is to walk through the streets (they call it marching) or to parade before Löwenstein[2] and bring shame to their own ranks. Long live the new reservists![3]

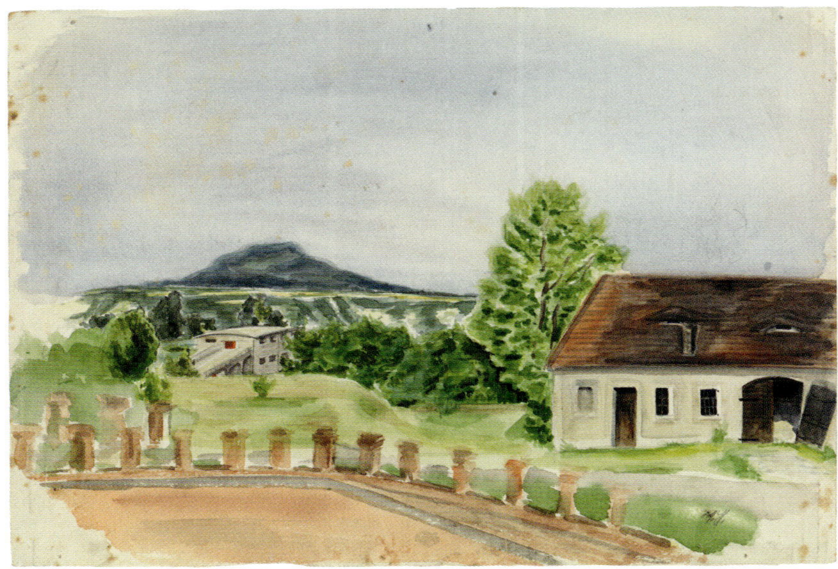

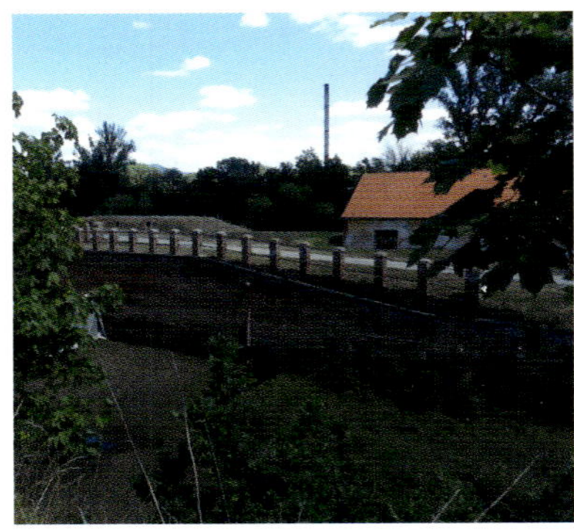

Fig. 4.8 The view from inside the ghetto as it is today
© Peter Tuka

20

View from inside the ghetto,
1942/43
Watercolour on paper
Signed at lower right 'MH'
PP.2005.68.2

Farmhouse on the right, on the left possibly the torture prison, Kleine Festung *(Small Fortress).*

Marianne's paintings show her fascination with the ghetto's exit gates as well as views of the outside world seen from Theresienstadt's walls. This view is from the north-east bastion, looking towards the Ohře river and the Křemín hill. Pictures such as this express the most basic longing for freedom and a life beyond the ghetto walls. In her diary, fellow prisoner Nava Shean noted on 8 March 1942, 'I can see mountains around me, and it brings me a sense of serenity.'[4] However, the presence of Kleine Festung is a sinister reminder of the punishment that faced those who opposed their Nazi oppressors. Artists like Leo Haas, Otto Hungar, Bedřich Fritta and Ferdinand Bloch were tortured there in the summer of 1944.

O. Guttman wrote in the magazine *Vedem*:

'Early in the morning, as usual, I go to work in the garden. I'm given tools and I leave along the long wall of the bastion. The green bushes tremble in the cold wind, a bird cheeps here and there. The sun's rays shine on the budding trees and green flowering shrubs. I see fields in the distance, mighty mountains and small houses. Nearby is a grey winding asphalt road that leads to us. Late in the evening, as we prepare to leave for the ghetto, heavy footsteps are approaching from afar. Here we see a long line of convicts who are led to the Small Fortress. It's a strange feeling to see so many convicts with heads shaven. I leave with a sad look and think of the poor convicts, but I believe that one day we will all be free.'[5]

21

Villa Kursawe, 11 October 1943
Watercolour on paper page from spiral
bound notebook
Signed and dated at lower right '11.X.43
Ter./MH'
PP.2005.38.3

*View of outside the Theresienstadt ghetto
showing the dwelling house taken over by
the German officers. As more transports
arrived bringing in Jews from Austria
and Germany too, the Czech population
within the walls of the ghetto was moved
elsewhere.*

Villa Kursawe, situated at the south
gate to the ghetto, beyond the inner
fortifications, used to belong to Karel
Kursawe, the SS commander in charge
of the camp's agriculture. In the summer
of 1943, a railway line into the ghetto
was built to make transports in and out
easier, and to conceal them from locals.
Before, prisoners had to walk to or from
a station two kilometres away. The
railway passed directly behind the villa
as Marianne shows. She also depicts at
the upper left the ghetto's columbarium
where the wooden, and later paper,
cinerary urns of the Jewish dead were
placed. At the end of October 1943, the
villa was transferred to the management
of the ghetto's Jewish Council and
turned into a hospital for children
infected with tuberculosis and typhus.

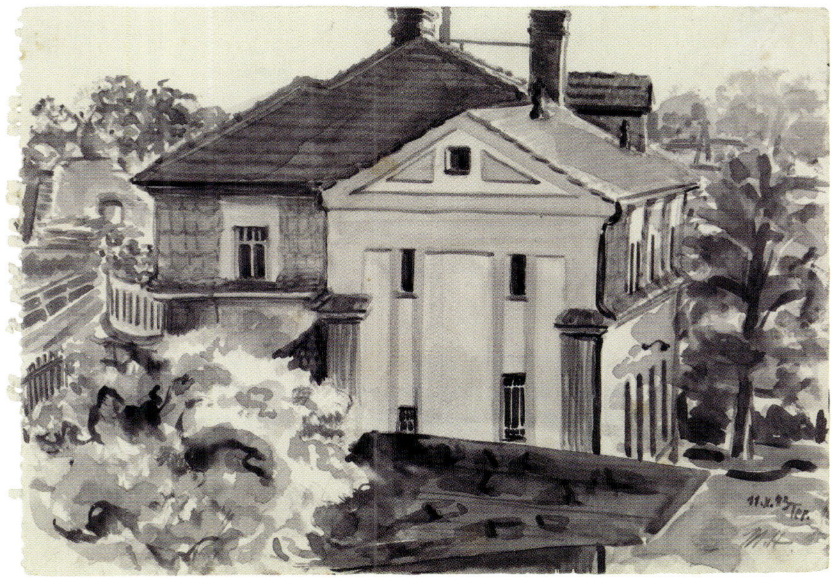

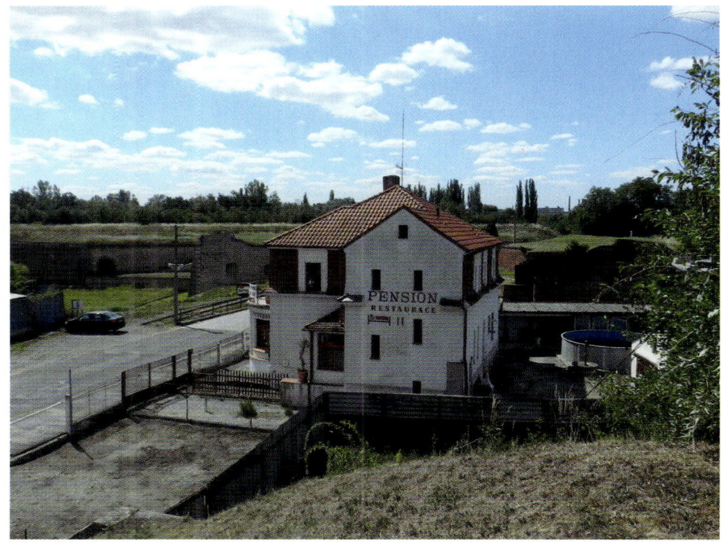

Fig. 4.9 Villa Kursawe as it is today
© Peter Tuka

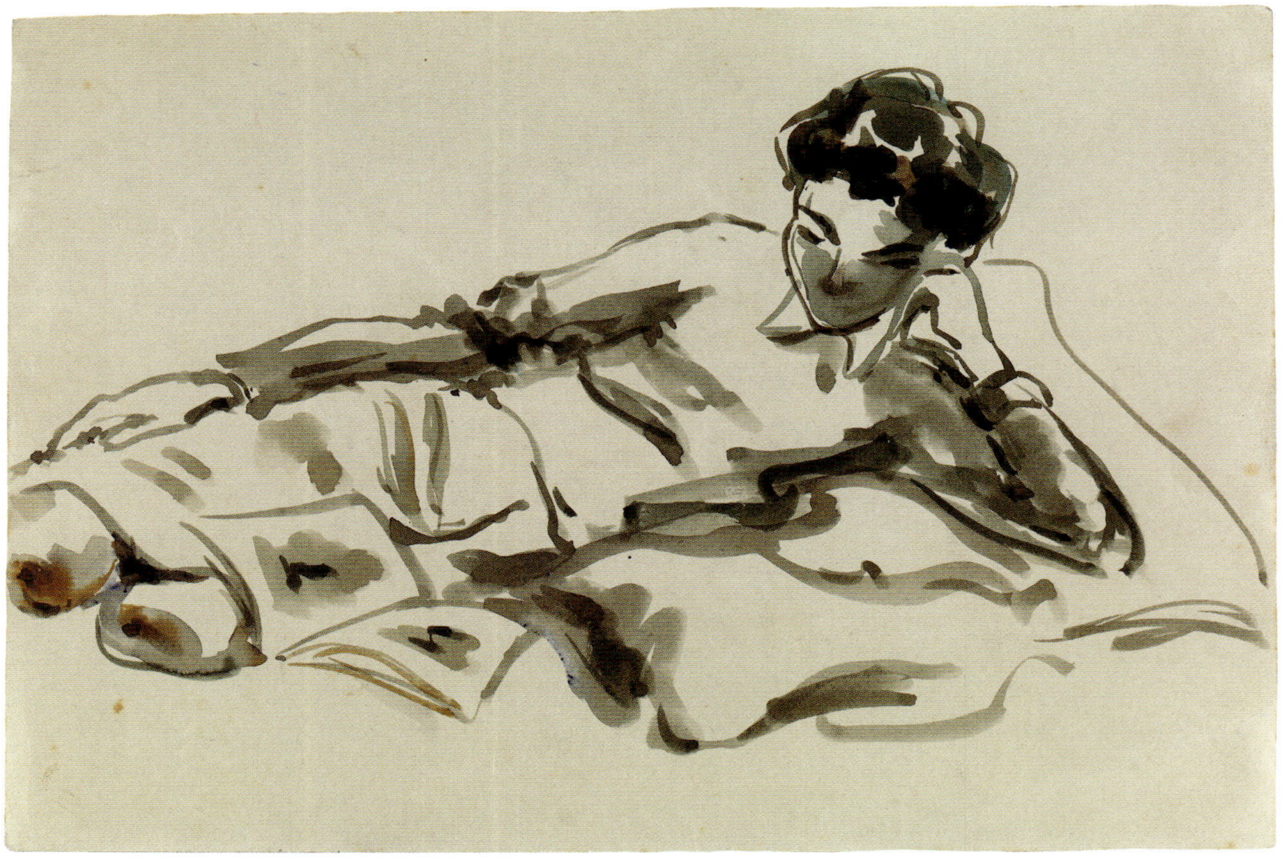

22
Ruth relaxing, 1942/43
Watercolour on paper, double-sided
Signed on reverse at lower right 'M.H.' and inscribed
in pencil at a later date 'Ruth Bondy Bashan/Ramat Gan.'
and in pen 'drawn in Theresienstadt./Ruth Bondy'
PP.2005.38.20

*Ruth Bondy survived and went on to become one of Israel's top
journalists and writers. She was the only girl to survive, along
with me, from the youth agricultural labour group I was in
before we were transported to Theresienstadt.*

Ruth Bondy (1923–2017), later Bashan, and Marianne were
both active members in the Zionist youth movement and
took part in Hachshara (agricultural training) before being
deported to Theresienstadt. Like Marianne, Ruth worked as
one of the leaders in the ghetto's vegetable gardens, and
after Theresienstadt was sent to Auschwitz-Birkenau, then

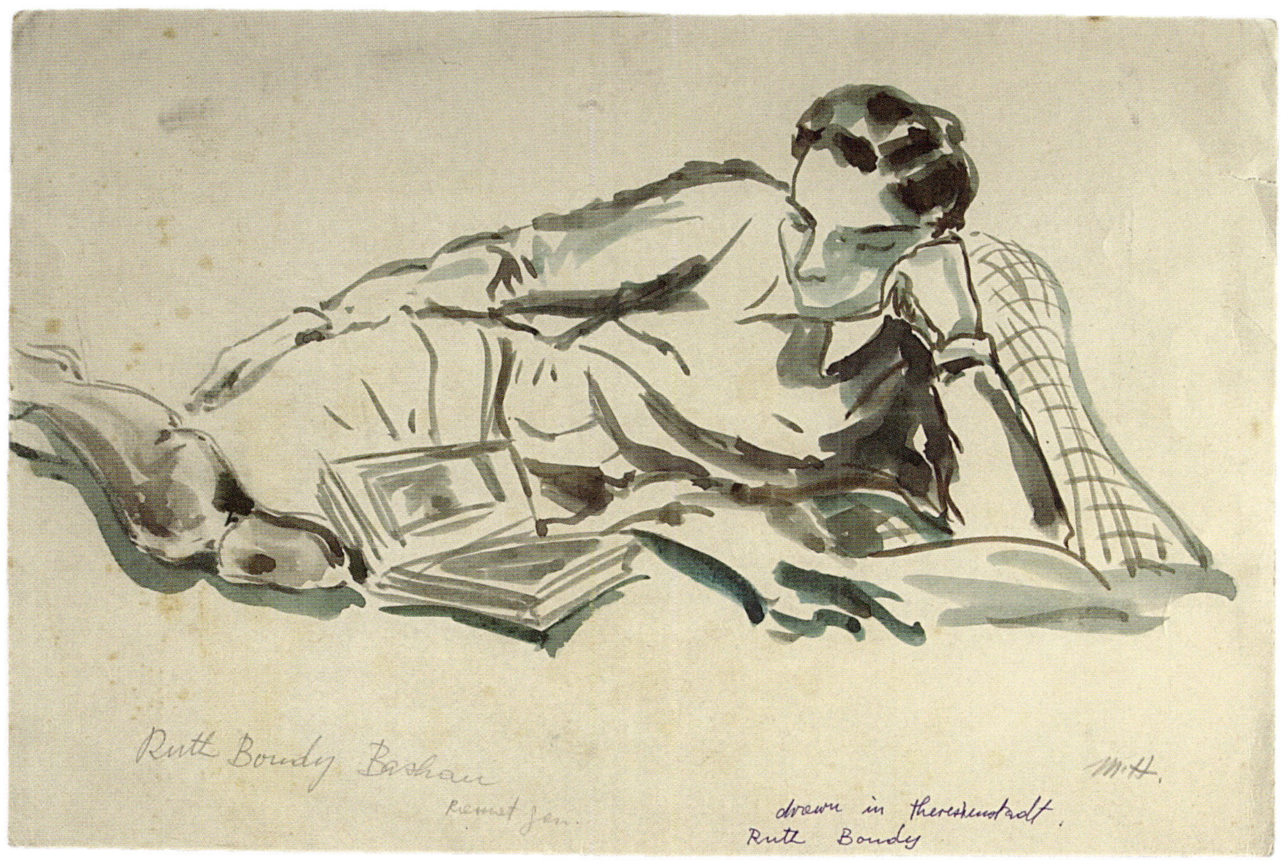

to slave labour camps in Germany, and finally to Bergen-Belsen. In 1948 Ruth emigrated to Israel, where she worked as a journalist and translator of Czech literature into Hebrew, living in Ramat Gan, a suburb of Tel Aviv. She published many scholarly articles and books on the Holocaust, including a famous biography of Jacob Edelstein, chairman of the Jewish Council in Theresienstadt. She received multiple awards and was the first woman to win The Sokolow Prize, an Israeli journalism award.

Marianne shows Ruth lying, resting her head on her hard, as she reads a book probably borrowed from Theresienstadt's prisoner-run library which opened in November 1942. The imaginative power of books allowed a degree of escapism and intellectual freedom. Ruth wrote: 'I would like the Terezín ghetto to be remembered the way it was: a place of uplifted spirit as well as toughness, of pettiness and of generosity, of mutual help and of ignoring the suffering of others – a kaleidoscope of human beings trapped in a disrespectful situation, most of whom knew how to preserve human dignity, who were not cruel to one another, who hoped to hang on until the yearned-for end of the war, which for the majority came too late.'[6]

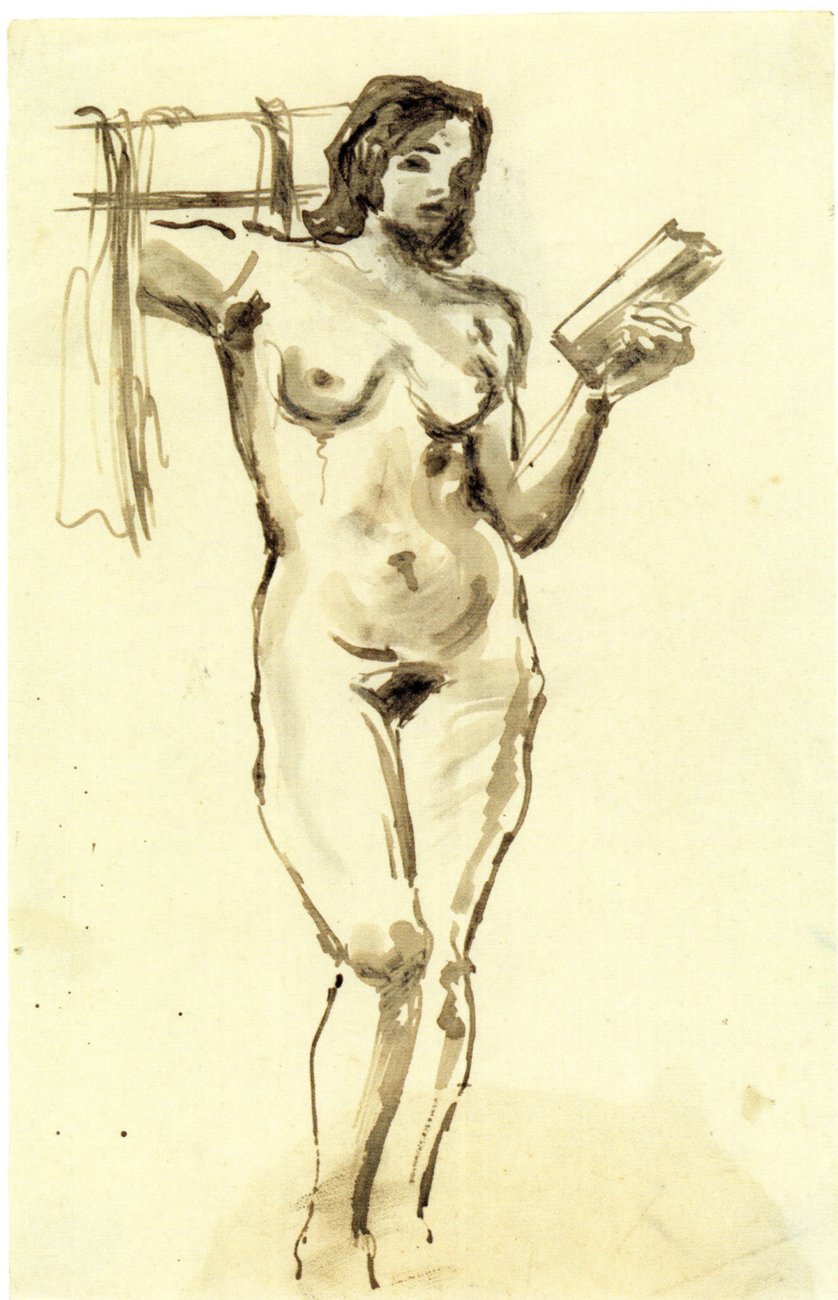

23
Nava Shean modelling for
Marianne in the loft of the
Magdeburger Barracks,
1942/43
Watercolour on paper
Unsigned
PP.2005.38.22

She was an actress learning her lines for a play. I was desperate for a model, as I did not want to lose my art skills. There were a lot of artists and musicians, and the Germans used them to prepare for the Red Cross visit. After the war she became one of Israel's leading actresses.

Life drawing is the bedrock of art training. Marianne, eager to develop as an artist, found a willing model in actor Nava Shean (1919–2001), who posed for her on several occasions.[7] Born Vlasta Schönová in Prague, Shean was very active in Theresienstadt's many theatre productions. Particularly outstanding were her performances of Jean Cocteau's monodrama *The Human Voice*, and her dramatization of Jan Karafiát's classic children's story *Broučci* (*The Fireflies*) which was performed under her guidance by children in the ghetto. Both drawing and acting were a form of covert resistance against the Nazis and a statement of creative resilience. Nava Shean wrote in her notebook diary in Theresienstadt in November 1942: 'The theatre is not an amusement for me, it is a necessity.'[8] The title *Fireflies* evokes light and beauty in dark times. Shean, who went on to find success with Israel's national theatre and the Munich State Theatre, wrote in her autobiography:
'All this was performed within the daily struggle between life and death. The camp was swamped with disease, lice and fleas. Transports with people from the camp were sent to the east; transports with new people arrived. Within all that, the theatre lived, survived and helped others survive.'[9]

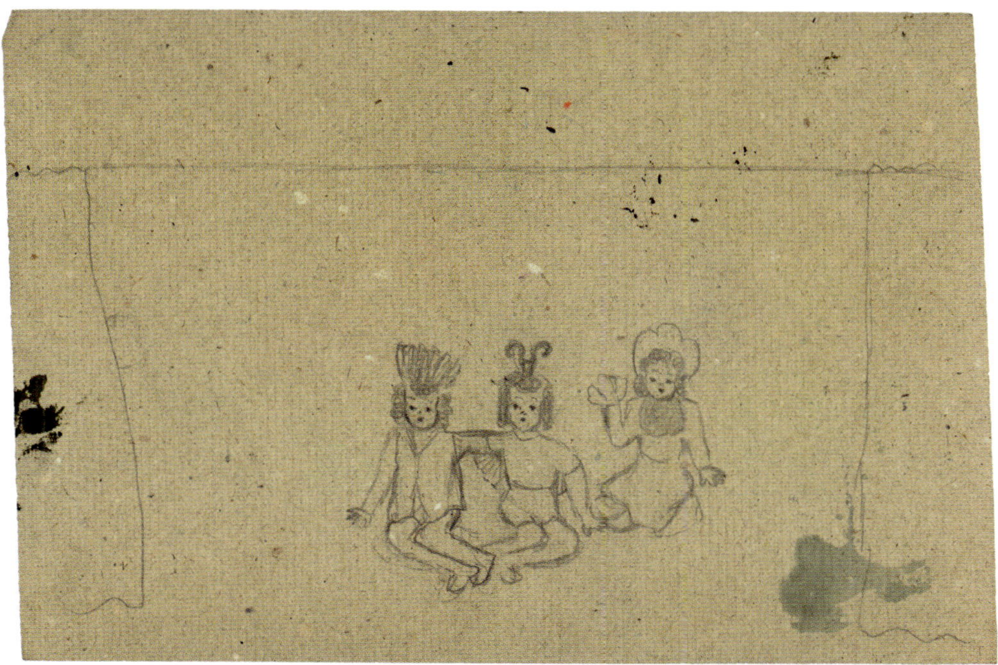

Fig. 4.10
Unknown artist
Theatre performance – The Fireflies, 1943–44
pencil on paper

This drawing shows a group of children dressed up as fireflies in the eponymous play performed in the ghetto. Jan Karafiát's stories about fireflies are among the most popular Czech children's tales, in which little fireflies learn how to fly at night and light up the world for human beings. From the collections of the Jewish Museum in Prague (acc. no. 130.588)

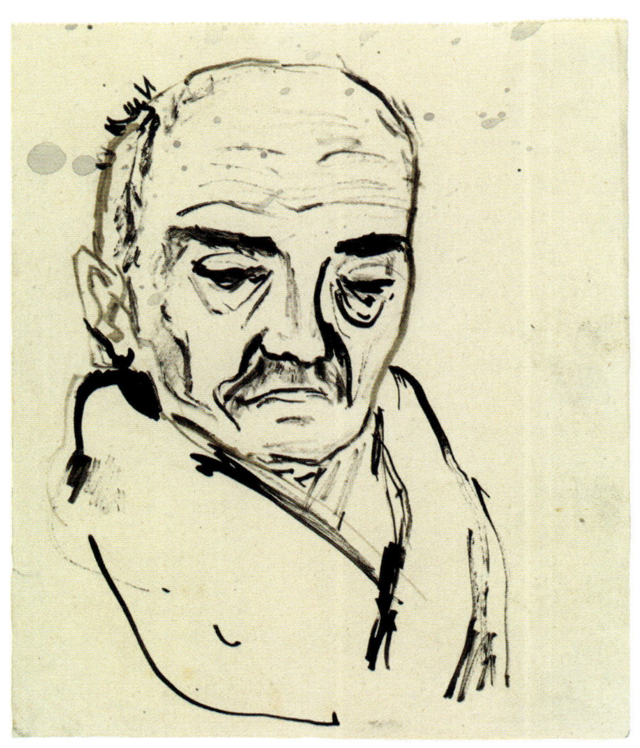

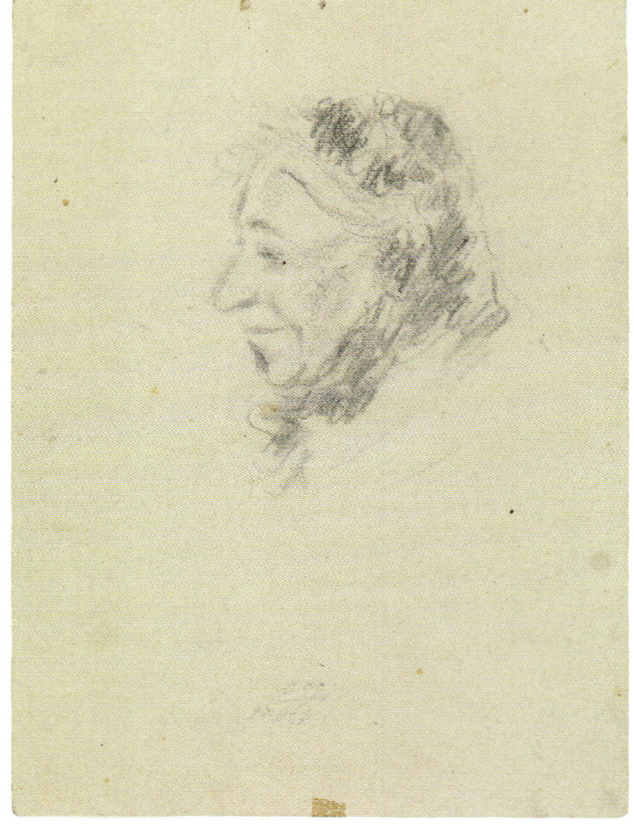

24
Sketch of old German or Austrian man in the mock café, 1943
Indian ink on paper page from notebook
Unsigned
PP.2005.38.7

25
Sketch of old German or Austrian woman in the mock café, 1943
Charcoal on paper
Unsigned, 'inscribed on reverse 'Jsem na balkóně' (I am on the balcony)
PP.2005.38.8

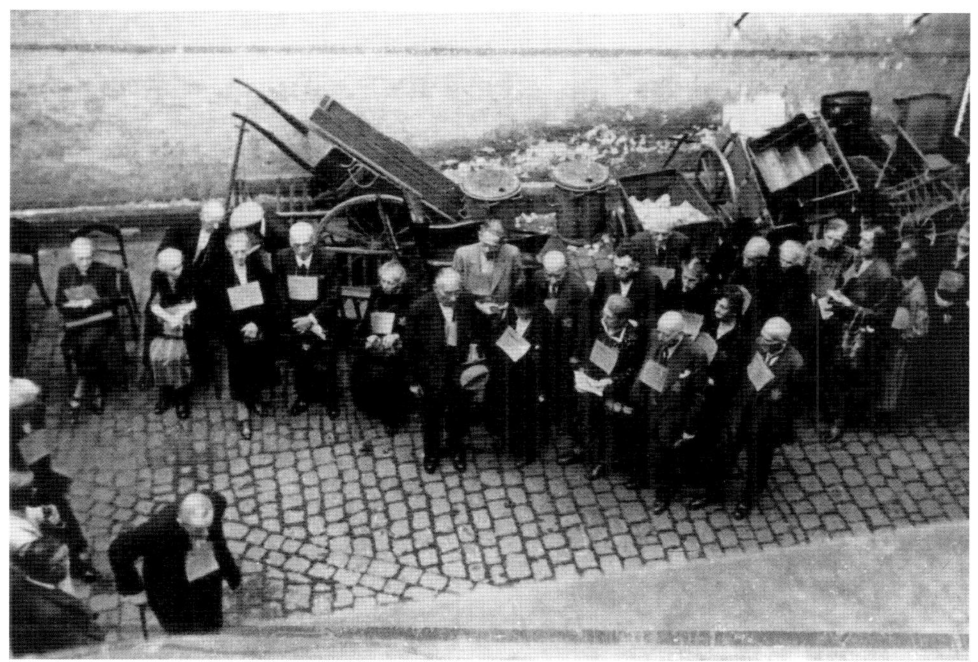

Fig. 4.11   German Jews in Wiesbaden, Germany, wearing identification tags, before deportation to Theresienstadt. August 1942.
© bpk image agency

In the autumn of 1942, the Nazis began transporting Jews from Germany, Austria, the Netherlands and Denmark to Theresienstadt. These were mainly elderly people and World War I veterans of a higher social status who had been fooled into believing they were coming to a retirement spa town, for which they had handed over their life savings. Many did not survive the long and exhausting transport, and even more died when they arrived at the ghetto due to poor hygiene and malnutrition. Marianne was among those who volunteered to help them. She also drew their portraits in the mock café that opened on 8 December 1942.

The mock cafés were set up for a Red Cross visit to demonstrate the good treatment of the ghetto dwellers. There was nothing to eat there. The drink was a brew made from acorns.

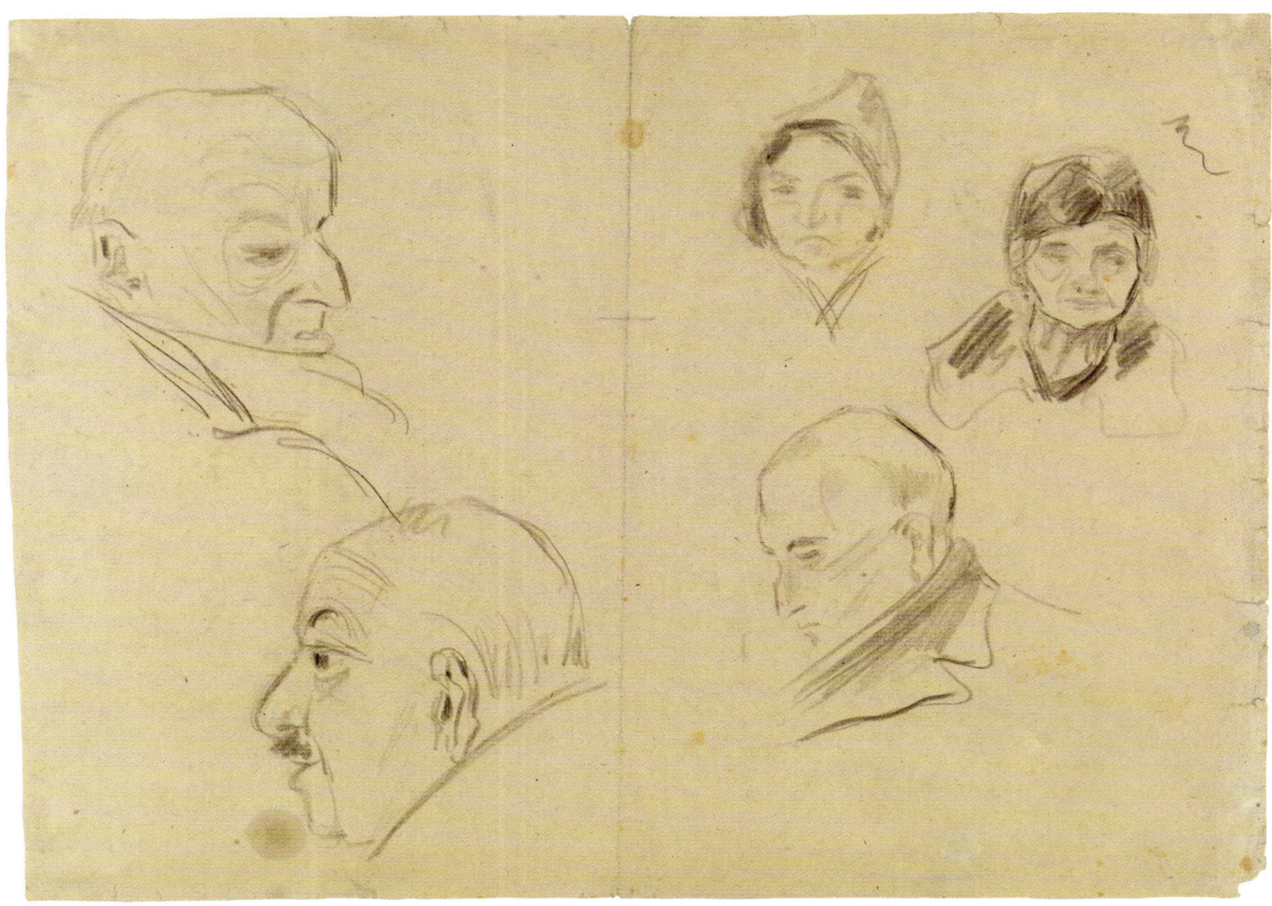

26 (above)
Sketch of old German or Austrian people in the mock café, 1943
Coloured pencil on paper
Unsigned
PP.2005.38.9

27 (opposite)
Sketch of old German or Austrian women in the mock café, 1943
Coloured pencil on paper
Unsigned
PP.2005.38.10

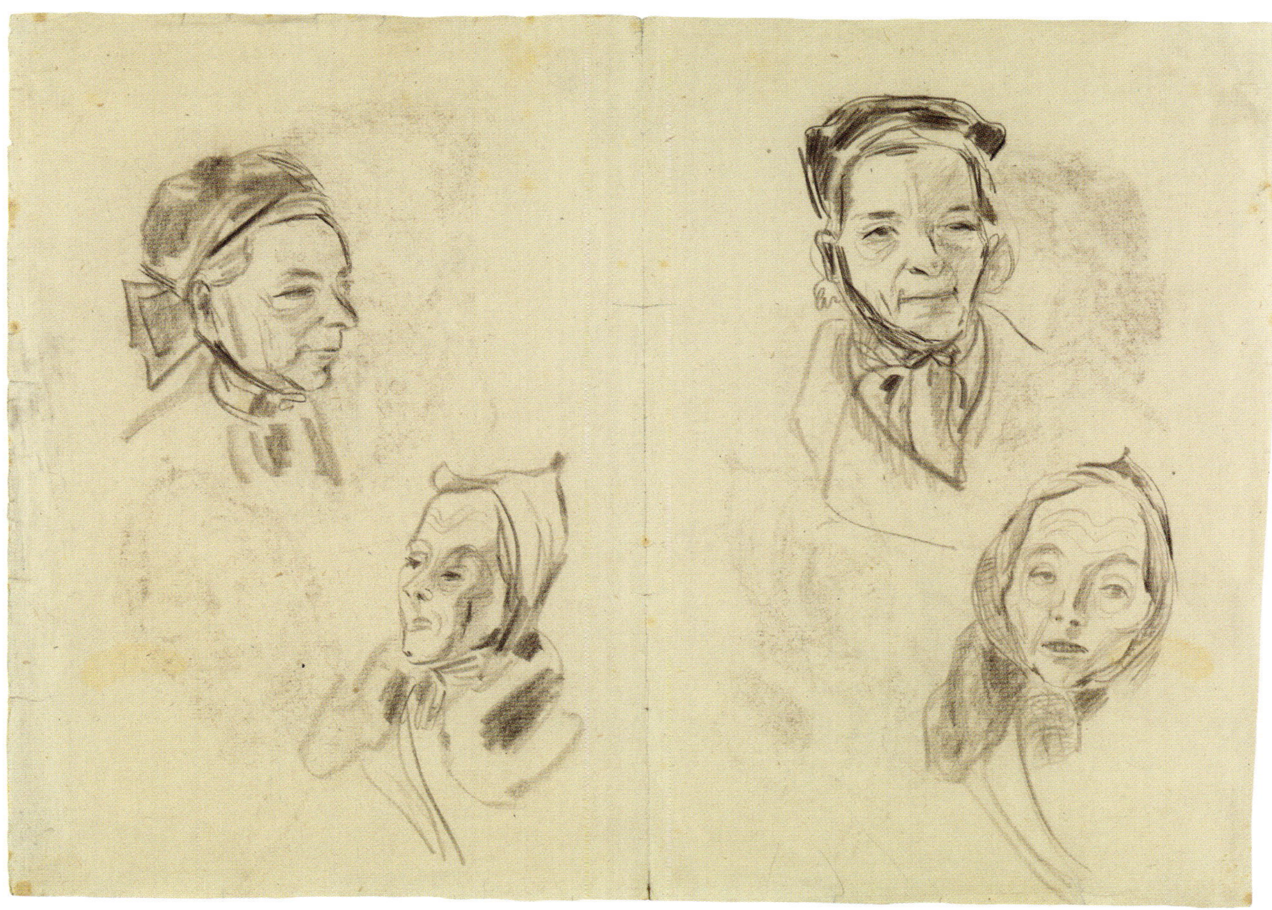

Portraits were the most common type of art produced in the camps. They emphasized the value of an individual life and strengthened the sense of community. Marianne's portraits of the elderly in the mock café of Theresienstadt are empathetic and dignified, although they are also a record of physical and emotional suffering. Faces are haggard and gaunt. Eyes look down or stare into space, lost in thought. Some artists in the camp were commissioned by the SS to paint portraits for them in return for privileges, such as more provisions, better quarters or protection from transportation east. In contrast, Marianne's modest unsolicited drawings quietly recorded lives, ensuring their survival on paper, although the reality was that the elderly who survived Theresienstadt were immediately selected for the gas chambers on arrival at Auschwitz.

In her Theresienstadt diary, Nava Shean wrote about the elderly Jews arriving there: 'At first glance they all look the same. They are all equally wrinkled, shrivelled and grey. But each one of them manifests a complete life that is over, the life of a particular person.'[10]

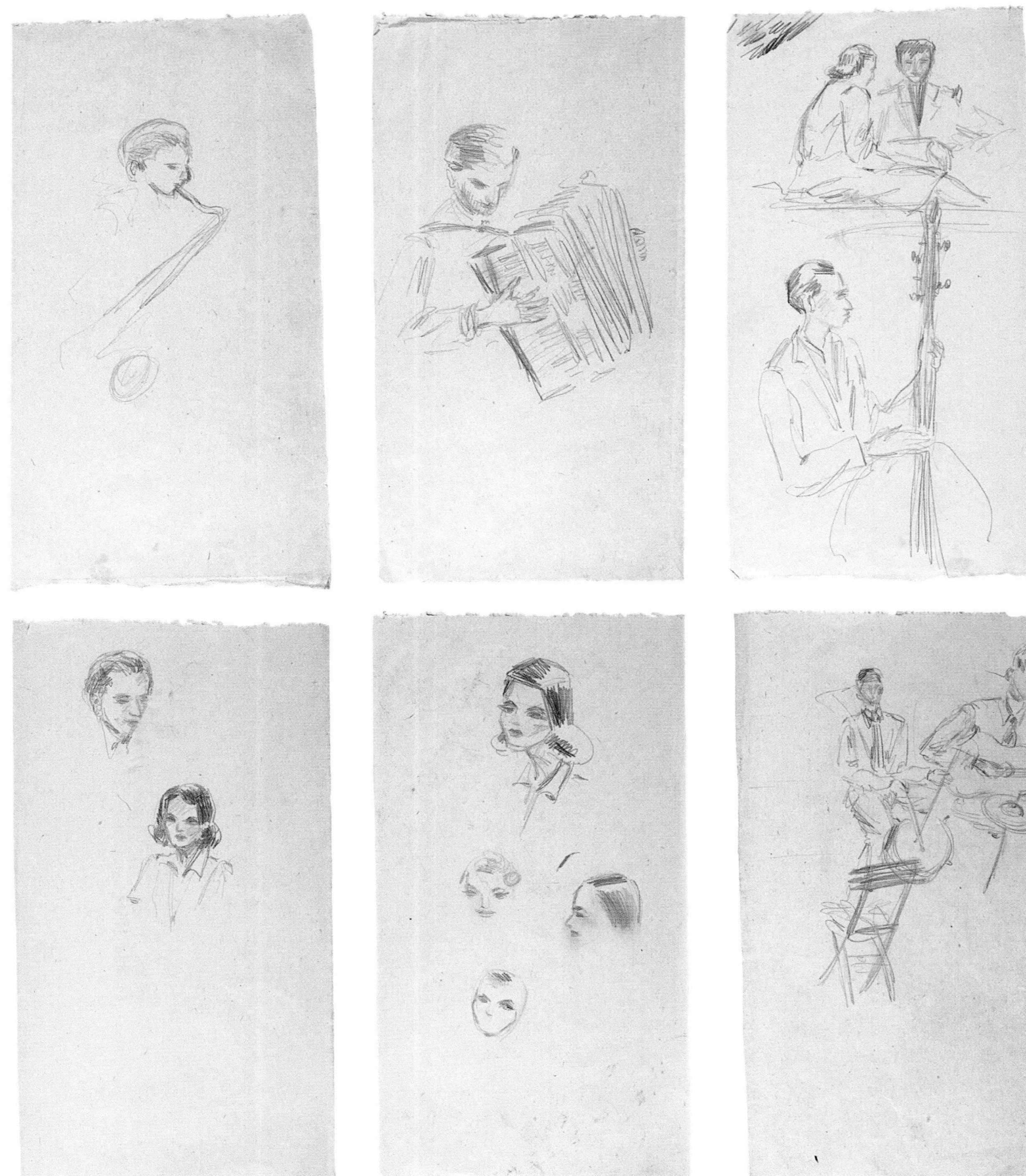

28

Sketches of musicians and people in the propaganda mock café, 1943
Pencil on paper, folded sheet, double-sided
Unsigned
PP.2005.38.11

A large number of professional singers, musicians and composers were imprisoned in Theresienstadt, resulting in a thriving musical scene. At first, instruments were confiscated but were later permitted for propaganda purposes. All kinds of musical groups were active in the camp: choirs, orchestras, operas and jazz cabarets. Lessons were given and new pieces of music written and premiered. Performances were repeated many times, due to demand. Joseph Spier's hand-coloured lithograph of a concert in Theresienstadt's 'coffee' house, from an album commissioned by the Nazis as a souvenir for Red Cross delegates, is deceptively idyllic. Czech cartoonist Fritz Taussig's satirical drawing is equally political, the vacant misery of the audience set against a guarded barbed wire fence. Marianne's sketches of musicians playing and individuals quietly listening offer a straightforward account of performances which helped keep spirits up and brought hope in the most difficult of conditions.

In preparation for the Red Cross visit, a series of mass deportations to Auschwitz was initiated in September 1943 in order to reduce Theresienstadt's over-crowding. Marianne's mother was selected for one of these transports. This was the fourth time she had been selected, and Marianne could not get her off the list, refusing to sleep with Dr Benjamin Murmelstein (1905–89), an elder in the Jewish Council, despite his pressured seduction and promises of help. Murmelstein, nicknamed 'Das Schwein' ('The Swine'), was known for his sexual predation. Marianne, who would not leave her mother, jumped on the departing cattle trucks and was taken to Auschwitz with her.

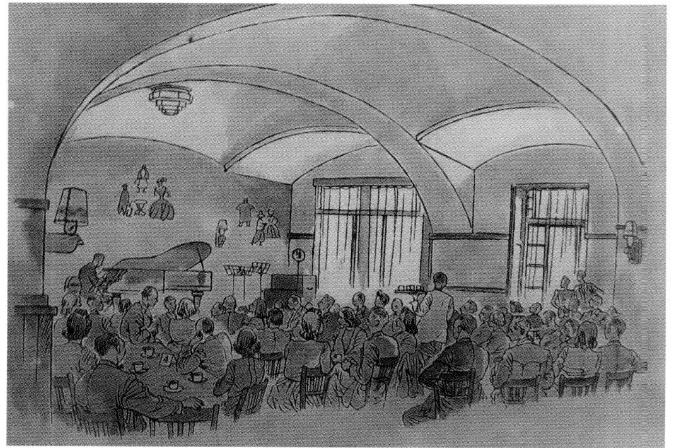

Fig. 4.12   Joseph E.A. Spier, *Kaffeehaus* from *Bilder aus Theresienstadt*, 1944, lithograph and watercolour on paper
© Stedelijk Museum Zutphen The Netherlands/heirs Jo Spier

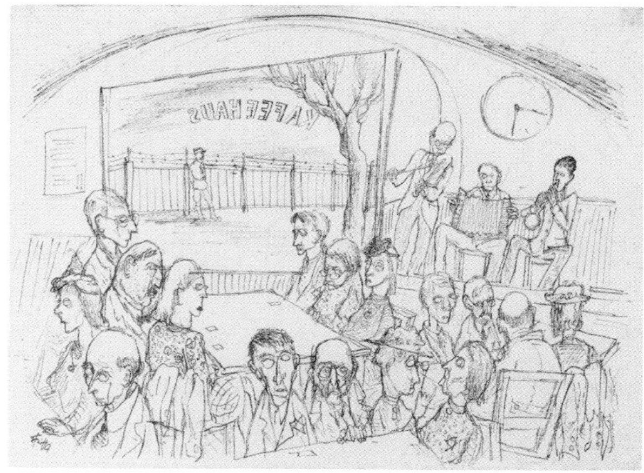

Fig. 4.13   Bedřich Fritta, *Café, Terezín*, 1943, pen and ink
Thomas Fritta-Haas, long-term loan to the Jewish Museum Berlin, photo: Jens Ziehe

Auschwitz Death Camp: 18 December 1943–July 1944

Transport designation Ds, 18 December 1943 from Theresienstadt to Auschwitz, 2015 murdered, 488 survived

THE AUSCHWITZ COMPLEX, set up by the Nazis in Poland, was an enormous network of over 40 camps and sub-camps that has come to symbolize the abject horror of the Holocaust. Auschwitz II Birkenau, which opened in March 1942, was the largest camp. Its purpose was extermination. The vast majority of Auschwitz victims, over 1 million, died in Birkenau; about 90% were Jews from Nazi-occupied Europe. Most were murdered in the gas chambers, while others died as a result of starvation, hard labour, infections or medical experimentation.

In September 1943, a special section within Birkenau was established for prisoners from Theresienstadt, the *Familienlager* (Family Camp), B/2/b. It had slightly different conditions from the rest of Auschwitz. Prisoners did not have their heads shaved on arrival, and families were kept together, although men, women and children slept in separate quarters. Marianne recalled that the children's barracks, Block 31, was relatively 'comfortable'. It was a temporary camp, created in anticipation of a Red Cross visit to Theresienstadt, should delegates want to see where people were being deported. Over 17,000 prisoners were transported from Theresienstadt in September and December 1943, and in May 1944. 'SB' and 'six months' were written in their papers, meaning *Sonderbehandlung* – special treatment for six months, after which the gas chambers without exception.

Marianne recalled: 'At some point we realized that this was a termination camp, a death camp, and people were gassed, as the bellowing chimney with black smoke and the stench of burning hair and flesh was all over the place. […] Sometimes the chimneys worked more than other times. Sometimes it was quiet and sometimes it was working at full capacity.'[11]

Of the first 5,000 prisoners deported from Theresienstadt to the Family Camp in September 1943, 3,800 were gassed in one night on 8 March 1944. Marianne remembers this most horrible event: 'The SS came into the camp, everybody was trembling. They removed all the adults and children who had been on the transport before us, and took them to the exit

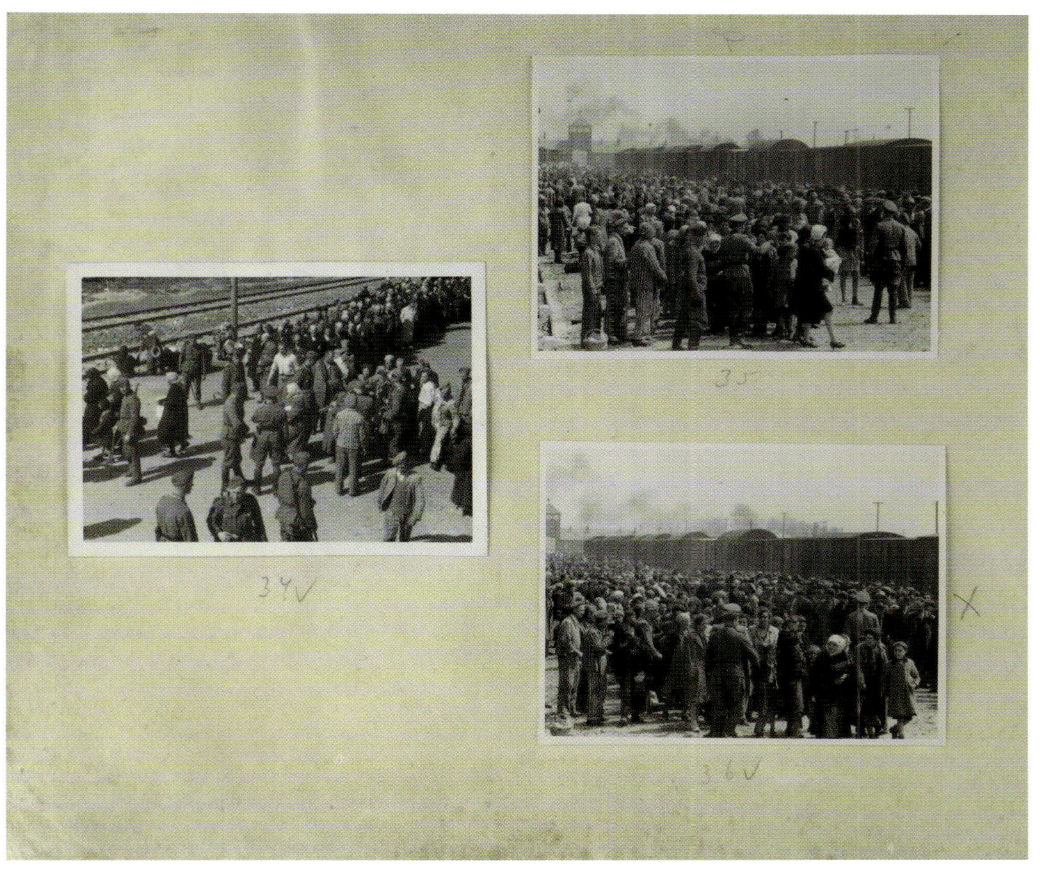

Fig. 4.14 Arrival of cattle wagons at Auschwitz-Birkenau. Selection was carried out immediately at the rail tracks. Auschwitz photo album, Yad Vashem collection

from the camp, and they wrote down each number of each person, like a register. And the sick people weren't allowed to come, only the healthy ones. So I had a sick girl who had been working with me, a youngster in Theresienstadt in the youth gardens, and she was very ill, so I took her to the *krankenbau*, the sick room. And I ran in that desolate place to the *schreiber*, who sat at a desk, the *schreiber* was a writer. He was also a Kapo [a Jewish person employed by the Nazis as a guard] in grey and blue and I said, "She is not coming. She is ill, she is in the hospital block, she can't come", and with that I saved her life.'[12] The girl's name was Hana Káňová (née Heitlerová), who survived the Holocaust, the only one from her large family. Interviewed in 2014 when she was in her 80s, Hana acknowledged that Marianne had saved her life, 'Mausi Hermannová … it was her who put me in the sickbay, it was her who saved me.'[13]

In June 1944, as Marianne's six-month period of 'special treatment' was coming to an end, Nazis decided to deport able-bodied prisoners from the Family Camp to labour camps in Germany. Marianne and her mother passed the selection for the transport and managed to escape the gas chambers. Everyone who remained was murdered, and the camp liquidated.

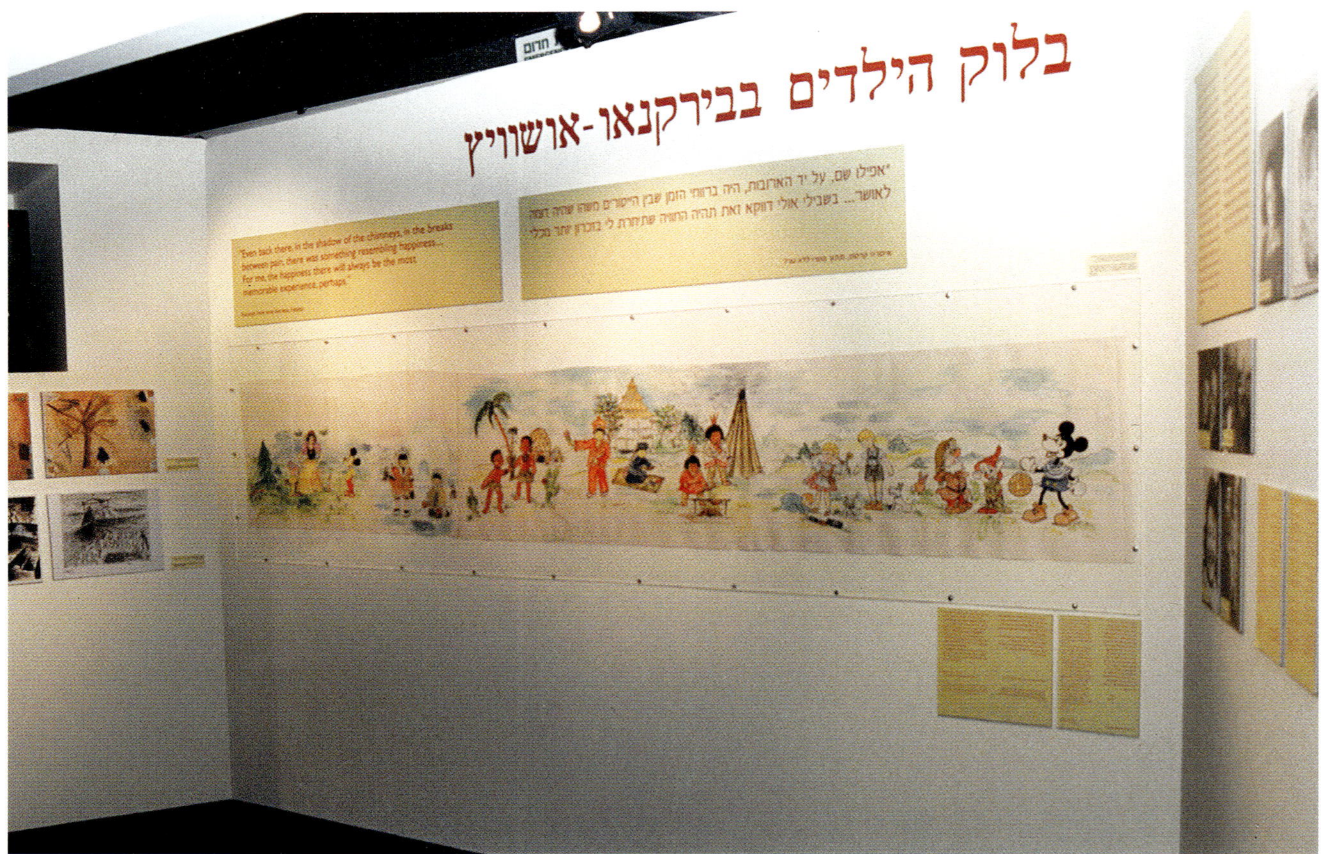

Fig. 4.15
Decoration for the Children's
Block in Auschwitz, 1997
Photographic print
PP.2005.38.27

While working with children in Block 31 of the Family Camp, Marianne and Dina Babbitt (née Gottliebová), another youth counsellor, were asked by youth leader Fredy Hirsch to decorate the walls. They painted children of the world and their favourite cartoon characters. Dina painted Snow White and the Seven Dwarfs and Marianne added her beloved Mickey Mouse and Bambi the deer. The murals did not survive, but Marianne recreated them from memory in 1997 for the exhibition *No Child's Play* at Yad Vashem, the World Holocaust Remembrance Center in Jerusalem.

Of the total number of estimated 155,000 Jews who passed through Theresienstadt, it is believed 12,171 were children. Despite the efforts of the Jewish leadership in the ghetto to safeguard these children from transports, 9,001 were taken to the death camps in the east. Of these, only 325 survived.

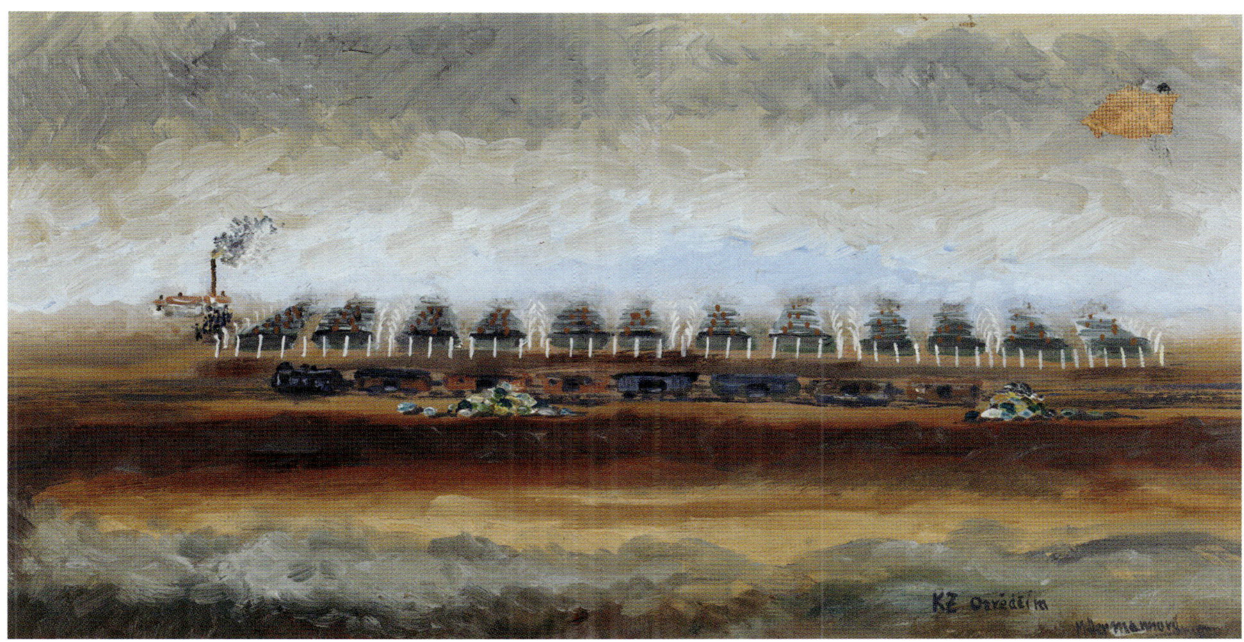

29

KZ Osvědčím, 1952
Oil on hardboard
Signed at lower right
'KZ Osvědčím/
M. Hermannová'
PP.2005.38.26

*Done after the war, in 1952
in Glasgow from memory.
View of Auschwitz-Birkenau
Familienlager (Family
Camp). The empty railway
track with left-over piles of
luggage. There is a hole in
the paint.*

This painting conveys the desolate forsakenness of Auschwitz. Marianne recalled: 'Auschwitz was yellow mud. Desolate. Not one bird was singing, not one tree […] you couldn't see anything but yellow mud.'[14] She depicted the rows of miserable barracks standing in the mud and, on the left, the gas chambers and crematoria that claimed the majority of those who did not succumb to starvation, disease or exhaustion.

Marianne painted this after the war when she was about to become a mother, a final reflection on Auschwitz before putting her Holocaust artworks to rest in a trunk in the attic for over 30 years. She signed it with her Czech maiden name and used the Czech name for Auschwitz (Osvětim/Osvěčím). The paint loss she refers to was where she removed the sun as it never shone in Auschwitz.

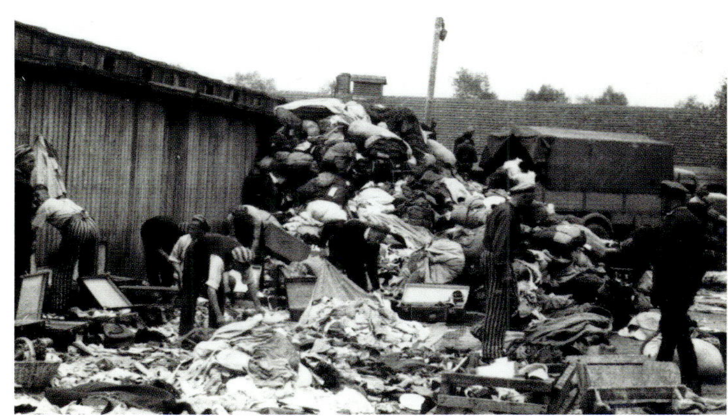

Fig. 4.16 Luggage confiscated from prisoners on arrival at Auschwitz being sorted by other prisoners for transfer to Germany. Yad Vashem, Photo Archive, Jerusalem

Slave Labour in Germany: Early July 1944–5 April 1945

NEUENGAMME CONCENTRATION CAMP in northern Germany was established as a subcamp of Sachsenhausen concentration camp by the SS in December 1938 on the site of an old brickworks on the outskirts of Hamburg. It grew, becoming a large central camp with more than 80 of its own subcamps, holding prisoners of war and political prisoners from Germany and its occupied territories, but comparatively few Jews (about 13,000). Prisoners were forced to work to support the German war machine, digging canals, working in clay pits and manufacturing arms. It was extermination through hard manual labour. Of the estimated 106,000 prisoners who passed through Neuengamme, nearly 43,000 perished due to malnutrition, disease, physical exhaustion, brutal punishments and medical experimentation. From 1942, the SS began systematically killing prisoners no longer capable of work by lethal injection or in the gas chambers.

Marianne and her mother were among the 1,000 Czech Jewish women from Auschwitz who, in early July 1944, were taken to Dessauer Ufer, the largest of Neuengamme's satellite camps for women, to carry out clearance work for Hamburg's oil refineries. In September 1944 they were moved to a smaller female labour camp, Neugraben, and then in February 1945 to another, Tiefstack. The work they were set included digging foundations for bunkers, laying water pipes and manufacturing concrete slabs for new housing. This was performed under daily threats of Allied air raids which killed many prisoners.

Despite everything, there was a supportive atmosphere among prisoners. On one occasion in Dessauer Ufer Marianne was working on a barge, collecting and transporting bricks cleared from buildings destroyed by Allied bombardments. As the air raid siren sounded and everyone hurried for shelter, Marianne fell into the water. Her friend Véra stayed at the quayside to help her. 'It was high up. I couldn't climb up so she bent down while the air raid went, the sirens went and she waited to pull me up. So that was a fantastic friendship'.[15] Marianne's artistic creativity continued to be in demand and she was commissioned by Germans at Neugraben to make toys, including dolls made from old tights, and rugs for Christmas presents, and was asked to decorate the walls of the officers' mess. This meant she could stay indoors, escaping the worst of the cold, and she was allowed to keep the art materials.

While working on a building site in Falkenberg near Hamburg, Marianne befriended a young German woman who gave her something to eat each day. Marianne painted this cheerful image of herself in work overalls and headscarf, and the woman in a fresh white apron and dress, with her little son in a pram, and gave it to her as a thank you. Forty years later, the painting appeared in a leaflet published to celebrate the anniversary of the housing estate. The little boy, now a grown-up man, contacted Marianne and sent her this photograph and a copy of the leaflet.

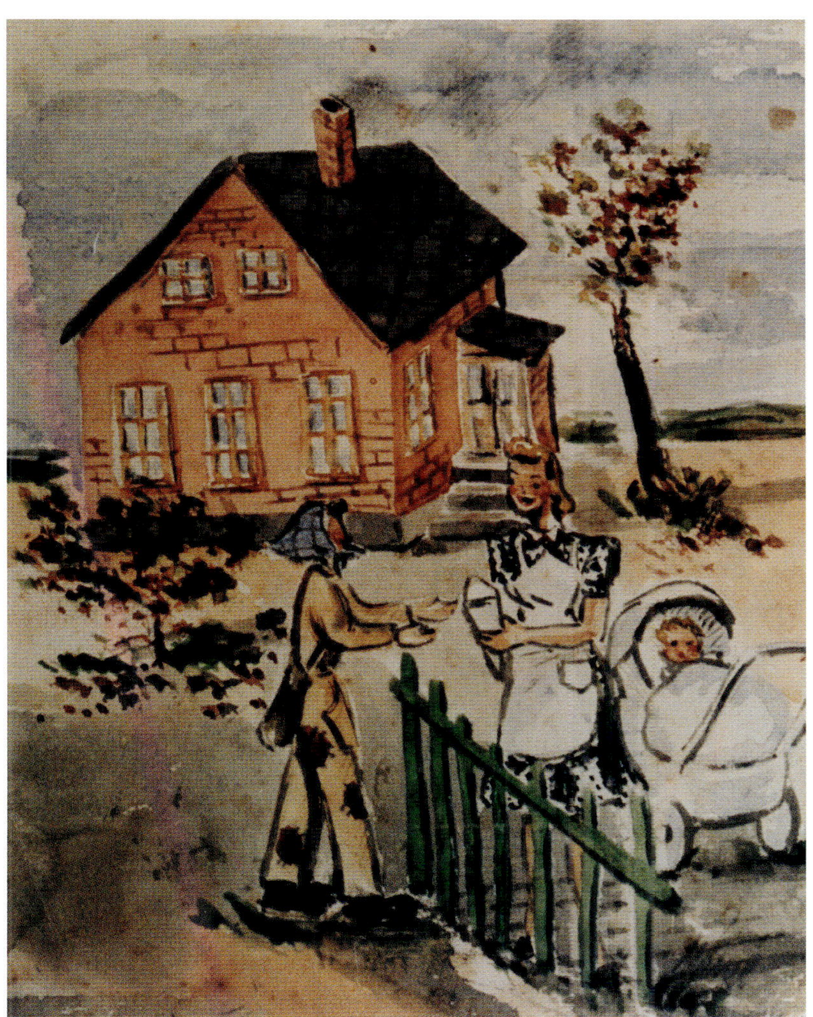

Fig. 4.17
Caricature made as a gift for a woman who gave me an apple or sandwich, 1944
Photograph of original watercolour on paper
PP.2005.38.28

Bergen-Belsen Concentration Camp: 5 April 1945–July 1945

BERGEN-BELSEN WAS A NAZI concentration camp located south-west of the towns Bergen and Belsen in northern Germany. It was established in 1940 as a prisoner-of-war (POW) camp, but it also held criminals, political prisoners, Roma, Jehovah's Witnesses and gay men. In 1943 it became a concentration camp and began to receive Jewish prisoners evacuated on foot from camps closer to the Front Line. These were the so-called death marches. As new prisoners arrived, camp numbers soared. Whereas in July 1944 there had been 7,300 inmates, by April 1945 there were 60,000. With insufficient food and water rations, abysmal

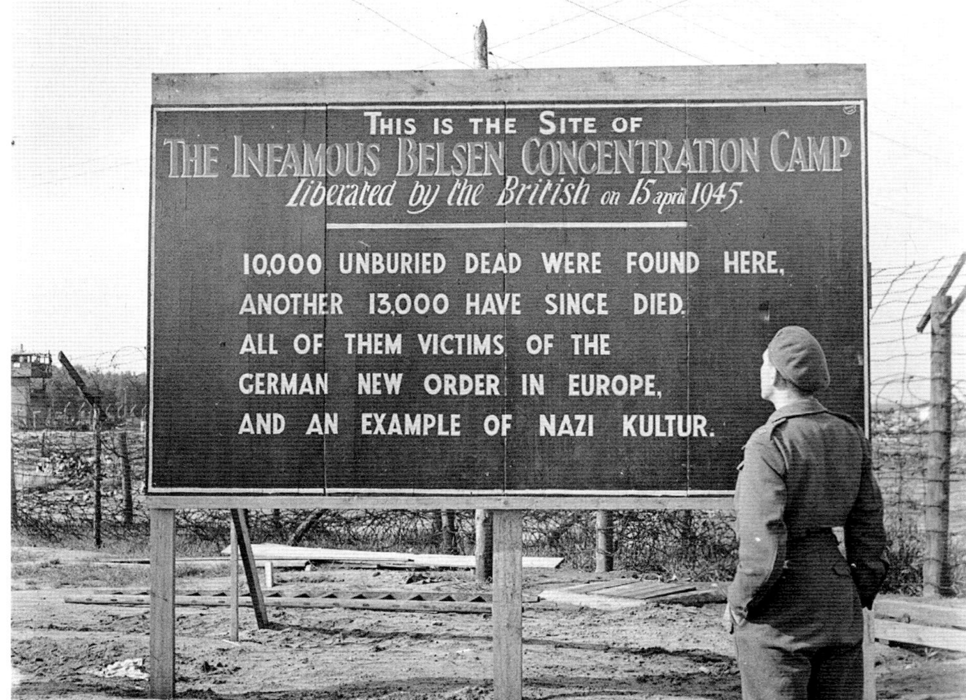

Fig. 4.18   A sign erected by British forces at the entrance to Bergen-Belsen concentration camp, Germany, 29 May 1945
© IWM (BU 6955)

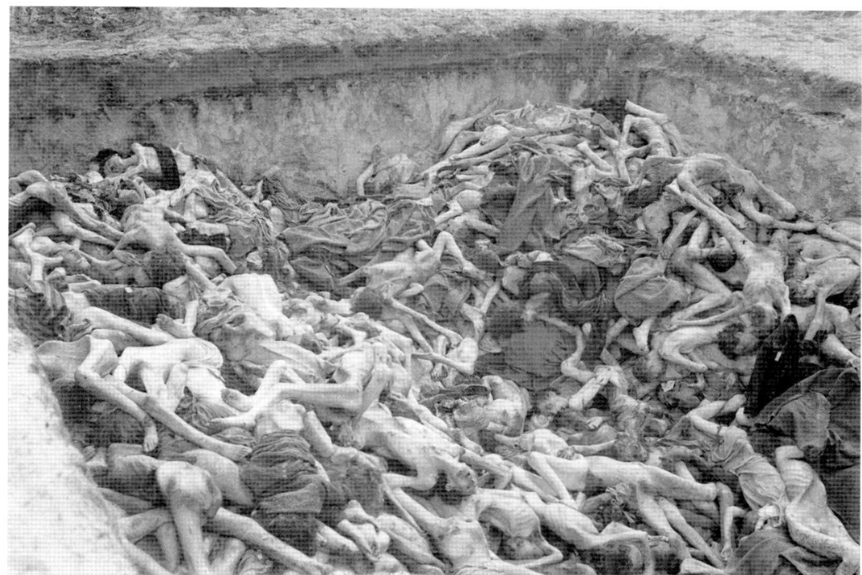

Fig. 4.19 One of the mass graves at Bergen-Belsen
© IWM (BU 3741)

sanitation and severe overcrowding, diseases such as tuberculosis, typhus, typhoid fever and dysentery spread, killing hundreds of starving and exhausted people every day. Over 36,000 prisoners died there in the spring of 1945. The famous Holocaust diarist Anne Frank (1929–1945) succumbed to typhus only a few weeks before the camp's liberation. The daily death toll was so enormous that the retreating Nazis stopped burying bodies and just left them lying in piles around the camp.

In January 1945 a large women's camp (*Grosses Frauenlager*) had been set up in a northern section of the complex. This housed women evacuated from Neuengamme, like Marianne and her mother, who arrived on 5 April 1945. They were shocked by what they found, thousands of dead and dying lying untended and unburied. Marianne had brought with her the watercolours and paper that she had received from the German guards in Neuengamme and began to draw the horrors around her.

Bergen-Belsen was the first major Nazi concentration camp to be liberated by the Western Allies, on 15 April 1945. Photographs soon appeared in newspapers worldwide. Marianne's drawings powerfully record the direct experiences of a person who lived through this human tragedy and despite it all did not lose the will to survive. Recognizing the importance of not forgetting, some soldiers commissioned drawings from Marianne; other drawings she gave away as reminders. When Marianne left Bergen-Belsen with the Red Cross to recuperate in Sweden, she took her remaining drawings with her.

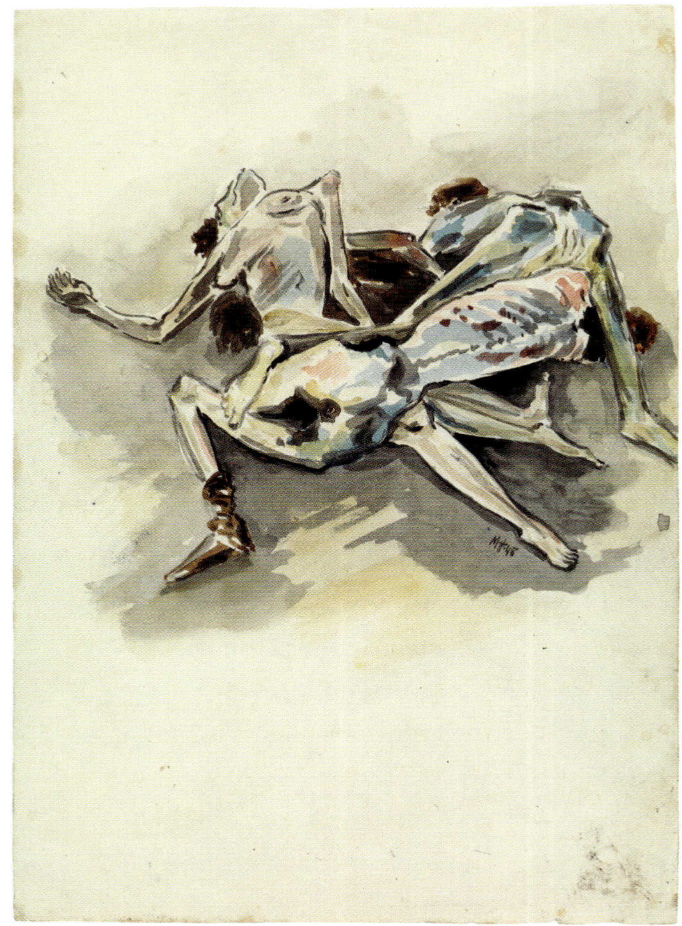

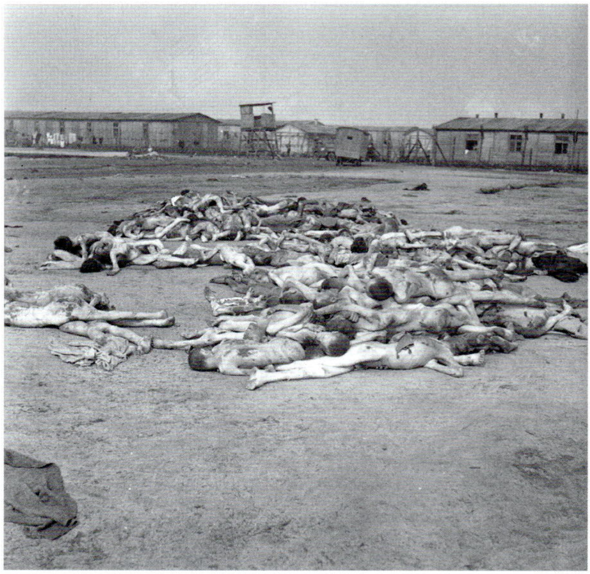

Fig. 4.20   Photograph taken by the British shortly after liberation, showing the unburied dead
© IWM (BU 3770)

30
Pile of dead bodies,
1945
Watercolour on paper
Signed and dated at
lower right 'MH/45'
PP.2005.38.35

In this disturbing watercolour Marianne shows naked, broken bodies thrown on top of each other like animal carcasses. The single stocking on an otherwise naked figure draws our attention to the bodies as individuals, now dehumanized and humiliated, but once clothed. With limbs bent at unnatural angles, their degradation is summed up in the soiled anus of the figure at the centre of the composition. The touches of yellow and blue suggest decomposition, implying that these bodies have been dead for some time. The artistic detachment in works such as this is astounding.

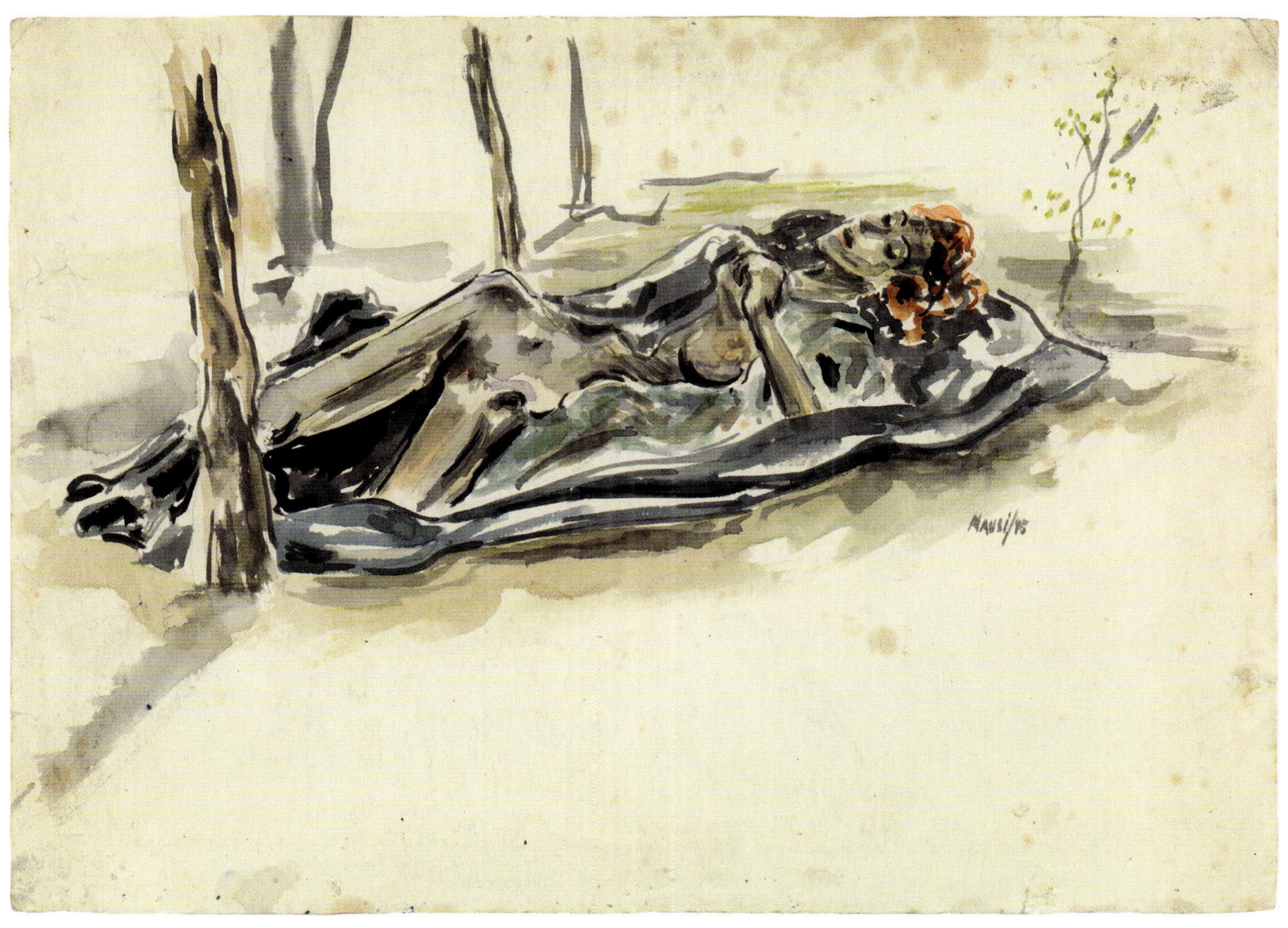

31

Dead body of young woman with red hair, 1945
Watercolour on paper
Signed and dated at lower right 'Mausi/45'
PP.2005.38.36

My mother and I shared one beetroot per day between us. There were no rations, no bread, no soup. I went on painting dead bodies. Between the young birches a beautiful young red head caught my eye.

The situation in the camp was desperate. The only food available was a store of beetroots and potatoes guarded by Hungarian militia with machine guns who shot at anyone attempting to get near. Extreme starvation even led to cannibalism among some inmates, as Marianne's friend Dita Kraus (née Polachová; b. 1929) recalled.[16] In this context it is all the more significant that Marianne focused on the person as an individual in this watercolour, finding beauty even in suffering and degradation. The young birch saplings are a reminder of the continuation of life.

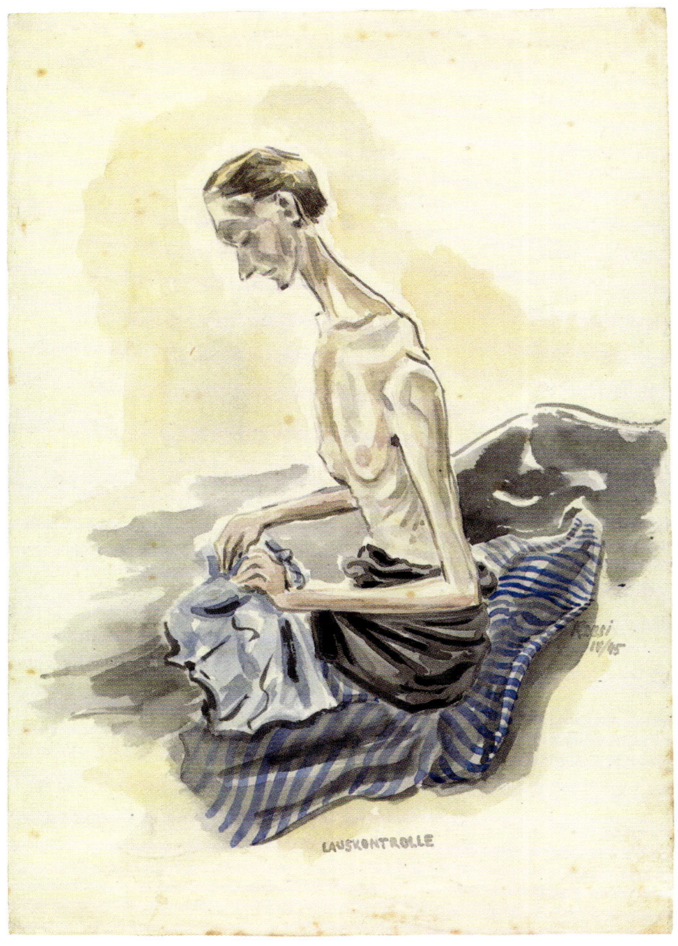

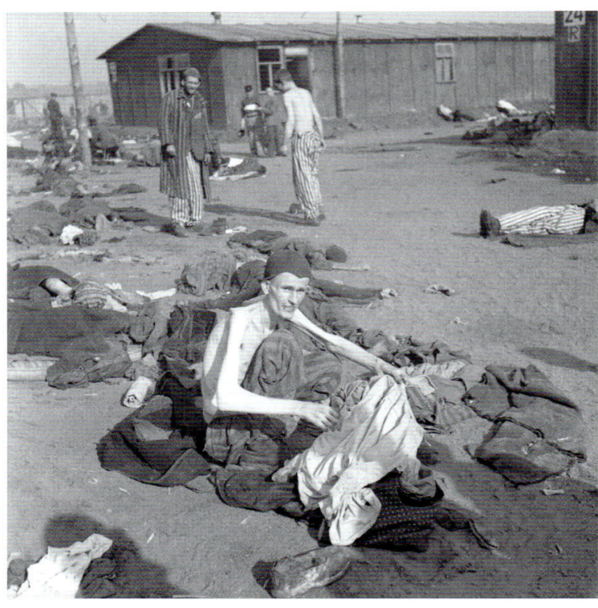

Fig. 4.21   Photograph taken by British forces shortly after liberation of the camp. A camp inmate checks his clothes for lice.
© IWM (BU 3765)

32

Lauskontrolle,

April 1945

Watercolour on paper

Inscribed lower centre 'LAUSKONTROLLE', signed and dated at right 'Mausi IV/45'

PP.2005.38.34

Lauskontrolle, checking our garments for lice (the carriers of typhus). Our daily task.

A typhus epidemic broke out in Bergen-Belsen in early 1945, claiming the lives of thousands. Delousing of clothes was crucial to minimizing the spread of the disease. The extremely emaciated woman in this watercolour methodically checks her official camp-issued striped uniform for lice. The taking away of civilian clothing and its replacement with standard issue prison wear had been intended to further humiliate inmates and strip them of their personal identity. Yet Marianne gives this woman, absorbed in her simple task, as much dignity as that found in traditional painted domestic scenes of women sewing.

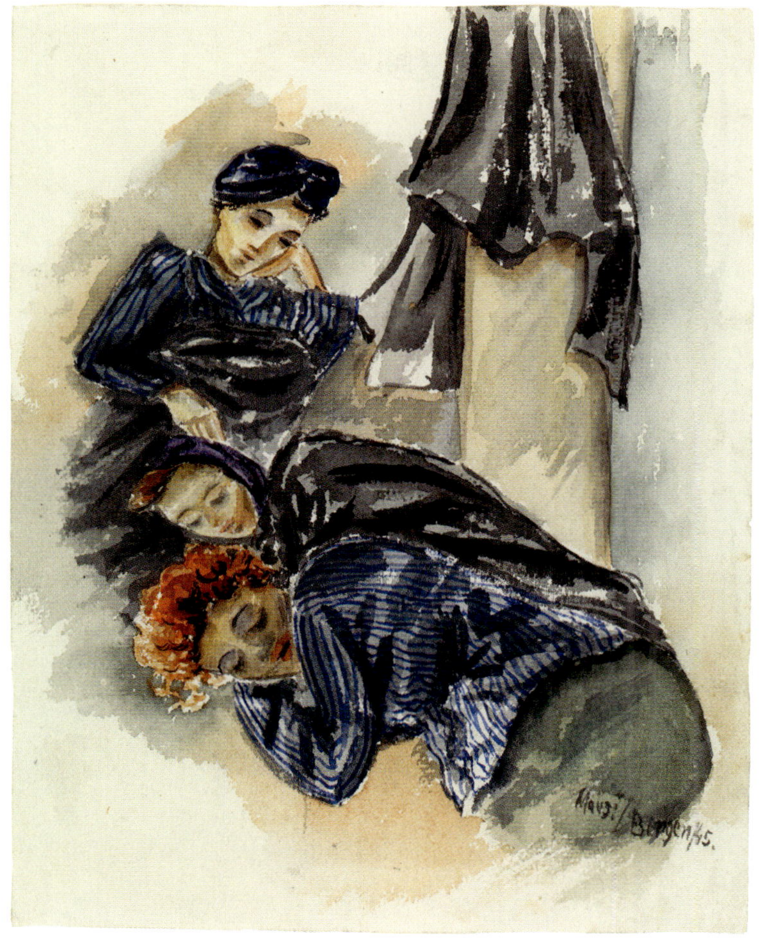

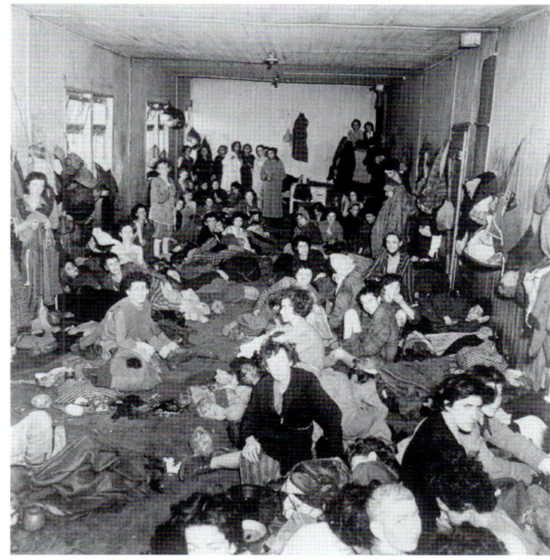

Fig. 4.22   Photograph inside a hut at Bergen-Belsen, taken by the British shortly after liberation
© IWM (BU 3805)

33

Inside the dwelling hut, 1945

Watercolour on paper
Signed and dated at lower right 'Mausi/ Bergen/45'
PP.2005.38.30

Inside the dwelling hut, showing the people already inside the hut when we arrived. People sleeping and ill, before Montgomery's army liberated the camp.

Marianne recalled that the women inside the huts had sickly yellow faces: 'Some were alive still, but barely moving and we slept with them.' Whereas previously the women had been used as forced labourers, now that the SS had surrendered there was nothing to do. Marianne shows one woman wearily leaning on her hand, eyes downcast, as the two women beside her sleep. Because of the terrible smell and threat of infection, Marianne and her mother eventually decided to sleep outside.

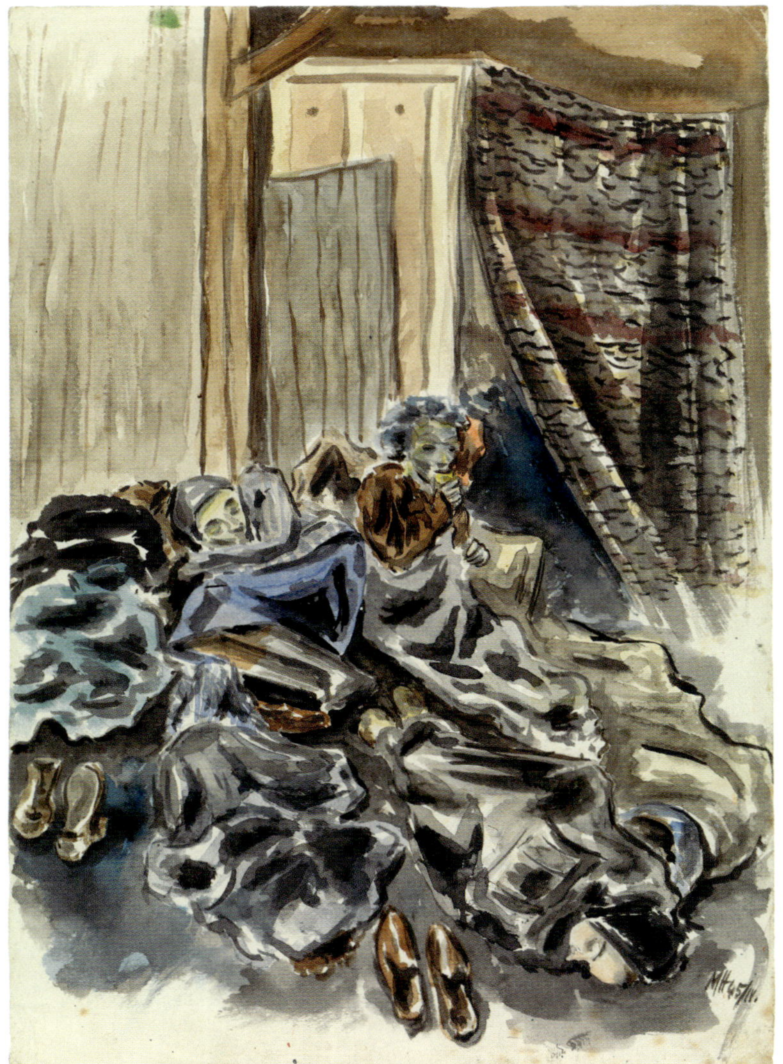

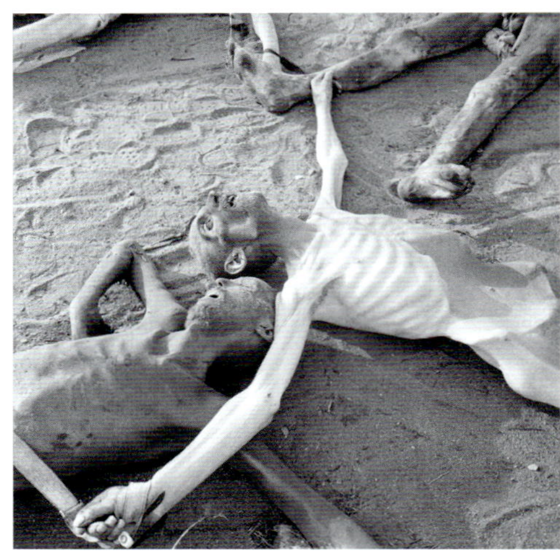

Fig. 4.23 Photograph of dead bodies at Bergen-Belsen, taken by the British shortly after liberation
© IWM (BU 3760)

34

People dead and dying inside the hut due to typhus and malnutrition, April 1945
Watercolour on paper
Signed and dated at lower right
'MH 45/IV'
PP.2005.38.29

Bodies lie huddled together under makeshift bedding. The shoes in the foreground may belong to one of the sleeping figures but, empty, they are a visual suggestion of human loss. British soldier William Arthur Wood described what he saw on entering the camp: 'Outside the huts were piles and piles of dead bodies, and living ones, we didn't know which were which. In the huts themselves, equally, you didn't know who was dead and who was alive unless they made, there was some movement you could see, because the dead and the living were all together – they hadn't the energy to take the dead out'.[17]

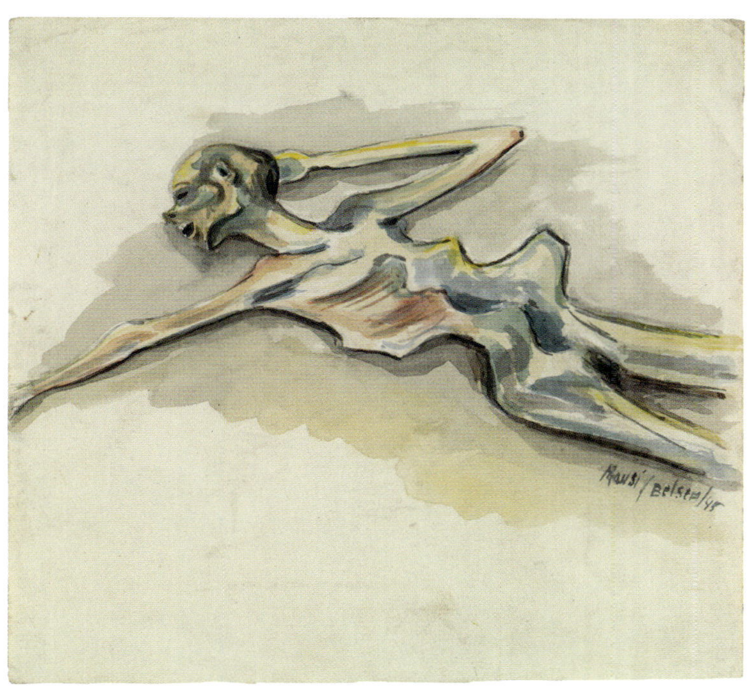

35 (above left)
A dead body, 1945
Watercolour on paper
Signed and dated at lower right 'Mausi/Belsen/45.'
PP.2005.38.33

36 (above right)
Sketch for 'A dead body' (cat. 35), 1945
Pencil on paper
Unsigned
PP.2005.38.32

The jutting bones of this skeletal man are harrowing to see, but Marianne recognized the importance of creating a visual record of the atrocities and inhuman conditions at Bergen-Belsen. Her watercolours correspond closely with contemporary photographs and witness statements. Wood again: 'We'd been trained for war wounded, we were used to terrible wounds […] But I'm afraid when we got to Belsen we hadn't been trained for this, and it was so, so different to, well to anything. I can't explain it, it was so terrible and so different from anything we'd seen in our move up from D-Day onward. We'd seen distressed people about, people walking from town to town, but nothing like this.'[18]

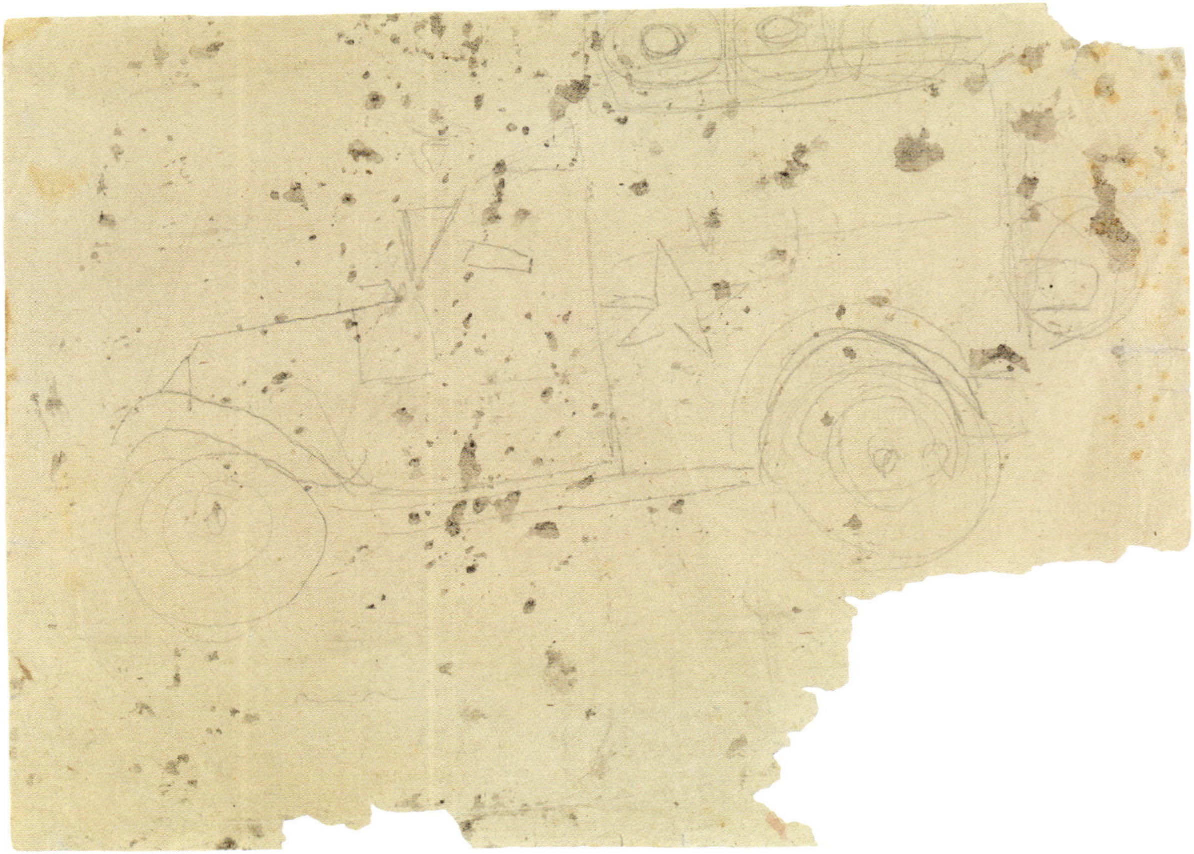

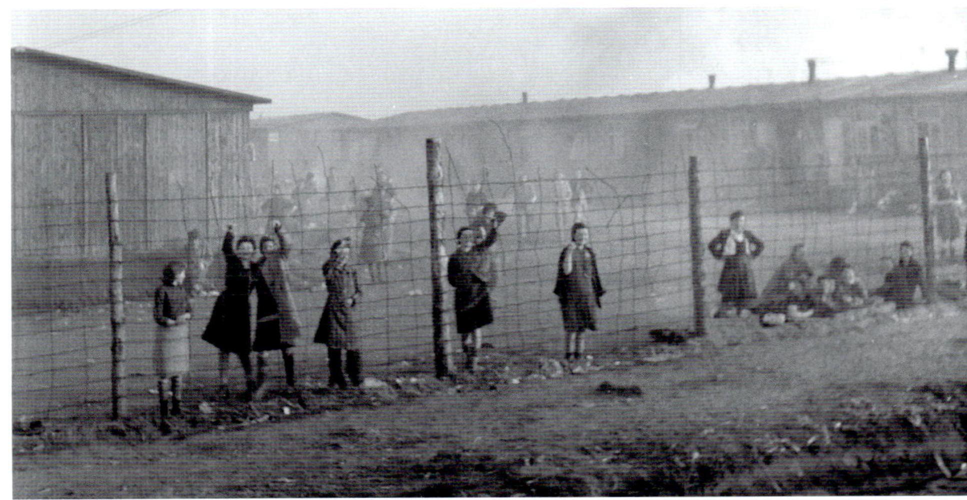

Fig. 4.24 Photograph of inmates welcoming the liberation army, taken by the British shortly after arrival
© IWM (BU 4043)

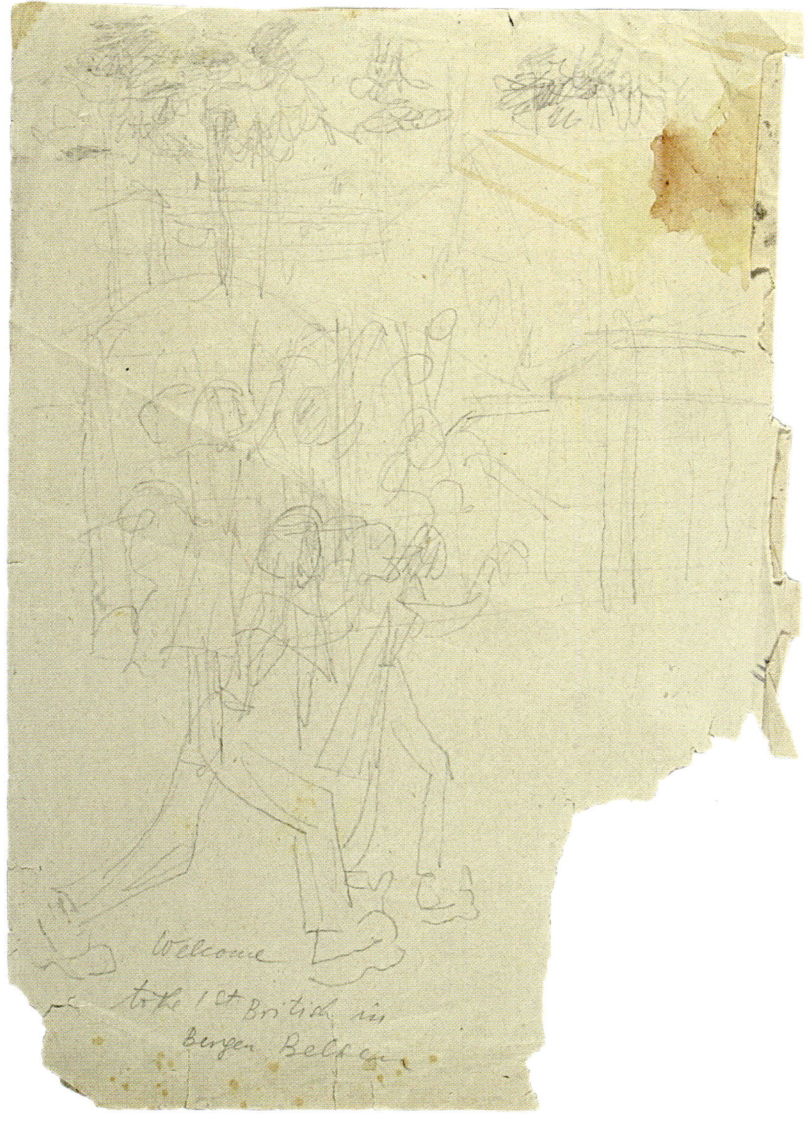

37 (opposite)
British army arriving, April 1945
Pencil sketch and mud on paper
Unsigned
PP.2005.38.37 (front)

38 (above)
**Welcome to the first British in
Bergen-Belsen**, April 1945
Pencil sketch on paper
Inscribed at the bottom 'Welcome to
the 1st British in Bergen Belsen'
PP.2005.38.37 (reverse)

This image [opposite] *is splashed with
Bergen-Belsen mud.*

The British 11th Armoured Division led
by Field Marshal Montgomery entered
the camp on 15 April 1945 after the
retreating Germans surrendered
peacefully. Marianne recalled that
the earth trembled as the British
army approached. She recorded the
moment of their arrival on this torn
piece of paper. Her supplies of art
materials must have been low by
this time. Wasting no precious paper,
she drew on the front and back.
These quick sketches in pencil were
made on the spot and were splashed
with mud. As Marianne and other
survivors remembered, this truck
with loudspeakers on its roof was the
first to enter the camp, announcing
the arrival of the British army and the
camp's liberation. Marianne recalled
it was a most emotional moment.
On the reverse she drew prisoners
running and cheering, conveying their
elated feelings in quick lines. Marianne
later remembered a celebration
where she danced with Montgomery.
However, for thousands of inmates
at Bergen-Belsen freedom came too
late and, despite the tremendous
efforts of the Allied army to arrange
rapid medical aid, about 500 people
continued to die every day during the
first month after liberation.

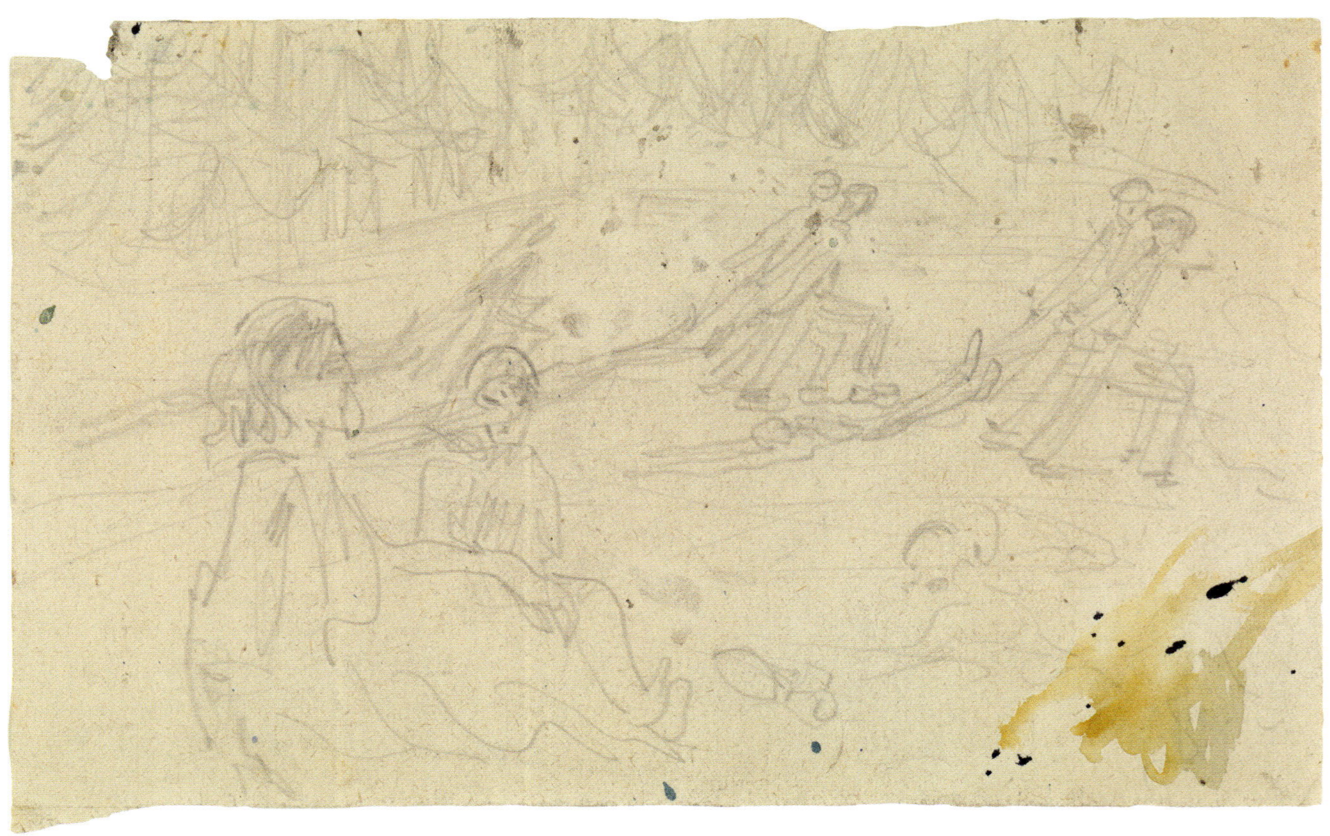

39
**Germans made to drag away
the dead bodies**, 1945
Pencil on paper
Unsigned
PP.2005.38.38 (front)

German soldiers strain as they pull corpses behind them; in the foreground are the sick and the dying. Immediately after their arrival, the liberating army faced the task of burying over 13,000 dead in various stages of decomposition. Initially, surrendered German soldiers were forced to clear the camp, but soon bulldozers had to be employed. Marianne's friend Dita, who also survived Bergen-Belsen, recalled: 'The dead bodies were scattered everywhere. Everywhere you looked there were corpses. When the British arrived, they could not bury them individually. They had to use bulldozers to clear away the bodies and put them together into huge graves'.[19]

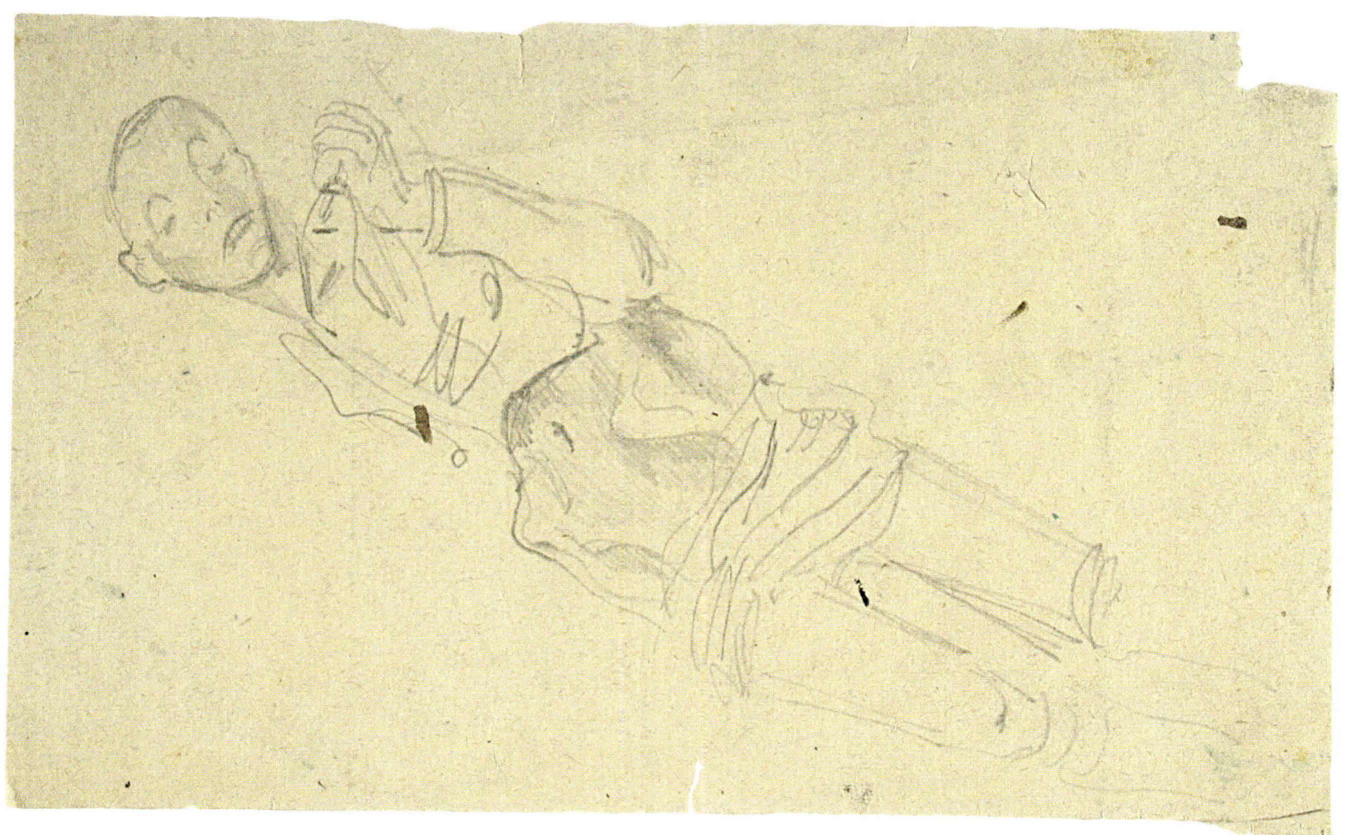

40

Sketch for 'Dead body of Belsen camp' (cat. 41), 1945
Pencil on paper
Unsigned
PP.2005.38.38 (reverse)

The British established a Displaced Persons (DP) Camp in nearby barracks, formerly the quarters of German and Hungarian soldiers. Inmates from Bergen-Belsen were temporarily rehoused there. Marianne and her mother shared a room with Dita and her mother. It was here that Marianne started working for the British as a translator, signwriter, and distributor of cigarette rations to the soldiers. In her spare time she continued drawing dead bodies, commissioned by soldiers so that they would never forget what they had witnessed in Bergen-Belsen. This drawing is a sketch for one such image.

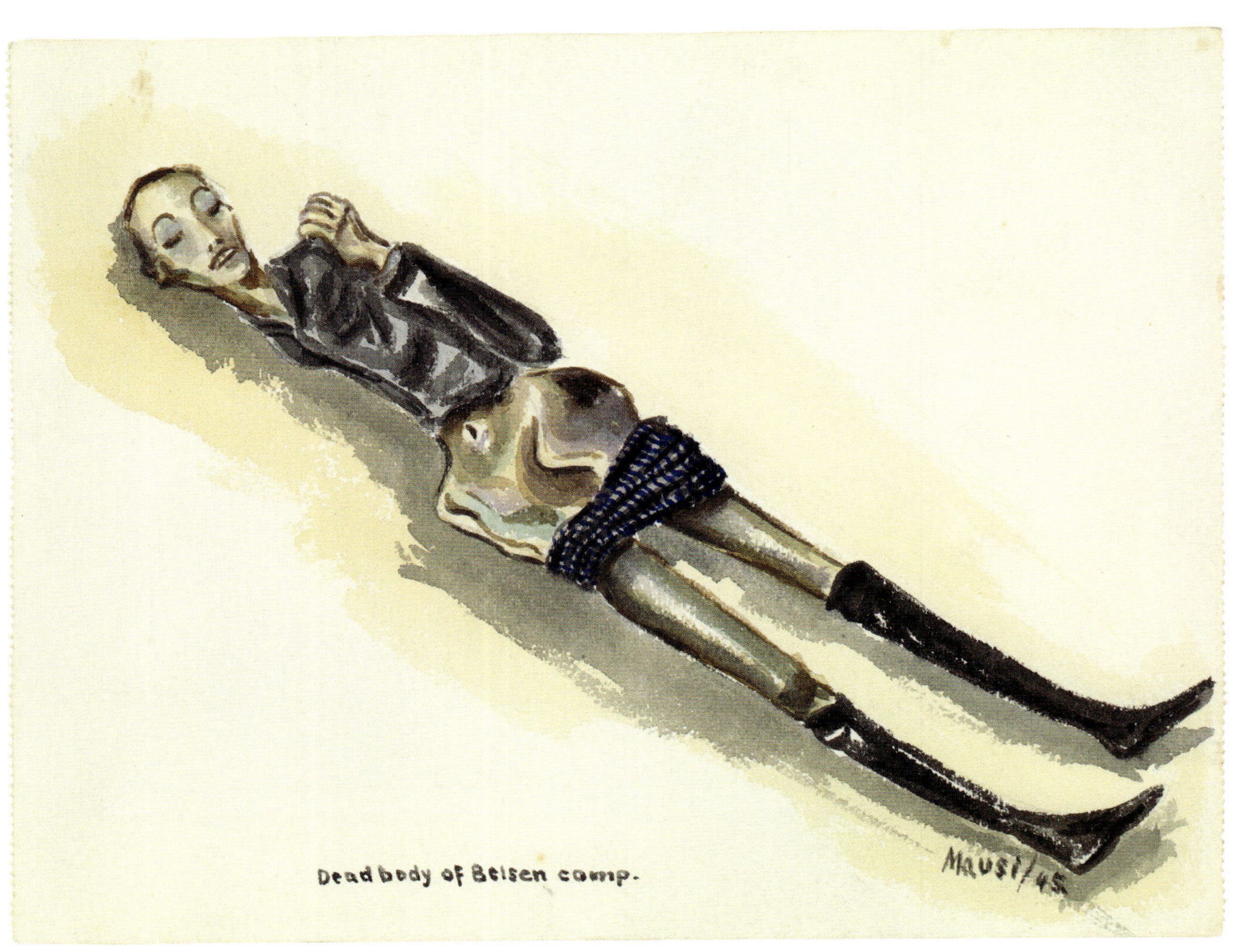

Dead body of Belsen camp.
Mausi/45.

41

Dead body of Belsen camp,
1945
Watercolour on paper
Inscribed 'Dead body of Belsen
camp.' Signed and dated at lower
right 'Mausi/45.'
PP.2005.38.31

A likely victim of the typhus epidemic, this woman lying in a dishevelled state of undress, white teeth bared in a final grimace, is nevertheless a visceral reminder that women prisoners were often subject to sexual violence within the camps.

Another copy of this painting, given by Marianne to Major Charles Philip Sharp (1913–1998), is now in the collection of the United States Holocaust Memorial Museum. Sharp was one of the first British officers to arrive at Belsen on 17 April 1945. As his unit had been vaccinated against typhus it was selected to bury corpses to prevent the typhus contagion from spreading across Europe.

Sharp was stationed in Bergen-Belsen for five weeks and kept a detailed diary. On 22 May he wrote in his diary: 'Marianne, the little Czech artist presented us with a picture of a body in No. 1 "To the Commandant so that he will never forget Belsen" – as though I could. She used to do cartoons and gay pictures before she was taken – now see what she does. We are using her as a sign writer so she apologized that this drawing was not as detailed as she would have liked it to be, but nevertheless it brings back the atmosphere at once.'[20]

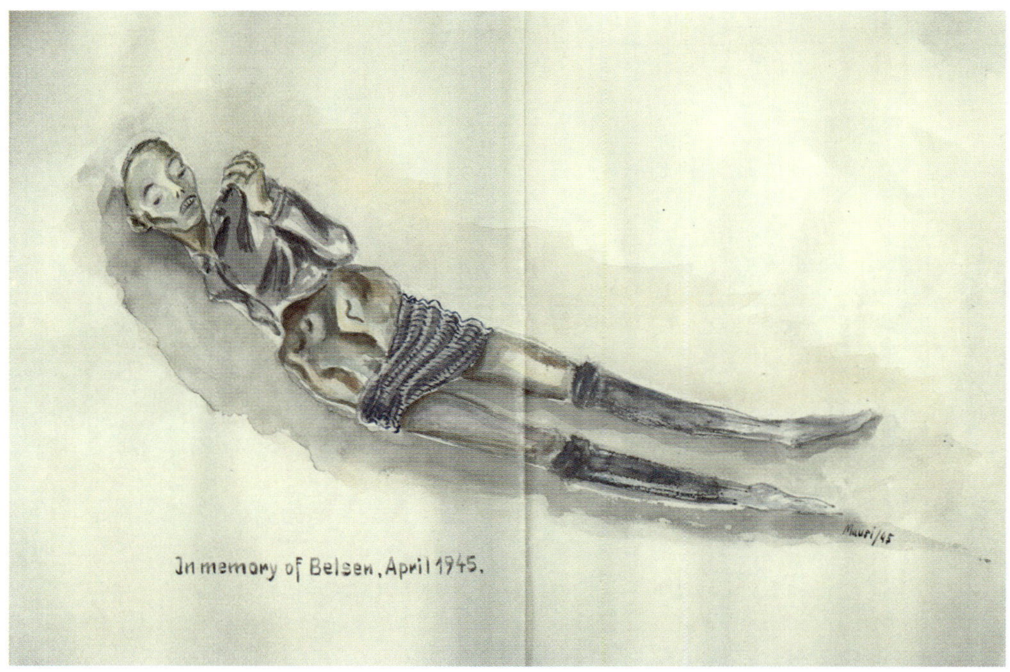

Fig. 4.25
In Memory of Belsen,
May 1945
watercolour on paper
United States Holocaust
Memorial Museum
Collection
Gift of Peter Stevens
2004.570.1

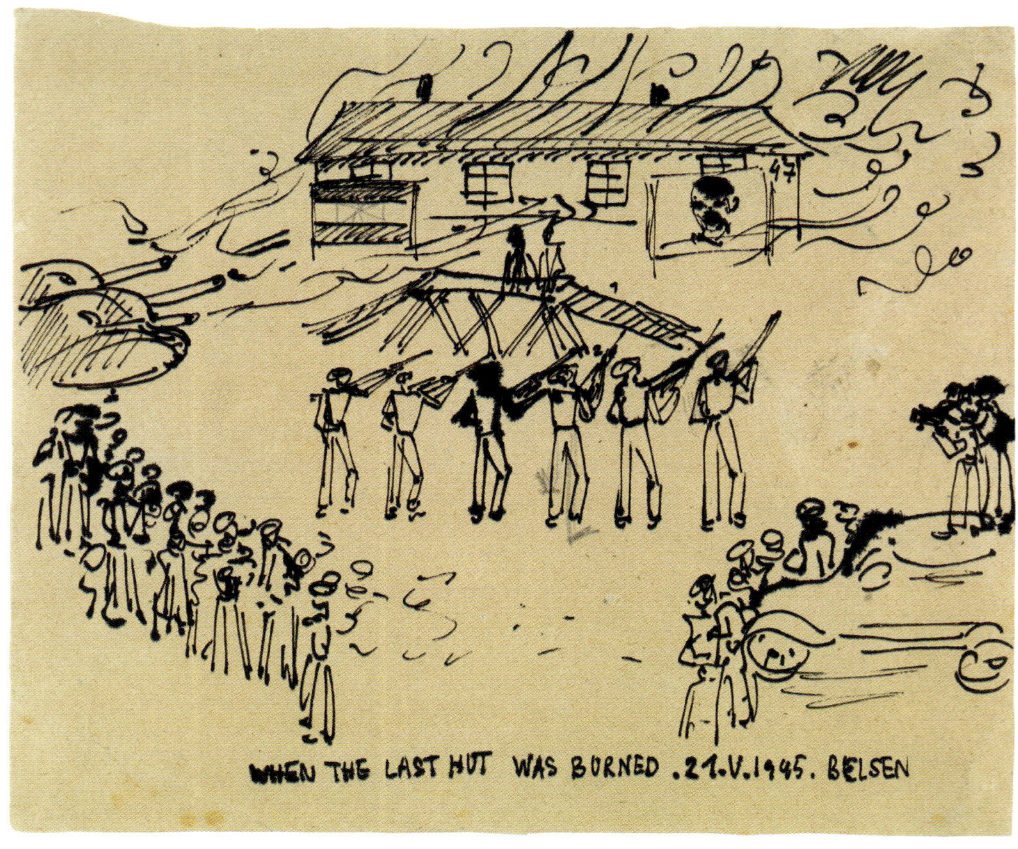

42

When the last hut was burned,

21 May 1945

Ink and pencil on paper

Inscribed 'WHEN THE LAST HUT WAS BURNED .21.V.1945. BELSEN'

PP.2005.38.39

Ceremony when the last hut at Belsen was burned by the British on 21 May 1945. As the whole camp was infested it had to be destroyed.

This quick on-the-spot sketch shows soldiers and tanks firing on Hut no. 47, from which Hitler's portrait and the German war ensign (1933–35) are hung, watched by former inmates, while a film crew records the event. In the middle distance is a small stage erected for speeches.

The Scotsman newspaper reported: 'At 6:00 last night the last traces of the notorious Belsen Camp were burnt in a ceremony attended by former prisoners […] Just before the news was received of the final destruction of the camp, a cable from Reuter's correspondent at S.H.A.E.F. [Supreme Headquarters Allied Expeditionary Force] said the horror camp's death-rate has been reduced by 80 per cent in a month. Forty thousand inmates were disinfected within 15 days of the camp being liberated, and hospital accommodation for 17,000 patients was organized.'[21]

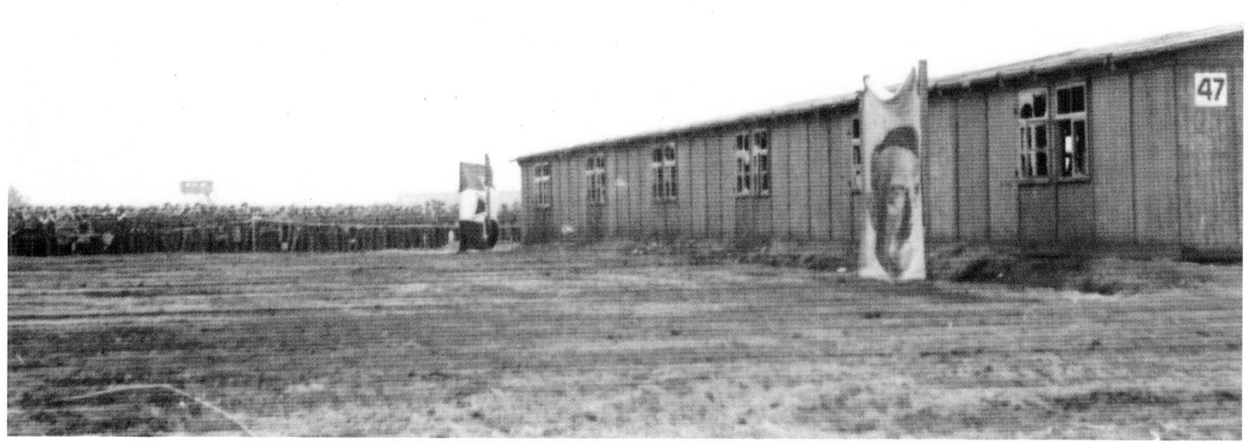

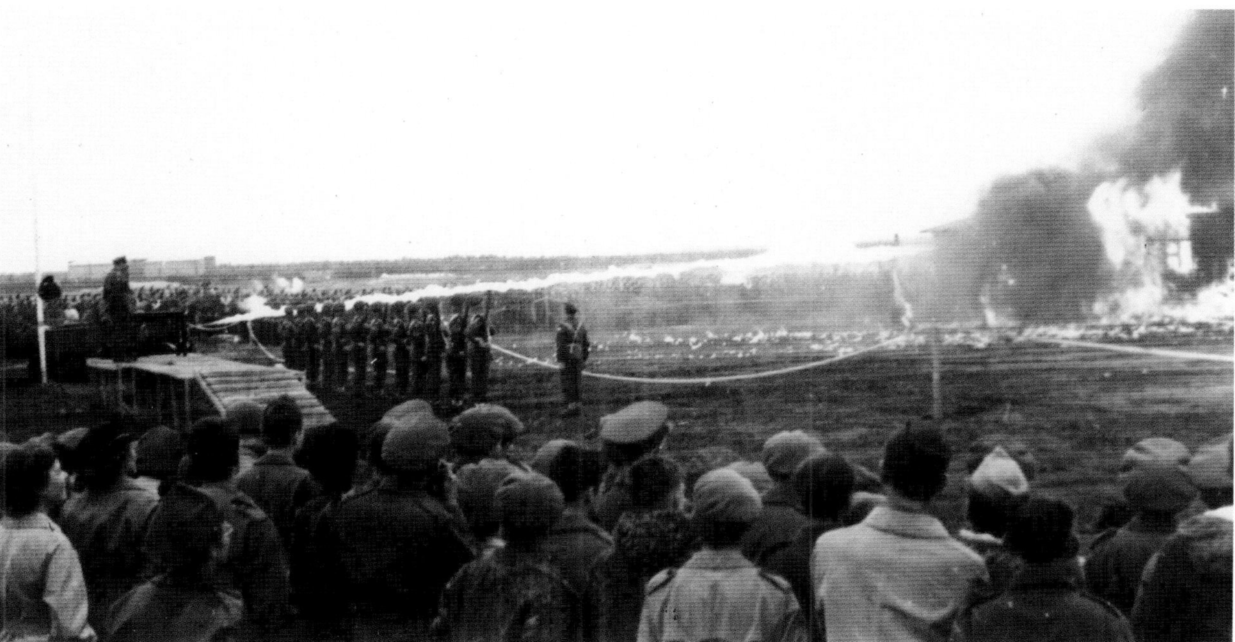

Figs. 4.26 and 4.27   Photographs of the event captured by British Reverend Charles Martin King Parsons (1899–1953) who entered the liberated Bergen-Belsen with British troops

Sweden: 11 July 1945– September 1951

In March 1945 Sweden, which had remained a neutral country throughout the war, began to negotiate the release of Scandinavian nationals from Nazi concentration camps. The rescue mission widened to include other prisoners. In the end Sweden accepted nearly 5,000 Holocaust survivors and supported their rehabilitation and return to normal life.

Marianne described Sweden as 'the only land in the world where the state dictates and advertises help and pro-Jewish feelings towards immigrants.'[22] The Jewish Telegraphic Agency in New York reported on 17 May 1945:

> Three thousand Jewish refugees liberated from German concentration camps have arrived in Sweden within the past few days. Among them are 1,500 Jews from Poland, 400 from Holland, 200 from France, 800 from Hungary and 150 from Germany and Austria.
>
> Many of the arrivals are ill and most have been separated from their families… The misery and sufferings they have undergone are indescribable.[23]

Marianne had wanted to return to Prague, but her mother was too ill and Dr Sean Styles, an Allied doctor, warned of famine in Europe. Assisted by the United Nations Relief and Rehabilitation Administration (UNRRA), which had been set up to repatriate refugees displaced by the war and to tackle food shortages, Styles got them on a Red Cross hospital ship to Sweden. Marianne and her mother were taken by ambulance train to a Swedish transit hospital in Lübeck. Before their boat sailed, Marianne met an American from Chicago, probably Fred Hoehler (1893–1969), Director of the Division on Displaced Persons for UNRRA. Examining some of Marianne's Bergen-Belsen watercolours, he expressed interest in exhibiting her work in New York.

When Marianne arrived in Malmö, she was welcomed by members of the Swedish Women's Voluntary Defence Organization and initially quarantined in a school before being placed at Robertshöjd 1, a former holiday camp turned refugee camp near Gothenburg. Evacuees were encouraged to work, and Marianne found ill-paid employment painting ceramics. She later undertook more fulfilling design work with a screen-printing company in

Alingsås and a cabaret theatre in Liseberg Park in Gothenburg. Although she initially planned to emigrate to Israel, Marianne came to appreciate the quality of life in Sweden. After leaving the camp, she took a cheap room near the harbour with her mother, before settling in a small flat just outside the city and establishing her own design studio, employing a small number of staff.

Marianne showed some of her Bergen-Belsen drawings in an exhibition headed by the German anti-fascist artist Hans Tombrock (1895–1966) which was held at the workers' education union Arbetarnas Bildningsförbund (ABF) in Gothenburg in November and Malmö in December 1945. She was disappointed that her Theresienstadt artworks, in the safekeeping of Petr Erben, did not arrive in time to be included.

Marianne expressed admiration for Tombrock's work, which spoke out vehemently against Nazi abuse, but in Sweden she found she did not want to revisit the horror of the camps in her art. The work she produced here was consciously cheerful and unpolitical. She wrote, 'I managed to get through it all with such an iron energy and strong will, in the end, for the better times.'[24]

By the end of the 1950s, large numbers of Jewish refugees had been integrated into Swedish society. Others emigrated to the United States, Canada and Israel. After becoming engaged to her pen friend, German Jewish refugee Jack Grant, in the summer of 1951, Marianne travelled with her mother to Scotland, was married in London in September and settled in Battlefield on the southside of the city of Glasgow.

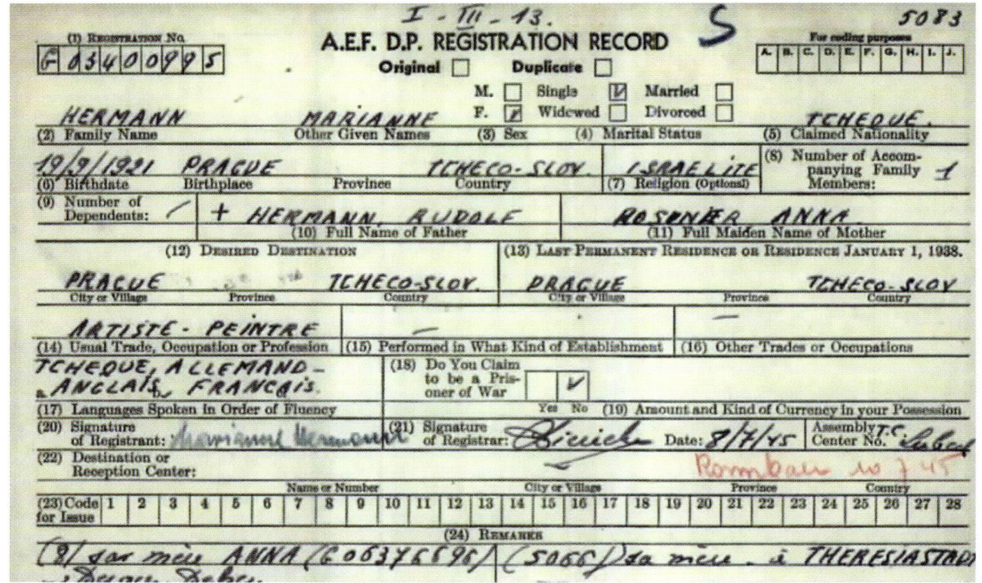

Fig. 4.28 After liberation, Marianne was registered as a Displaced Person by the Allied Expeditionary Force. She was no longer a mere number but recognized as an individual. This is the card she was issued with in Lübeck. She gave her profession as 'Artist-Painter'. Arolsen Archives: International Center on Nazi Persecution, doc. 67345705, Marianne Hermann

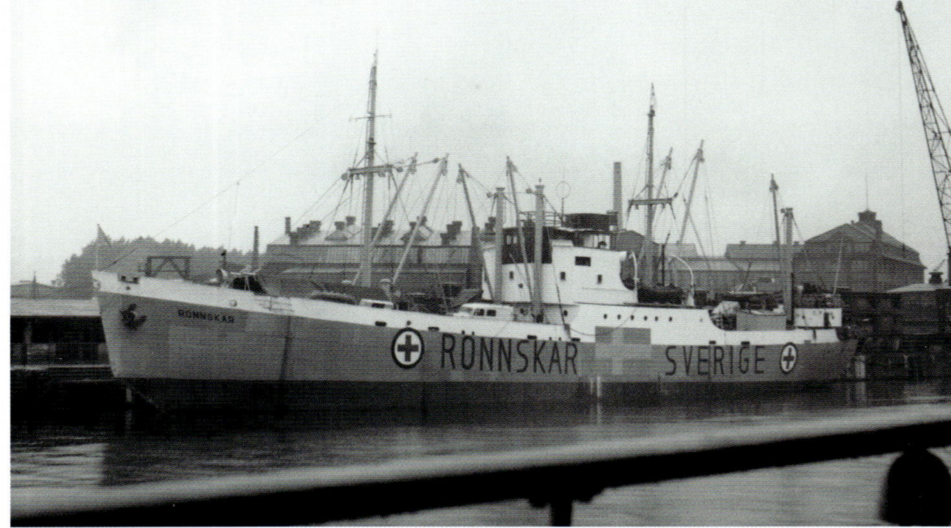

Fig. 4.29 (right)
Marianne sailed from Lübeck for Malmö on 10 July 1945 aboard M/S *Rönnskär*, one of four Swedish merchant ships and one naval vessel kitted out with medical equipment and supplies to evacuate refugees. They were accompanied by minesweepers.

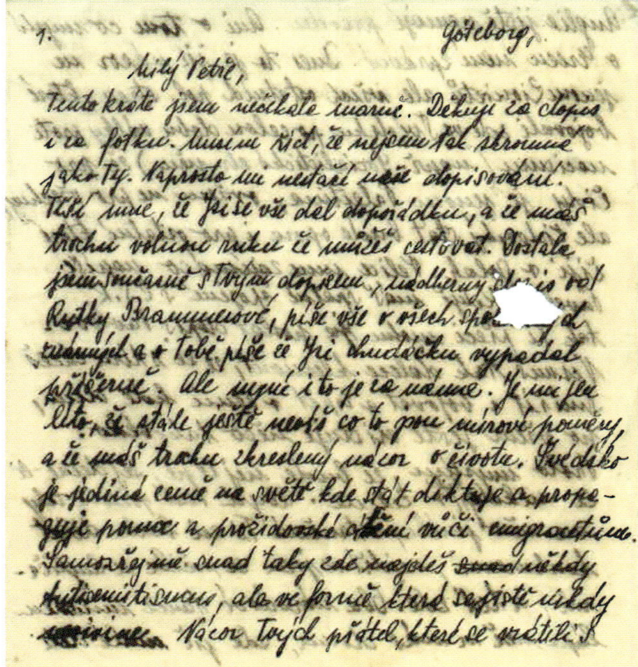

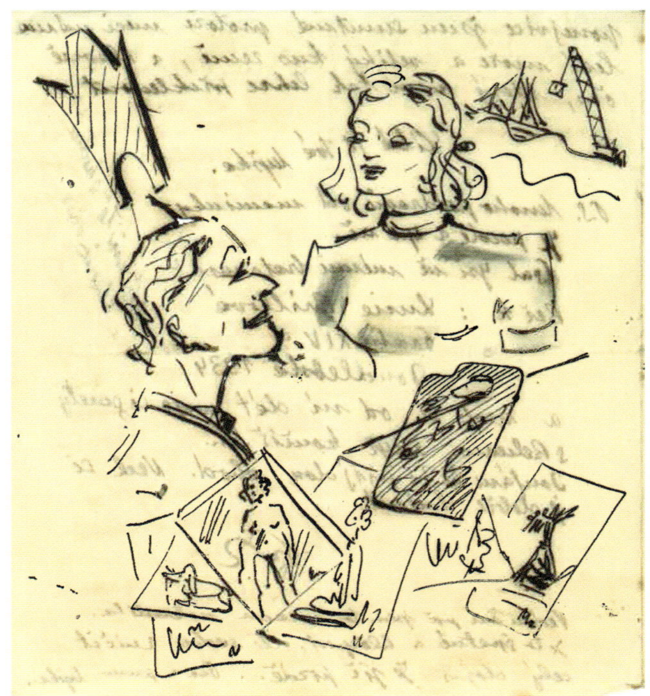

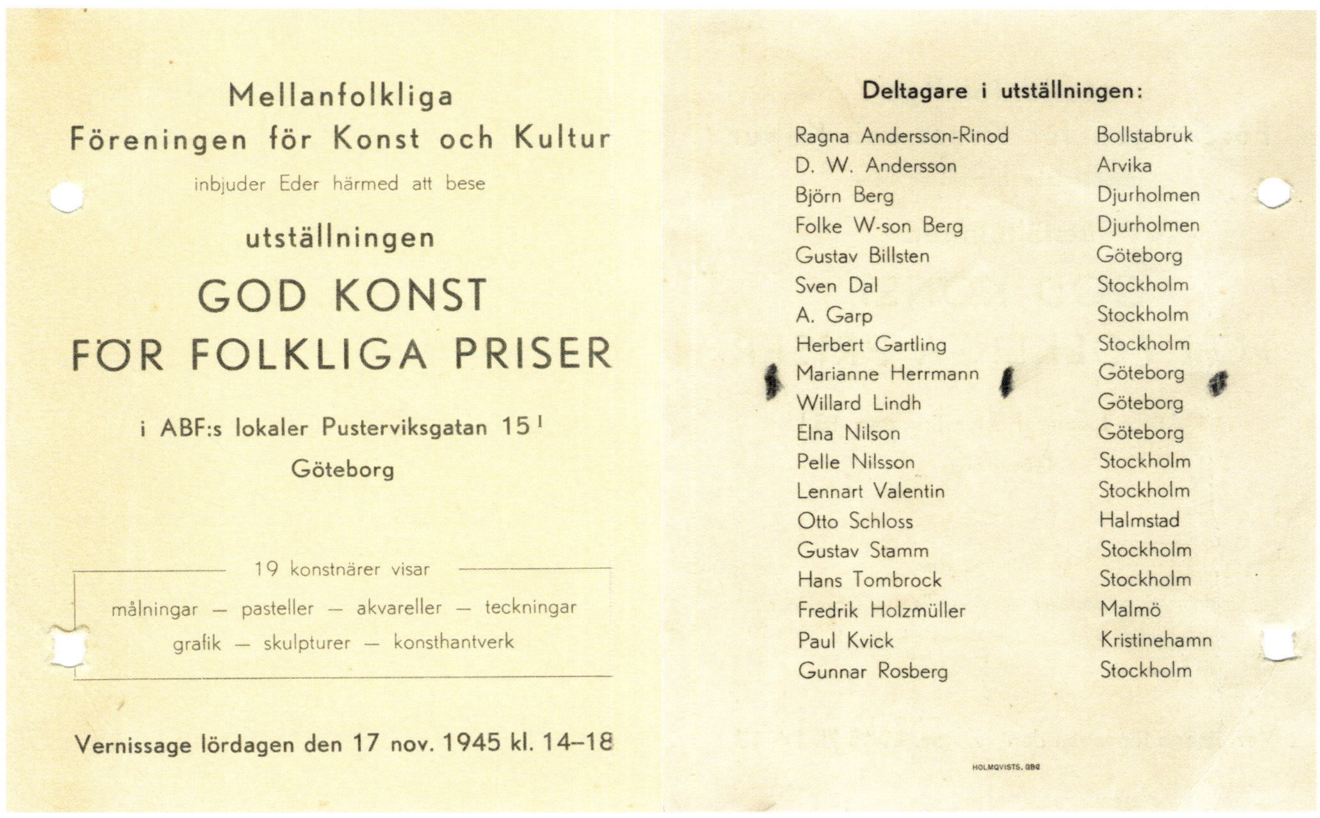

Mellanfolkliga
Föreningen för Konst och Kultur

inbjuder Eder härmed att bese

utställningen

GOD KONST
FÖR FOLKLIGA PRISER

i ABF:s lokaler Pusterviksgatan 15 I

Göteborg

19 konstnärer visar

målningar — pasteller — akvareller — teckningar

grafik — skulpturer — konsthantverk

Vernissage lördagen den 17 nov. 1945 kl. 14–18

Deltagare i utställningen:

Ragna Andersson-Rinod	Bollstabruk
D. W. Andersson	Arvika
Björn Berg	Djurholmen
Folke W-son Berg	Djurholmen
Gustav Billsten	Göteborg
Sven Dal	Stockholm
A. Garp	Stockholm
Herbert Gartling	Stockholm
Marianne Herrmann	Göteborg
Willard Lindh	Göteborg
Elna Nilson	Göteborg
Pelle Nilsson	Stockholm
Lennart Valentin	Stockholm
Otto Schloss	Halmstad
Gustav Stamm	Stockholm
Hans Tombrock	Stockholm
Fredrik Holzmüller	Malmö
Paul Kvick	Kristinehamn
Gunnar Rosberg	Stockholm

HOLMQVISTS, GBG

Fig. 4.30 (opposite, bottom)
Letter dating from autumn 1945 from Marianne to Petr Erben in which she talks
about Sweden welcoming Jews and exhibiting with Tombrock. She drew herself
in Gothenburg and Petr in Prague with her artwork, an unsubtle reminder that
she wanted her drawings back.
Family archive

Fig. 4.31 (above)
Leaflet advertising the Public Association of Art and Culture exhibition of pastels,
watercolours, drawings, prints, sculpture and craft at the ABF in Gothenburg
in November 1945, to which Marianne contributed, along with Tombrock and
Gothenburg-based artists Gustav Billsten (active 1945), Willard Lindh (1918–
2007) and Elna Margareta Nilsson (1910–1983).
Family archive

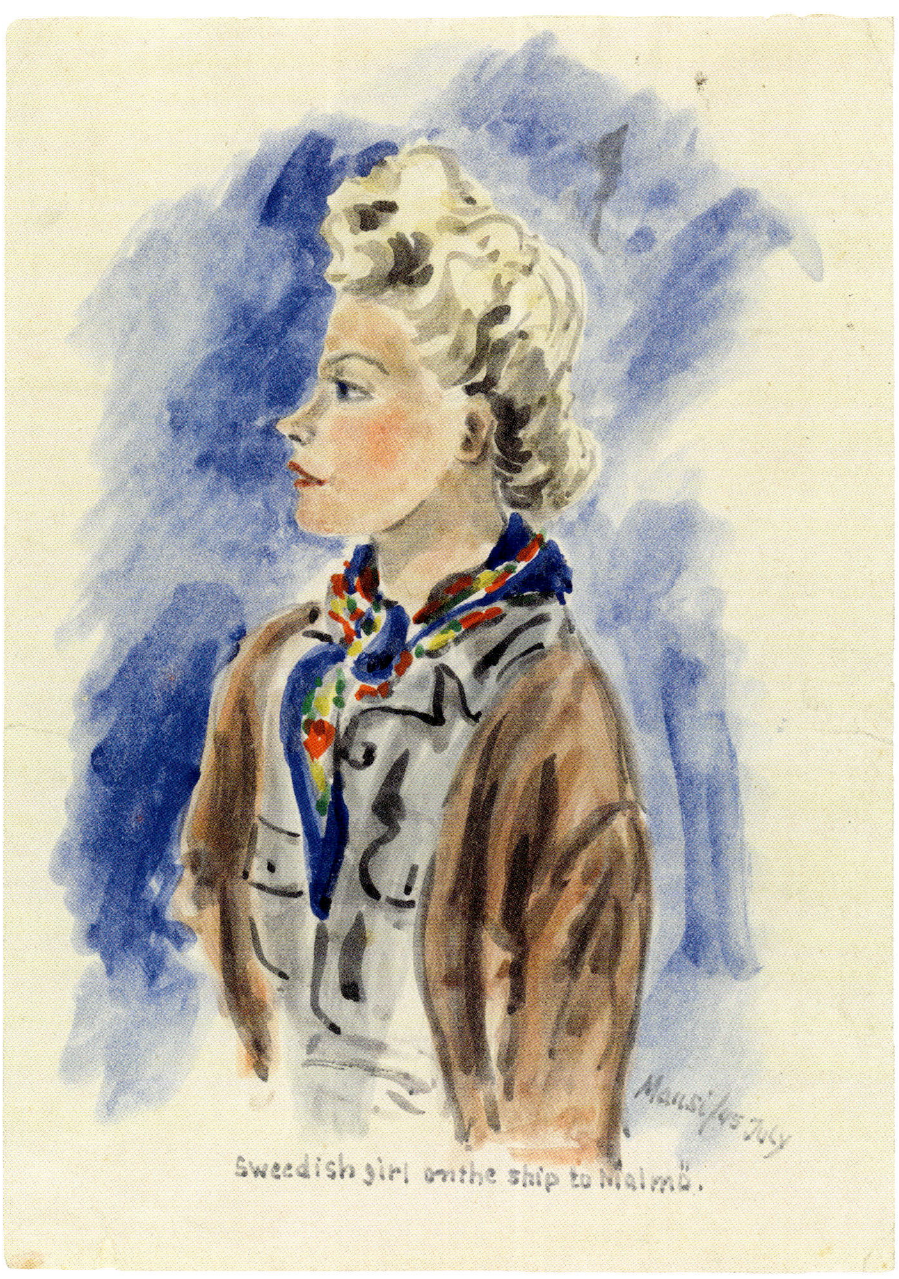

43

A Swedish girl on the Red Cross boat to Malmö, Sweden, July 1945
Pencil and watercolour on paper
Inscribed 'Swedish girl on the ship to Malmö.' Signed and dated at lower right 'Mausi/45 July'
PP.2005.38.40

About three months after liberation, my mother and I left Bergen-Belsen. We went by train to Hamburg and sailed to Malmö in Sweden on the Red Cross boat.

While at sea, Marianne made friends with this Swedish nurse. There were many very sick and weak people on the boat and Marianne, always looking for opportunities for useful employment, volunteered as a helper. And she continued to draw. Her buoyant mood is expressed in the bright colours of this watercolour, the nurse's vibrant floral scarf at the centre, and the whole set against an optimistic blue background.

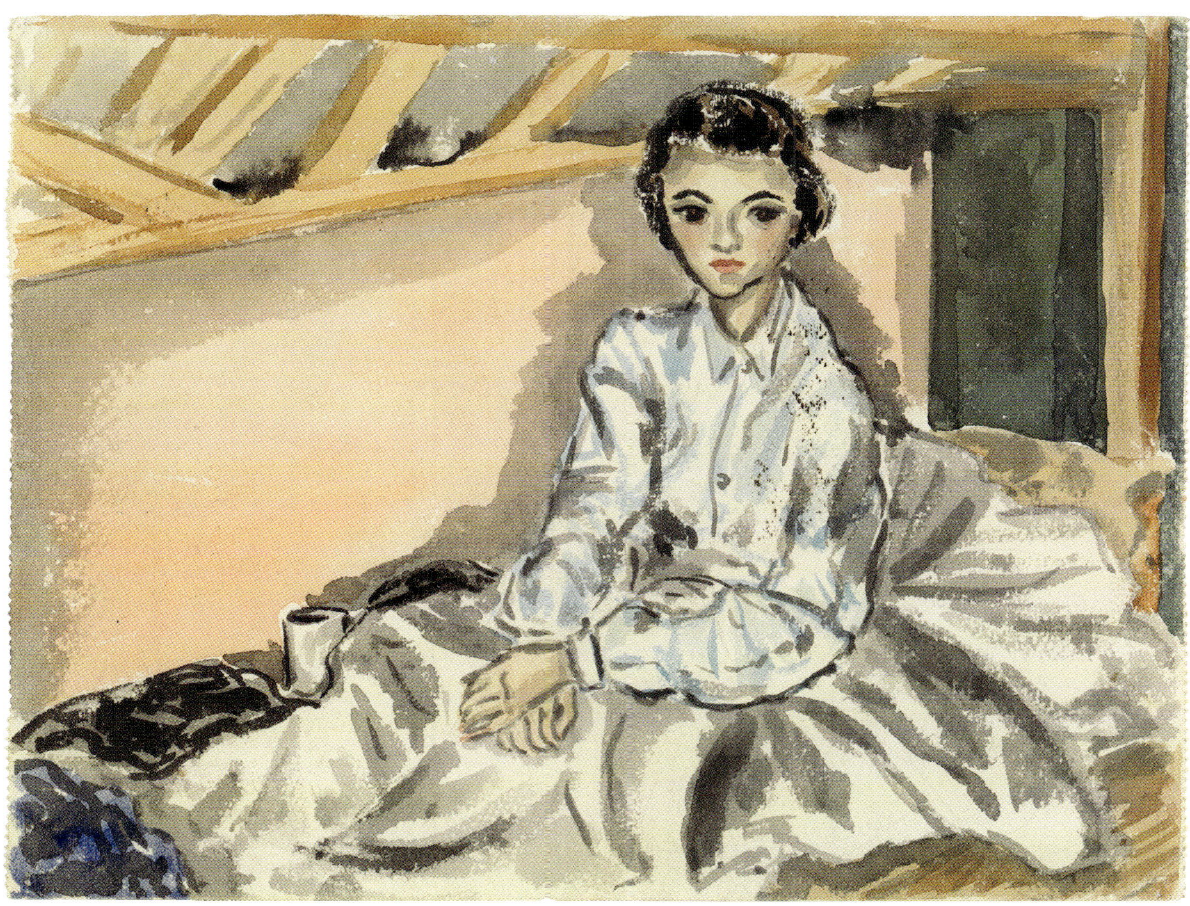

44

**On the Red Cross boat to
Malmö, Sweden**, July 1945
Watercolour on paper
Unsigned
PP.2005.38.41

*A young Jewish Dutch girl
from Bergen-Belsen. She was
dying from tuberculosis.*

Marianne also made friends with this young Dutch girl. Her attentive pose and the mug beside her suggest that Marianne had been doing her best to look after and entertain her, although her illness was terminal. The *Rönnskär* had 258 beds for very sick evacuees, as well as space for about 200 'walking wounded'. Bed sheets were made of paper to avoid contagion.

Everyone arriving in Sweden had to be disinfected and quarantined before being moved to refugee camps and sanatoria. Marianne, who had already endured bathing and disinfection with DDT by German soldiers in Lübeck, found the experience harrowing: 'They washed us 10 times, dusted us and cleaned us with spirit until I came out of there half dead, and it was all happening even though I was completely healthy.'[25]

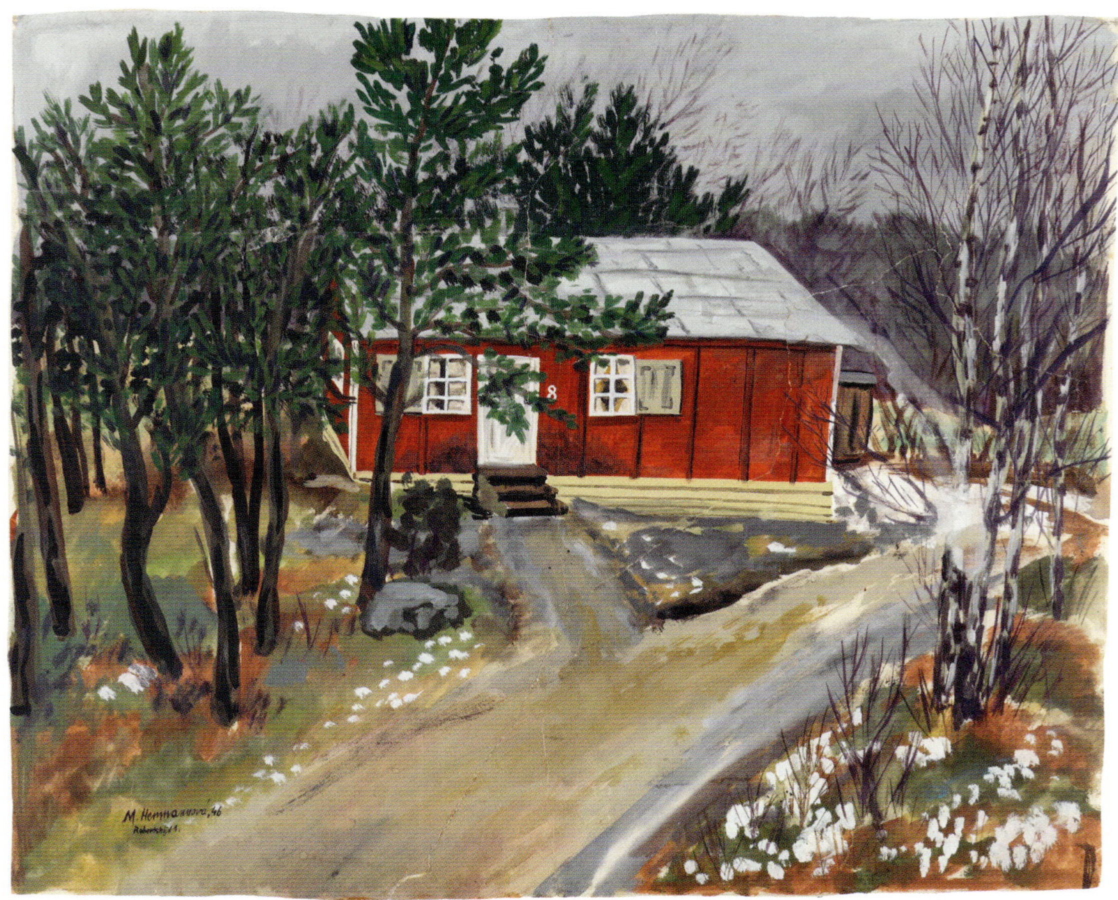

45

Hut 8 at Robertshöjd 1,
early Spring, 1946
Watercolour and gouache on paper
Signed and dated at lower left
'M. Hermannová, 46/Robertshöjd 1'
PP.2005.38.42

*Most of the refugees here were
Hungarian Jewish girls.*

In November 1945 Marianne wrote to her friend Petr: 'I live in a small house with two bedrooms. One big, in which 8 girls stay, and one smaller where I live with my mum. It is very simple, iron beds, mattresses filled with wood wool, 2 sheets – you lie on one and cover yourself with the other (that's the Swedish habit) and also blankets. Also, there are 4 wardrobes, but very narrow, you know like those in swimming pool or tennis court locker rooms. A few little chairs without backrests, table, a huge stove that overheats that little room terribly, and 3 windows. In the corner I paint and some of my pictures always hang there, and it is always messy there (or at least Mum says so, I don't mind paints and dirty brushes) and it smells of turpentine. I hope you can imagine it all. We eat at a canteen which is quite inconvenient because it rains badly all the time.'[26]

Despite this, there is obvious pleasure expressed in Marianne's work; the red chalet nestles among silver birches and evergreens.

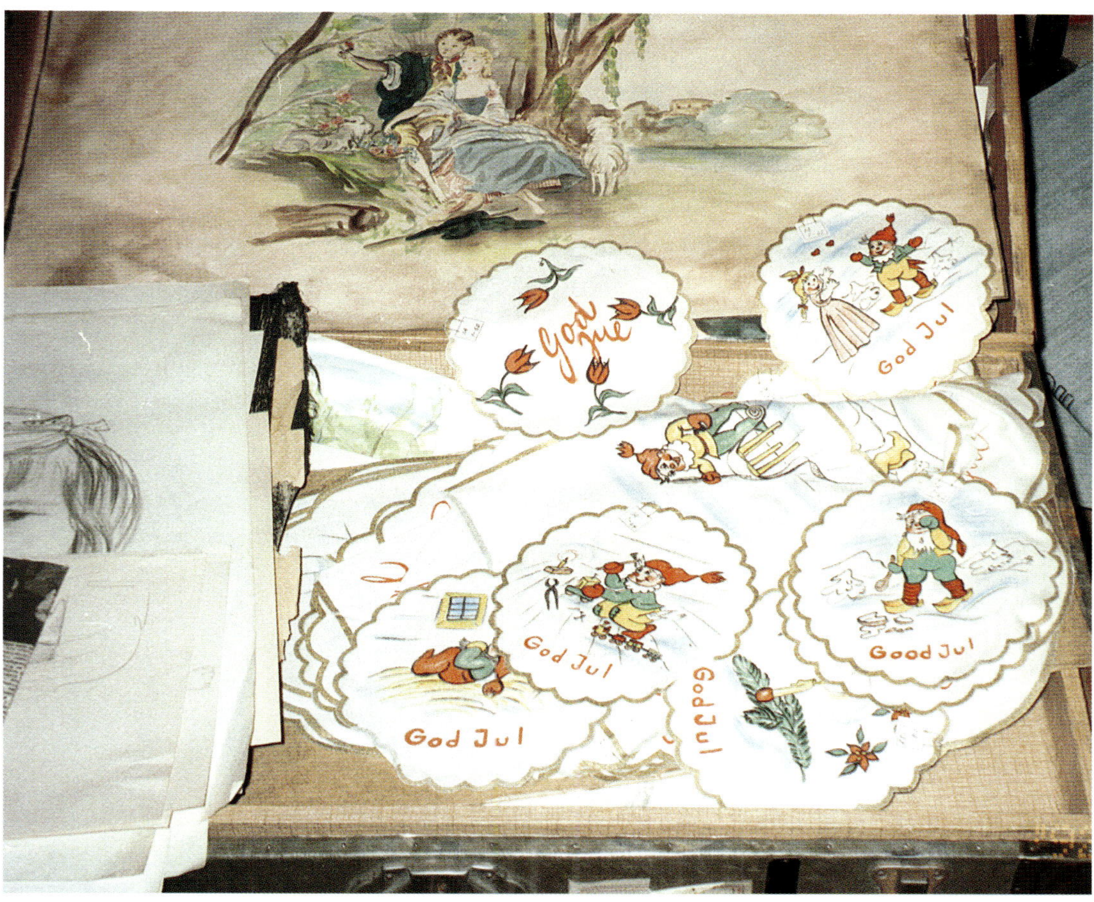

46

Swedish Christmas Mats,
between 1946 and 1951
Painted textile
PP.2005.38.57–77

In July 1945 Marianne applied to spend two months in Paris in the studio of the textile designer Pierre Kittler but her visa request was denied. However, she was tenacious and did not give up. These hand-painted Christmas placemats inscribed 'God Jul' (Merry Christmas) are typical of the work she produced in her own design studio which she went on to set up in Gothenburg. They show Jultomte (also called Tomte), a Swedish folk figure with a long white beard and red pointed hat who rides a sleigh and visits children's homes, handing out presents at Christmas. Marianne's cheerful designs demonstrate how adept she was at integrating into different cultures, and her desire to bring joy through her art, particularly to children. They are a story of rehabilitation, of determinedly looking forward to a brighter future.

The photograph shows the mats in the trunk in which they were locked away for decades, along with Marianne's other artworks, until she finally made the decision to talk about her Holocaust experience.

Notes

1 Marianne Grant, letter to Petr Erben dated 30 November 1945, Family archive. (All letters translated from the Czech by Peter Tuka.)

2 Dr Karl Löwenstein (1887–1976) was made the chief of the ghetto police, and thus was one of the top officers in Theresienstadt's inmate hierarchy. Many survivors remember him as being very militant and strict in enforcing an anti-corruption policy in the ghetto in order to stop the black market and ensure fair distribution of the scarce resources. Source: https://wiener.soutron.net/Portal/Default/en-GB/RecordView/Index/71026 (last accessed 22/10/2021).

3 Page from *Vedem*, vol. 7, published 29.1.1943. This scan was downloaded from the following webpage, where all issues of the magazine have been published with permission of the Terezin Memorial Museum, which holds the originals: Collection of Terezin Memorial, id.no.:1317 (http://archive.pamatnik-terezin.cz/vyhledavani/listiny/detail.php?table=Evidencni_karta&col=id&value=7552 last accessed 22/10/2021). *Vedem* was a clandestine magazine published in the ghetto by a group of teenage boys from Youth Home L417 between 1942 and 1944. Translated from the Czech by Peter Tuka.

4 Nava Shean, Theresienstadt notebook, November 1942 entry, quoted in *To Be an Actress*, translated from Hebrew by Michelle Fram Cohen, Lanham: Hamilton Books, 2010, p.25.

5 O. Guttman, 'Mé Dojmy' [My Impressions] in *Vedem*, May 1944, 1. p. 35. Collection of Terezin Memorial, database no. 1317, link: http://archive.pamatnik-terezin.cz/vyhledavani/listiny/detail.php?table=Evidencni_karta&col=id&value=7552&offset=621 (last accessed 22/10/2021). Translated from the Czech by Peter Tuka.

6 Ruth Bondy, 'The Changing Image of the Terezín Ghetto' in Ruth Bondy, *Trapped, Essays on the History of the Czech Jews, 1939–1943*, Jerusalem: Yad Vashem, 2008, p.13.

7 Another of Marianne's drawings of Nava Shean is in the collection of Beit Terezin, and there is also one in Marianne's family's archive.

8 Nava Shean, Theresienstadt notebook, November 1942 entry, quoted in *To Be an Actress*, translated from Hebrew by Michelle Fram Cohen, Lanham: Hamilton Books, 2010, p.27.

9 *Ibid* p.32.

10 *Ibid*, p.36.

11 *Marianne's Story*, interview by Rex Bloomstein, Nucleus Production for Glasgow Museums, 2002. Marianne Grant Collection Archive, Glasgow Museums, GMA.2021.1.

12 *Ibid*.

13 Hana Káňová, interviewed for the project *Memory of Nations*, 20.4.2014, Translated from the Czech by Peter Tuka https://www.pametnaroda.cz/cs/kanova-hana-20140314-0

14 Excerpt from *Marianne's Story*, interview by Rex Bloomstein, Nucleus Production for Glasgow Museums, 2002, tape 5. Marianne Grant Collection Archive, Glasgow Museums, GMA.2021.1.

15 *Ibid*.

16 Dita Kraus, interview recorded for the project 'Memory of Nations' (a co-production with Czech television), 28.10.2015. http://www.pametnaroda.cz/witness/recording/id/3683?locale=en_GB (Last accessed 19.08.2021).

17 William Arthur Wood, British soldier interviewed for the collection of IWM (IWM SR 15427).

18 *Ibid*.

19 Dita Kraus, interview recorded in the framework of the project 'Memory of Nations' (a co-production with Czech television), 28.10.2015. http://www.pametnaroda.cz/witness/recording/id/3683?locale=en_GB (last acessed on 08.05.2018). Translated from the Czech by Peter Tuka.

20 Charles Phillip Sharp, *Personal Diary*, p.131, in the United States Holocaust Memorial Museum, Charles Phillip Sharp collection, Accession Number 2004.664.3; Series 4: Personal Items, 1945; Diary, 1945; item no: 2004.664.3_001_013_0345 https://collections.ushmm.org/search/catalog/irn531154#?c=3&m=0&s=0&cv=344&xywh=-235%2C0%2C1200%2C799 (last accessed 22/10/2021).

21 'END OF BELSEN CAMP, Former Inmates at Final Burning Ceremony' in *The Scotsman*, Tuesday 22 May 1945, p.5.

22 '3000 Jews Released From German Concentration Camps Arrive In Sweden, More Expected' in *JTA Daily News Bulletin* Vol. XII, No. 112 (27th year), Thursday, May 17 1945, p. 2 http://pdfs.jta.org/1945/1945-05-17_112.pdf (last accessed 5 October 2021)

23 *Ibid*.

24 Marianne Grant, letter to Petr Erben, undated, autumn 1945. Family archive.

25 Marianne Grant, letter to Petr Erben dated 18 October 1945. Family archive.

26 Marianne Grant, letter to Petr Erben dated 16 November 1945. Family archive.

Epilogue

Geraldine Shenkin

My mum Marianne's courage, determination and amazing artistic talent saved her and my grandma's lives. We as a family have always felt the importance of ensuring her legacy lives on for future generations. In continuing Mum's work by visiting and telling her story in schools around Scotland over the last few years I have been overwhelmed by the schoolchildren's knowledge and keen interest in the Holocaust.

It is very ironic that Mum was blessed with twins, my brother Garry and myself, after many times having to record by drawing the gruesome experiments performed on twins in Auschwitz by Josef Mengele, the 'Angel of Death'.

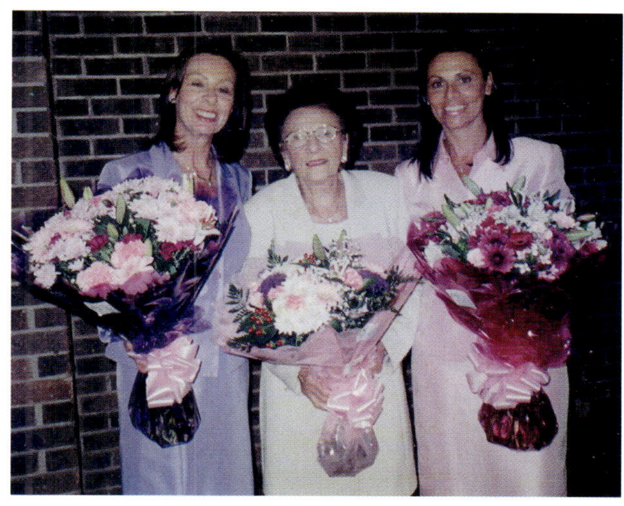

Marianne with her two daughters, Susan (left) and Geraldine (right), when she was made a Freeman of East Renfrewshire in 2003

My dear sister Susan Slater, who sadly passed away in April 2020, like myself was extremely keen for Mum's book to be republished. I know she would be so happy that this project has come to fruition, and our family are so proud of Mausi and her achievements and are delighted that her story can be shared far and wide.

I want to thank the whole team who helped make this book a reality. A special thanks to Jo Meacock, Peter Tuka, Paula Cowan, Susan Pacitti, and of course Deborah Haase, who was instrumental in the creation of the original book. In working with the team on this project, many interesting new facts and stories were discovered, and I am grateful that this opportunity arose.

With thanks to all the family for their continued support: my husband Michael, Garry Grant, Hayley and Steven Groden, Katie and Tim Goodman, Martin Slater, Simone and Elliot Wilson, and Tali and Dani Kramer.

Timeline

Year	Marianne's Life	Holocaust History
1921	19 September: Marianne Hermann/Mariana Hermannová (nicknamed 'Mausi') is born to banker Rudolf Hermann (*c*.1888–1938) and milliner Anna Hermann (née Rosner; 1889–1973). They live at Nové Město, Vyšehradská 5, Prague. Marianne nearly dies because of a milk allergy.	
1927	A local paper publishes some of Marianne's drawings, submitted by her eye specialist. Marianne begins to attend a German primary school.	
1930	The family moves to a spacious, modern apartment with electricity, provided by the bank, in Schnirchova, Holešovice, a fashionable neighbourhood near Stromovka Park.	
1935	Marianne attends a private German girls' high school in Prague.	September: Reichstag (German parliament) adopts the Nuremberg Racial Laws, turning Jews into second-class citizens and unleashing arrests, denunciations and other decrees and anti-Jewish measures.
1936	Marianne spends one year at an English grammar school in Prague.	
1937	Marianne enrols at Studio Rotter in Prague.	
1938	April: Marianne's father Rudolf dies. Her mother Anna sends small amounts of money every day to help her sister Terez Rosner and her family in Austria save funds to get to London safely. Marianne joins the Zionist Youth Movement El Al. They meet once a week and learn Hebrew and Jewish songs.	12 March: Germany annexes Austria. 1 October: Following the 'Munich Agreement' Germany occupies Sudetenland (the borderland of Czechoslovakia with Germany). December: Prague is full of Jewish, Communist and political refugees.
1939	Marianne and Anna are forced to move to a flat in a poorer area, Smíchov, Žižkova 12; this is smaller but closer to relatives. Marianne is not allowed to graduate from Studio Rotter. A cousin gets a place on the Kindertransport and other family members flee overseas. Marianne and her mother unsuccessfully apply to many embassies for a visa, including the British embassy, but quotas are full and Marianne does not have employment to go to. She applies for positions as a dog walker and nurse. Marianne's mother obtains a place for Marianne to study at Bezalel Academy of Art and Design in Jerusalem for two years, but Marianne refuses to be separated from her.	14 March: Slovakia declares independence and becomes a Nazi satellite. Czechoslovakia falls apart. The first Kindertransport train rescuing Jewish children from Czechoslovakia leaves Prague. 15 March: German troops occupy the remainder of Czech lands (Bohemia and Moravia), creating the so-called 'Protectorate of Bohemia and Moravia'. 16 March: Many Jewish professionals (teachers, lecturers, scientists, civil engineers) are prohibited from practising, while others (doctors, dentists, vets, lawyers, journalists) face restrictions in numbers and can only work for Jews. 21 June: A decree defining 'Jews' is passed in the Protectorate, based on the Nuremberg Race Laws, the principles of which are gradually extended over the occupied land, and regulations enforce the registration and liquidation of Jewish property. 14 August: Jewish people in the Protectorate are prohibited from using most restaurants, cafes and public sport facilities. They are also to be segregated in hospitals and care homes for the elderly. September: A curfew is imposed, and Jews in Prague are forbidden to leave their homes after 8pm. 1 September: Germany, the Soviet Union and Slovakia invade Poland. 3 September: Britain and France declare war on Germany. October: Two transports with 1,300 Jews from Moravia leave for a concentration camp in Nisko, Poland.
1940	A Jewish friend of Marianne's breaks the rules and goes to the cinema. He is arrested and killed. Marianne's mother Anna has an operation to remove a benign tumour.	20 February: Czech Jews are excluded from attending the cinema and theatre performances.

Year	Marianne's Life	Holocaust History
1940 **contd**		17 May: Jews are forbidden to enter Prague's public parks. 22 June: France surrenders to Germany. Germany attacks the Soviet Union. 5 Aug: Jews are restricted to shopping between 11a.m.–1p.m. and 3–4.30p.m.
1941	Marianne and her Jewish Zionist group are directed by the Jewish Council to work on farms in Bohemia and Moravia under the pretext that it is part of their Hachshara. 1 September: Marianne is forced to wear the yellow star. In secret Marianne teaches teenage Jewish girls fashion design and gains studio experience with a Czech sculptor. She takes lessons in underwear making and ceramic restoration, part of a retraining programme supported by the Central Bureau of Emigration in Prague.	Germans demand Jewish agricultural labourers replace Czech farmers sent to work in coal mines and munition factories. 31 March: Jewish businesses in the service, travel, insurance, banking and real estate sectors are forbidden. Only manual labour is unaffected by labour laws. In a decree issued by Reinhard Heydrich, the Protector of Bohemia and Moravia and Head of the Central Office for Reich Security (RSHA), all Jews above the age of six are forced to wear a yellow badge. 6 September: Jews within the Protectorate are forbidden to use public libraries. October: Systematic deportations of Jews from the Protectorate begin. 10 and 17 October: Heydrich, Adolf Eichmann and other leaders of the Nazi occupation force meet in Prague to discuss the Jewish question in the Protectorate. It is decided that Terezín (German Theresienstadt) will be converted into an assembly and transit camp for the Jews on their way to extermination in the east. 22 November: Jews are prohibited from using buses unless blind or a war invalid. 24 November: First transport to Theresienstadt with 342 Jewish men from Prague. 4 December: Jews within the Protectorate are forbidden to visit museums, galleries and archives. 20 December: Sewing machines are confiscated from Prague's Jewish population.
1942	Knowing they are to be taken to some kind of work camp, Marianne and her mother pack suitcases and make warm clothing. They entrust their jewellery and valuables to local Czech families. 28 April: After spending a night in the Art Nouveau exhibition centre Výstaviště Praha Holešovice ('The Fairground Palace') in Prague, Marianne and her mother are taken by rail to Theresienstadt. Marianne chooses to work in the Youth Garden. June: Marianne, along with the entire population of Theresienstadt, is made to stand outside without food or drink for a full day while Nazis shout through loudspeakers demanding information on Heydrich's assassination. Many inmates collapse and some die. Marianne volunteers to help elderly German and Austrian Jews who are dying from dysentery. Marianne becomes very ill with hepatitis.	9 January: First transport east to Riga ghetto, in modern-day Latvia, departs Theresienstadt. 20 January: At the Wannsee Conference Nazi officials plan the murder of millions of Jewish people. It is decided that Theresienstadt will be presented as an *Altersghetto*, a retirement home for elderly Jews from Germany and Austria, to conceal from the Reich's population the true purpose of the deportations. 27 May: Attempted assassination in Prague of Reinhard Heydrich. 4 June: Heydrich dies from his injuries. In retaliation, the Nazis destroy the two Czech villages of Lidice and Ležáky, executing or imprisoning all citizens. June: First transports with Jews from Germany and Austria arrive in Theresienstadt. September: Overcrowding in Theresienstadt reaches its peak, with nearly 60,000 inmates crammed in every corner of the small town. Insufficient hygiene and lack of food result in nearly 4,000 deaths that month alone.

Year	Marianne's Life	Holocaust History
1942 contd		26 October: The first transport from Theresienstadt to Auschwitz-Birkenau. 8 December: A fake café opens in Theresienstadt in house Q418 with music and cabaret performances.
1943	15 December: Marianne's mother is selected for transport east. Marianne is unable to get her off the list and so follows her. They travel separately on packed cattle wagons. There is no food, water or sanitary provision. People die on the journey. 17 December: Marianne arrives in Auschwitz-Birkenau. She meets Gusta who used to come for lunch in Prague while learning to be a blacksmith. He helps keep her money and watch from being confiscated. Marianne searches for her mother until she finds her. 18 December: In freezing temperatures everyone is stripped of their clothes and selection for the gas chambers takes place. Disabled people and those with scars from operations are immediately selected. The rest are given random, second-hand clothes to wear. Marianne offers to work as an unofficial teacher in the Children's Block. A Slovak guard asks Marianne to make illustrated books for his children for Christmas. She also paints a Roma girl for him.	2 February: German 6th Army surrenders at Stalingrad. 5 September: The first of two transports with 5,007 prisoners from Theresienstadt depart for the newly formed 'Family Camp' at Auschwitz-Birkenau. December: 'Beautification' of Theresienstadt begins in preparation for the potential International Red Cross visit the following year. 15–18 December: Further transports of 5,007 people to Auschwitz from Theresienstadt.
1944	Marianne's leather boots are stolen and she gets frostbite and almost loses her toes. Fritzi Mautner, Marianne's friend from school, commits suicide on the electric fence. Marianne suffers from pleurisy. Her life is saved by the Slovak guard who brings her medicine, fruit, bread, butter and an egg. Marianne is forced to draw for Mengele. She gets permission to decorate the walls of the Children's Block, with Dina Babbitt (née Gottliebová). 8 March: Jewish youth leader Fredy Hirsch dies, possibly poisoning or deliberate overdose. Marianne saves 14-year-old Hana Káňová (née Heitlerová), whom she knew from the Youth Garden in Theresienstadt, from death in the gas chambers, demanding she be taken to the hospital because she is sick. Another child, Peter, a favourite of Marianne's from Theresienstadt, is murdered, aged 8. Marianne describes him as 'one of my beloved children […] a lovely boy with large black eyes and black hair […] Whenever I was home after work he came to see me and I gave him titbits and we were just great pals. I loved that little boy.' July: Marianne and Anna pass selection. They are stripped and searched to make sure they have no personal belongings with them and are given overalls to wear. They are sent to Dessauer Ufer, a woman's camp, part of Neuengamme Concentration Camp in Hamburg. They live in old grain stores and are made to clear factories devastated in Allied bombing raids. September: Marianne and Anna are moved to a smaller female labour camp, Hamburg-Neugraben. When it is discovered that Marianne is an artist, she is asked to decorate the mess hall and make Christmas presents for the officers' families. Pregnant Jewish women are sent back to Auschwitz and killed. One conceals her pregnancy but her newborn baby is euthanized by Jewish doctor Goldie on SS orders. Anna gets hit by a brick on the foot, requiring an operation. She survives. A young German mother befriends Marianne and gives her occasional apples and sandwiches. The camp is bombed and some inmates are killed.	March: The surviving prisoners who were deported to the Family Camp in Auschwitz in September 1943 are ordered to write postcards to their families in Theresienstadt and to post-date them so that the Red Cross delegation can see they are alive and well. 8 March: All these prisoners are gassed without selection. 6 June: D-Day, Allied invasion of Normandy. 23 June: International Red Cross Delegation visits Theresienstadt in order to investigate the living conditions and treatment of Jewish people. The visit is brief, and the delegates are taken only to pre-selected parts of the camp, where the prisoners are instructed on how to behave and are forced to give positive reports of their living conditions. 17 July: A number of Jewish artists in Theresienstadt, including Leo Haas, Otto Ungar, Bedřich Fritta and Ferdinand Bloch, are arrested and tortured in the Small Fortress at Theresienstadt for depicting the camp's true conditions in their art.
1945	February: Marianne and her mother are sent to Hamburg-Tiefstack concentration camp. 5 April: Marianne and Anna are moved on foot and by rail to Bergen-Belsen concentration camp. Marianne notes that the SS are already wearing white arm bands. There is nothing to eat in the camps. Piles of dead bodies lie unburied. 15 April: Marianne and Anna witness the liberation of Bergen-Belsen. They are rehoused in the former barracks of Hungarian soldiers and share a room with Dita Kraus and her mother, who dies.	January: Germans begin to abandon the concentration camps close to the advancing front lines. The SS drive columns of prisoners in so-called 'death marches'. Some are transported in freight trains. 27 January: Auschwitz is liberated by the Soviet army. February 1945: Famous diarist Anne Frank dies of typhus in Bergen-Belsen, aged 15.

Year	Marianne's Life	Holocaust History
1945 contd	Marianne works as an interpreter for the British army. She also distributes cigarette rations and is commissioned to make drawings of dead bodies. Marianne is offered jewellery from plundered German homes. She takes only a plain wedding band for her mother and a watch for each of them to replace those lost. Anna catches typhoid and is looked after by Dr Sean Styles in an isolation hospital. 21 May: Marianne witnesses the burning of the last Belsen hut along w th Hitler's portrait and a German war ensign. July: Marianne and Anna journey by rail to Hamburg, Dr Styles having arranged their passage on a Swedish Red Cross boat. 10 July: They sail aboard the M/S *Rönnskär* from Lübeck to Malmö, Sweden, arriving 11 July. Marianne is initially housed in a school before being taken to Robertshöjd 1 refugee camp near Gothenburg. Anna is sent to a sanitorium. Marianne is visited by the local Jewish community, most notably Herbert Sterner, vice-chairman of the Jewish Committee in Gothenburg, and his daughter Myrre, who becomes Marianne's friend. 10 October: Marianne talks of possibly emigrating to Israel to join a kibbutz. 17 October: Anna leaves the sanitorium and joins Marianne at Robertshöjd 1. 18 October: Marianne is too late to apply for Czech repatriation. She considers emigrating to London where her cousin Egon Rosner lives. November: Marianne is employed painting tiles and making stuffed toys. She paints a landscape scene for her boss. She also starts work with a screen-printing company in Alingsås, an hour's commute from Gothenburg. 17 November: An exhibition organized by the Public Association of Art and Culture, hosted by Arbetarnas Bildningsförbund (ABF), opens in Pusterviksgatan, Gothenburg. It includes some of Marianne's Bergen-Belsen watercolours. 30 November: Marianne receives her Theresienstadt artworks from Petr Erben, too late to be included in the exhibition. December: The exhibition opens in a second venue, Malmö. Marianne attends. Anna is admitted into hospital for an operation after having been given the wrong medication. Marianne is employed by a cabaret theatre in Liseberg Park, Gothenburg, until autumn 1946. She sells several of her landscape paintings	March 1945: Swedish Red Cross begins rescuing Scandinavian concentration camp survivors. 15 April: Bergen-Belsen is liberated by the British army. 8 May: Germany surrenders and World War II ends in Europe. This day is remembered annually worldwide as Victory over Fascism Day. In the UK it is also known as VE Day (Victory in Europe). 9 May: Theresienstadt is liberated by the Soviet army. 18 October: The first Czech repatriation transport leaves Sweden.
1945– 1946		November 1945–1 October 1946: Nuremberg Trials - Nazi Germany leaders stand trial for crimes against peace, war crimes, and crimes against humanity. Twenty-two leading Nazis are tried; 12 are sentenced to death, 7 imprisoned, and 3 acquitted.
1946	Anna works as a milliner for a large department store. Marianne and Anna take a small room by the harbour before acquiring their own apartment on the outskirts of Gothenburg. Marianne starts her own graphic design business. Anna gives up work to look after her. January: Marianne goes to the British embassy in Stockholm to try to get a UK visa. December: Marianne visits Prague and is reunited with her student artworks.	
1947	Marianne and Anna visit Aunt Terez and her two sons Egon and Friedrich in London and return to Sweden via Prague. Marianne befriends a young Jewish couple, Helmut and Margit Silbermann. Helmut's mother and sister live in Battlefield, Glasgow. Marianne starts writing to their lodger, Jewish refugee Jack Grant (1921–86).	The Auschwitz-Birkenau Memorial and Museum opens.
1951	Summer: Marianne becomes engaged to Jack on holiday in Båstad, Sweden. September: Marianne and Jack marry in London and honeymoon in Bournemouth. They settle in Battlefield, Glasgow where they raise their family. Anna lives with them. Jack teaches children Jewish studies at Queens Park Synagogue.	

Year	Marianne's Life	Holocaust History
1952	Fay 'Susan' Grant (later Slater) is born.	
1950s	Marianne attends evening classes twice a week at The Glasgow School of Art.	
1957	Twins Geraldine Grant (later Shenkin) and Garry Grant are born.	
1960	Jack begins working for Newton Mearns Hebrew Congregation, having previously been headmaster at its Hebrew School.	
1973	Anna dies at the age of 83.	
1979		Auschwitz-Birkenau become a UNESCO World Heritage Site.
1984		First International Conference of Children of Holocaust Survivors is held in New York.
1986	Jack dies, aged 65.	
1994	Marianne takes her family to Prague. They visit Marianne's former home in Nové Město and meet up with Petr Erben and his wife Eva. They visit the museum at Theresienstadt.	
1997	Marianne recreates paintings she did in the Children's Block in Auschwitz for an exhibition at Yad Vashem, Jerusalem.	
2000		27 January: Representatives from 46 governments around the world meet in Stockholm and sign a declaration committing to preserving the memory of those murdered in the Holocaust.
2001	Marianne Grant is interviewed by curator Deborah Haase for Glasgow Museums, for the film *It Didn't Have to be Me*.	The first Holocaust Memorial Day is held in the UK.
2002	27 January: Marianne participates in the Holocaust Memorial Day ceremony in Glasgow Royal Concert Hall. 12 April–30 June: Exhibition of Marianne's artwork in Kelvingrove Art Gallery and Museum; this travels to the City Art Centre, Edinburgh, in 2003. Filmmaker Rex Bloomstein interviews Marianne for *Marianne's Story*, a Nucleus Production for Glasgow Museums.	November: The Scottish Executive distributes *The Holocaust: A teaching pack for secondary schools*, which is based on Marianne's testimony, to all Scottish secondary schools.
2003	The Freedom of the City (East Renfrewshire) is bestowed on Marianne, in recognition of her work in raising Holocaust awareness.	
2004	Glasgow Museums purchases The Marianne Grant Holocaust Artworks Collection with grant support from the National Lottery Heritage Fund, Art Fund and National Fund for Acquisitions. A selection of works is displayed in the McLellan Galleries, Glasgow.	
2005	Marianne attends reception for Holocaust survivors, hosted by the Queen at St James's Palace.	
2006	The first of an annual rotation of the Marianne Grant Holocaust artworks collection goes on display in the refurbished Kelvingrove Art Gallery and Museum, Glasgow. Marianne meets the Queen again at the reopening of the building.	
2007	11 December: Marianne Grant dies at the age of 86.	
2013		The International Holocaust Remembrance Alliance (IHRA) adopts a working definition of Holocaust Denial and Distortion.
2016		The UK government adopts the IHRA's definition of antisemitism.
2017		The Scottish government adopts the IHRA's working definition of antisemitism.
2018		UNESCO and the Organization for Security and Co-operation in Europe publish guidelines for addressing antisemitism through education.
2021		*Vision Schools Scotland* publishes a teaching resource for secondary schools based on Marianne's testimony.